D0897844

Soldiering in the Army of Tennessee

Larry J. Daniel

A Portrait of Life in a Confederate Army

The University of North Carolina Press   Chapel Hill & London

Soldiering
in the
Army of
Tennessee

© 1991 The University of
North Carolina Press
All rights reserved
Manufactured in the
United States of America

The paper in this book meets the guidelines for
permanence and durability of the Committee on
Production Guidelines for Book Longevity of the
Council on Library Resources.

95 94 93 92 91   5 4 3 2 1

Library of Congress Cataloging-in-Publication Data
Daniel, Larry J., 1947–
    Soldiering in the Army of Tennessee : a portrait of
life in a Confederate army / by Larry J. Daniel.
        p. cm.
    Includes bibliographical references and index.
    ISBN 0-8078-2004-0
        1. Confederate States of America. Army of
Tennessee. 2. United States—History—Civil War,
1861–1865—Regimental histories. I. Title.
E470.5.D36   1991
973.7′468–dc20   91-50250
                              CIP

For my children,

LAUREN & MARK

Contents

Preface, xi

Acknowledgments, xv

Introduction: The Army of Tennessee Will
Decide the Fate of the Confederacy, 1

Chapter 1
Certainly a Rough Looking Set, 11

Chapter 2
We Drill Seven Hours a Day, 23

Chapter 3
We Have Drew the Finest Arms, 39

Chapter 4
I Am Hearty as a Pig on Half Rations, 51

Chapter 5
The Aire Is a Right Smart of Sickness, 64

Chapter 6
I Will Have My Fun, 83

Chapter 7
I Saw 14 Men Tied to Postes and Shot, 101

Chapter 8
The Army of Tennessee Is the Army of
the Lord, 115

Chapter 9
We Are Dissatisfied and We Don't Care
Who Knows It, 126

Chapter 10
I Never Saw Braver Men, 148

Notes, 169

Bibliography, 199

Index, 223

Illustrations

Corporal John T. Killingsworth of the Seventeenth Tennessee, 4

Sanders Myers of the Fourth Florida, 7

Captain Calvin H. Walker and Sergeant James J. Walker of the Third Tennessee, 9

William Shores, drummer boy of the Sixth Arkansas, 12

Private Reuben McMichael of the Seventeenth Louisiana, 16

Private John Rulle of the Second Tennessee, 19

Private Wright P. Sandige of the Seventeenth Tennessee, 31

Confederates captured at Missionary Ridge, 33

Private N. H. Martin of the Twenty-second Tennessee, 35

Private A. H. Smith of the Fifty-first Tennessee, 41

Private W. F. Henry of the Sixth Tennessee, 44

Privates John W. Montjoy and Jarret Montjoy of the Third Kentucky Cavalry of Wheeler's Corps, 45

Captain Pleasant G. Swor of the Fifth Tennessee, 67

Privates William H. Landis and J. A. Landis of the Twenty-third Tennessee, 68

Andrew Jackson Vawter of the Twelfth Tennessee, 72

Robert Patterson of the Twelfth Tennessee, 74

Private Ancel Sawyer of the Tenth
Mississippi, 76

Private Columbus Tullos of the Eighth
Mississippi, 81

Camp of the Fourth Kentucky at Corinth,
Mississippi, 85

Members of the Ninth Mississippi
encamped at Pensacola, 86

Men of the First Alabama in their
Pensacola camp, 89

Troops of the Fifth Georgia in camp, 92

A group from the Fifth Company of the
Louisiana Washington Artillery, 121

Private W. J. Cocker of the Third
Tennessee, 131

Private Jeremiah Jaco of the Thirty-fifth
Tennessee, 142

Lieutenant Nathan M. Robertson on
horseback, 145

Lieutenant Lawrence M. Anderson of the
First Florida, 151

John M. W. Baird and Henry Clements of
the First Arkansas, 158

Private Thomas Murrell of the Sixth
Tennessee, 160

Lieutenant Robert B. Hurt, Jr., of the
Fifty-fifth Tennessee, 162

Map of the area of operations of the Army
of Tennessee, 2

Preface

In 1967 and 1974, Thomas L. Connelly published his two major volumes on the Army of Tennessee, *Army of the Heartland* and *Autumn of Glory*. In this work, Connelly accomplished for the western army what Douglas Southall Freeman did for the Army of Northern Virginia a generation earlier—a definitive command-level study. As yet untold, however, was the story of the army from the opposite view—the grass roots. This book was undertaken to show the perspective of the men in the ranks.

The starting point was Bell I. Wiley's classic *Life of Johnny Reb*. This extensive study humanized the common soldier and told of the emotions of men in combat. Wiley used material from about three dozen soldiers in the Army of Tennessee, but, because of space limitations, only about a dozen were portrayed extensively. James I. Robertson's more recent *Soldiers Blue and Gray* serves as a sort of

third volume to Wiley's two books on Southern and Northern soldiers, but, perhaps subconsciously reflecting Robertson's preference
for Virginia, sources from western Confederates are extremely rare.
Reid Mitchell's excellent study *Civil War Soldiers,* which explores
the expectations and views of Northern and Southern troops, does
include some western sources, but by its nature is broadly based.
Joseph A. Frank and George Reaves's book *"Seeing the Elephant"*:
Raw Recruits at the Battle of Shiloh, is a sociological treatment of
men experiencing combat for the first time. For a general understanding of soldiers' life, attitudes, and motivations for enlisting, the
reader should consult these sources.

I became convinced that there was yet another story to be told. As
I eventually uncovered and digested the letters and diaries of nearly
350 of the army's soldiers and scores more of memoirs, this conviction was confirmed. My mission was to discover exactly who were
the men of the Army of Tennessee. How did they feel about their
officers, the Yankees, and the course of the war? What occupied their
time? How well were they armed, clothed, and fed? I also wished to
delve into more substantive issues such as religion and morale.

Two themes thus emerged and are explored in this book. First,
though I found eastern and western Rebs to be more alike than
different, their variances in certain areas, such as refinement and
morale, were more than subtle. Second, the Army of Tennessee,
unlike its sister army in Virginia, could not maintain cohesiveness
through confidence in leadership and battlefield victories. It relied
instead on certain "glues" that bonded the men together at the lower
ranks. Thus the unity of the army can properly be understood only
from the bottom up, not the top down, as was the case in Virginia.

It was an unusually cold day in April 1987 when I walked through
the camps of Albert Sidney Johnston's army. What I saw, of course,
were reenactors, many of whom, I was told, had spent the previous
night in nearby motels rather than their wall tents. They had gathered near the Shiloh National Military Park for the reenactment of
the battle in honor of its 125th anniversary. As I saw them drill,
cook, engage in contemporary games, and, later that afternoon,
rehearse with their Federal counterparts, who were camped within
easy viewing distance, I realized that this was as close as I could ever
come to seeing what it all must have been like. Yet I could not help

but muse what the reaction of some of Johnston's soldiers might have been had they been able to accompany me that day.

I hope I have helped to demythologize the modern-day Civil War reenactors. I believe that the only way the historical soldier's true nature can be unveiled is to go back to the original sources and let these men tell their own story. Thus I have quoted extensively from their diaries and letters, using their own phonetic spelling with a minimal use of sic. I used the scores of memoirs I examined with great caution, finding them frequently colored with hindsight, sometimes chronologically incorrect, and often having a hidden agenda. With only a few minor exceptions, all quotes in this book were taken from material written during the war. Also, to ensure that I kept my study focused on those who were truly ordinary, I considered, with few exceptions, only the comments of those at the rank of captain or below. General, line, and staff officers had a view of the war that was larger than that of the common soldier and thus their remarks are generally outside the scope of this work.

The portrait of army life for the western soldier that emerges is often a depressing one. Yet reading how these men coped and formed their perceptions leads to an understanding of what motivated them to fight, despite numerous losses, and what led them, to an appalling degree, to desert. It is not my intention that the reader agree with what they did, only to understand why they did it. It is my hope that the following pages have in some small way helped save from obscurity the thoughts and feelings of the men who made up that valiant army.

Acknowledgments

Several years ago I drove from Memphis to Jackson, Mississippi, to hear Richard McMurry speak. I was so taken by his writing and knowledge of the western theater that I wanted to meet him in person. Little did I realize that this meeting was to be the beginning of a cherished friendship. Coincidentally, we shared an alma mater—Emory University in Atlanta—although I was across the quadrangle in the School of Theology. Richard offered critical advice on the manuscript and tried in every way to strengthen it. Any remaining weaknesses in it are mine.

A serious student of the Army of Tennessee will sooner or later encounter Dennis Kelly, historian at the Kennesaw Mountain National Battlefield Park. About the time I began writing this book, I learned that he was working on a somewhat similar project. To my complete surprise, he turned his set of note cards, perhaps two xvi thousand of them, over to me and encouraged me to carry the project to completion. His overwhelming generosity took a year off my research schedule.

Several individuals called my attention to material that otherwise would have been missed. These include Arthur Bergeron of Baton Rouge, Louisiana, Joseph Glathaar of the University of Houston, Albert Castel of Western Michigan University, Allen Whitehead of Greenwood, Mississippi, Douglas Hale of Stillwater, Oklahoma, and George Reaves of the Shiloh National Military Park. I extend my deep appreciation to these persons and to many others who offered encouragement and assistance.

Soldiering in the Army of Tennessee

Introduction

The Army of Tennessee Will Decide the Fate of the Confederacy

At Dalton, Georgia, in the spring of 1864, the Army of Tennessee was reborn—both spiritually and organizationally. Its three-year history had been turbulent. The army's dead now lay buried on the great battlefields of the West—Fort Donelson, Shiloh, Perryville, Murfreesboro, Chickamauga, and Missionary Ridge. Time and again the troops had displayed their valor, but this alone had been insufficient to offset the leadership of incompetent generals, such as former commanders Albert Sidney Johnston and Braxton Bragg, who almost always lost. The course of the war in the West had resulted in the loss of Tennessee, north Alabama, all but the eastern

Area of operations of the Army of Tennessee

portion of Mississippi, and some of north Georgia. Despite its dismal record, the Army of Tennessee always returned to fight. Out of the rubble of the Missionary Ridge disaster, General Joseph E. Johnston, the new commander, restructured the army's fifty-five thousand officers and men into one cavalry and two infantry corps.

It was a bright day in late April 1864 when Johnston held a grand review on an open plain at the east base of Taylor's Ridge to showcase his remodeled army. Some thirty-six thousand infantry were involved, and the line, in double column, covered a front of more than a mile. Scores of flags flapped in the spring breeze as the general, mounted on a splendid bay thoroughbred and accompanied

by his staff, appeared to the right of the parade line. Frank Roberts,
one of those viewing the scene from the ranks, was most impressed
with the elegant new uniforms of the officers. A blast from the
trumpets came from a band positioned on the right, and the review
began in earnest. Brigadier General Arthur M. Manigault was re-
minded of a similar panorama he once viewed in Paris. Although he
conceded that it was larger and more elaborate, "our men were far
superior physically, of greater height, and showed a more hardy
appearance."[1]

Lieutenant General William J. Hardee and his staff were the first
to pass in review. The nucleus of his corps had been organized at
Bowling Green, Kentucky, in the fall of 1861 and now consisted of
the divisions of Major Generals Benjamin F. Cheatham, Patrick
Cleburne, W. H. T. Walker, and William Bate. Cheatham's division
had its antecedents in the old Provisional Army of Tennessee, and
most of its regiments had fought in all the major battles of the West.
Typical among them was the Twentieth Tennessee, which was described by a member as nine-tenths "country boys." Though it had
been temporarily broken up by Bragg in the post-Chickamauga
reorganization, Johnston had reinstituted its historical organization.
In appreciation, the men in one impulse had marched to general
headquarters with brass bands playing. If any unit symbolized the
backbone of the Army of Tennessee, it was Cheatham's Tennesseans.[2]

Pat Cleburne had molded his command into a model division. A
company in one of his regiments, the Forty-fifth Alabama, was a
sober reminder of the youth who had been drained from the countryside to feed the war effort. Known as the "Boy Company," by
1864 it had a dozen members under age eighteen and as many under
fifteen. The division had a distinctly trans-Mississippi flavor; half of
its regiments came from Arkansas and Texas. Cleburne was the only
major general who would accept Thomas Churchill's Texas brigade
when it arrived at Tullahoma, Tennessee, in the spring of 1863.
There was great animosity against the Texans because of their previous surrender at Arkansas Post. After their exchange, they were
assigned to Bragg's army. The brigade had more than redeemed itself
when it, along with the rest of the division, had stood firm at

Corporal John T. Killingsworth of the Seventeenth Tennessee was wounded at Shiloh and later captured at Chickamauga. (Herb Peck)

Missionary Ridge. In its finest hour, the division performed a rear-guard action at Taylor's Ridge that probably saved the army. When Johnston attempted to standardize the battle flags of the army, Cleburne's men successfully petitioned to retain their distinctive dark blue with white "silver moon" flags.[3]

Walker's primarily Georgia division, initially at least, seemed out of place in the Army of Tennessee because three of its four brigades had transferred from the Atlantic coast. By 1864, with the exception

of one brigade, the troops had been acclimated to the West, having
fought at Chickamauga and Missionary Ridge. The exception was
H. W. Mercer's large brigade of four Georgia regiments, some 2,800
strong, which had been on garrison duty in Savannah since its
formation. The veterans called them "band box soldiers" and railed
at their new uniforms and regulation chevrons, the latter having
been largely discarded in the Army of Tennessee. An amazed Tennessee sergeant who viewed them remarked: "This morning I saw a
regt., 1400 strong [Sixty-third Georgia] just from Savannah. It has
been in service nearly three years but has never been in a fight! We
expect to show it the 'elephant' in a few days." It was a solid division,
and not long into the Atlanta Campaign one of Walker's Georgians
was convinced that "We, Walker's Foot Cavalry, have been doing all
the strategy for Gen. Johnston."[4]

Bate's division, which was formerly commanded by John Breckinridge, was a product of Bragg's post-Chickamauga reorganization.
It consisted of a mixed Tennessee-Georgia brigade, the Kentucky
brigade, and the Florida brigade. The Kentucky brigade had its
genesis in the Kentucky State Guard. By the end of 1860 more than
four thousand men had joined this force, which was clearly a cut
above the average state militia and had strong Southern sympathies.
It would prove to be the core of what would become known as the
Orphan Brigade. In training and esprit, it was unsurpassed in the
army. Less impressive was the Florida brigade. The Floridians had
not endeared themselves when, at Perryville, they had mistakingly
fired into some Mississippi regiments. Also, according to a captain
of an Alabama regiment, "it refused to fight at Murfreesboro, so the
rumor says."[5]

Next in review came the corps of Lieutenant General John Bell
Hood. His caustic comment that he had inherited "all of the untried
troops of the army" was not true, for most of his men were veterans. He had three divisions at his disposal, led by Major Generals
Thomas Hindman, Carter Stevenson, and Alexander P. Stewart.
Hindman's division, primarily of Mississippians and Alabamians,
was essentially Jones Withers's old division organized after Shiloh. It
consisted of outfits from Bragg's now defunct corps brought up from
Pensacola, five regiments transferred from coastal duty after Shiloh,

and half a dozen regiments organized after the spring of 1862. Particularly noteworthy in its drill performance was the Tenth South Carolina. One year earlier, when the regiment had passed in review at Shelbyville, Tennessee, Lieutenant General Leonidas Polk was heard to exclaim, "There is good stuff in that regiment." It was not unusual for the Tenth to attract a large audience at each drill. Yet the division's reputation had been stained at Missionary Ridge, when both W. F. Tucker's brigade and Z. C. Deas's brigade were reported as being the first to rout.[6]

Stevenson's division historically had been composed of mountaineer conscripts from east Tennessee, north Georgia, and north Alabama—"very ignorant men," according to one unimpressed Mississippi lieutenant who viewed them. The division was routed at Champion Hill in Mississippi and was subsequently captured at the siege of Vicksburg. After its prisoner exchange, it joined the Army of Tennessee in the fall of 1863, at which time one of Bragg's veterans noted, "I saw one of the Vicksburg regiments today, it was the 37th Ala. and would number about 600 for duty being the largest reg't I've seen in six months." An Atlanta editor defended the division and claimed that rumors of its poor fighting ability were unfounded. Nevertheless, Johnston made a readjustment, swapping one of its Georgia brigades with A. W. Reynolds's brigade of A. P. Stewart's division. Yet Reynolds's command also had its problems. Composed of two Virginia and two North Carolina regiments, it, too, had received bad press concerning its role in the Missionary Ridge disaster.[7]

Stewart commanded a nonhistoric, conglomerate division consisting of the Louisiana brigade, a Georgia brigade formerly of Stevenson's division, and two Alabama brigades. The latter had one regiment that had fought at Shiloh but consisted mostly of outfits organized in the spring of 1862 and three regiments that had transferred to the army from garrison duty in Mobile in early 1863. It was a sound division but had not yet coalesced.[8]

Some 120 pieces of artillery (the balance was at Kingston, Georgia, so that the horses could graze) were parked to the right of the parade line in the review. The long arm had come a far distance since one-third of its guns had been captured at Missionary Ridge. New consignments of twelve-pounder Napoleon guns and fresh artillery horses had been received by rail, which had measurably assisted in

Sanders Myers of the Fourth Florida was severely wounded and captured at Missionary Ridge. (Florida State Archives)

getting the batteries back to combat trim. Manigault, though generally giving the artillery low marks in performance, was impressed with Dent's Confederate Battery, Garrity's Alabama Battery, and Howell's Georgia Battery. Many of the cannoneers did not like Johnston's new battalion structure, one grumbling, "Our time is more employed in details etc. than when we were only an independent company."[9]

Most of Major General Joseph Wheeler's cavalry were at Kingston or on outpost duty, but what horsemen were present were to the
left of the line in the review. A few outfits, such as the Seventh
Alabama Cavalry and the Fifth Georgia Cavalry, recently transferred up from Florida, had no combat experience, but most of the
other troopers were veteran campaigners. A core of regiments had
ties with the army predating the 1862 Kentucky Campaign. The
most renowned of these was the Eighth Texas Cavalry, better known
as Terry's Texas Rangers. With an aura of superiority, one of their
number concluded: "The most of our cavalry are Georgians, Tennesseans, & Alabamians & as they are . . . indifferent riders we do not
estimate them highly." Most of the infantry held the cavalry in
contempt. In expressing his disdain, a Florida lieutenant, writing
of a February 1864 skirmish before Dalton, noted that the gray
troopers "fired one round at them [enemy] when about 1,000 yards
off and retreated shamefully. We had to get behind trees and stumps
to keep from being run over by them."[10]

About a month earlier and a week distant by rail, Lieutenant
General Leonidas Polk's corps was reviewed at Demopolis, Alabama. Called the Army of Mississippi, it was soon to be merged
into the Army of Tennessee as a third corps. The occasion of the
March 27, 1864, review was the arrival of a special train of women
that had come up from Selma. Both W. W. Loring's and Samuel
French's divisions were ordered into town.

Loring's division held one Alabama and two Mississippi brigades
and was the first to pass in review. A few outfits hailed from Breckinridge's old Reserve Corps at Shiloh. The Third Mississippi contained
fishermen, oystermen, and sailors from the Gulf coast, as well as half
a dozen regiments of Fort Donelson exchangees and five regiments
recruited in the spring of 1862. One unit, the Fifty-seventh Alabama,
was not organized until the spring of 1863 and had never seen
combat, but most of the troops were veterans, having seen action
at the battles of Corinth and Champion Hill. Lieutenant Colonel
Walter R. Roher, who witnessed the review, particularly praised the
Twelfth Louisiana of Tom Scott's brigade as being "composed of
Louisiana's best young men, such men as never desert nor run
away," although he dismissed the balance of the brigade as "some
Ala. Conscript regiments." W. S. Featherston's Mississippi brigade,
he thought, was "dressed [aligned] badly and did not pass well."[11]

Captain Calvin H. Walker and Sergeant James J. Walker, both of the Third Tennessee, were captured at Fort Donelson. (Herb Peck)

French's division was next in review. Roher believed the first brigade, mostly Texans, was "good in a fight but [they] are wild and wreckless and troublesome, hard to manage." There were also two North Carolina regiments in the brigade, one of which, the Thirty-ninth, had a company of Cherokee Indians. The pride of the division, indeed of the corps, was the Missouri brigade. With roots extending back to the old Missouri State Guard, the men, according to Roher, "fight better, drill better and look better than any other men in the army, clean clothes, clean faces and all in uniform and every man in *the step*." Like the Missourians, the men of C. W. Sears's Mississippi brigade were veterans of the siege of Vicksburg who had been captured and exchanged.[12]

Finishing out the corps were the horsemen of Brigadier General W. H. "Red" Jackson's cavalry division, consisting of Mississippians and Alabamians and one brigade of Texans. The latter troops had been dismounted when they crossed the Mississippi River in the spring of 1862 and fought at Corinth as dismounted cavalry. Much to their satisfaction, they were subsequently remounted. Unfortunately, Jackson's troopers were no better esteemed by the infantry than Wheeler's divisions. During the Atlanta Campaign, a Mississippi soldier jotted: "They [Jackson's division] are in pursuit of them [enemy] but they are so worthless that no one expects anything to be done."[13]

These, then, were the corps of the Army of Tennessee. Six regiments of infantry regulars, perhaps thirty-five hundred men, had never pulled a trigger, but the vast majority were veterans in the truest sense. Forty-nine regiments of infantry (28 percent of the total) had been captured, some more than once, and were now back fighting again. Despite the uneven quality of the divisions, the army that coalesced that spring was far superior, both in experience and in the fighting efficiency of the men, to its previous level. True, these men had lost battles, but they were battle hardened and combat smart. It was with a sense of destiny that an Alabamian wrote: "I can't get rid of the idea that the Army of Tennessee will this year decide the fate of the Confederacy."[14]

I

Certainly a Rough Looking Set

In September 1863 two divisions of Lieutenant General James Longstreet's corps of Robert E. Lee's Army of Northern Virginia reinforced the Army of Tennessee. One of Bragg's cannoneers was
stunned when he first laid eyes on the veterans from Virginia. "Our
first impression was partly caused by the color of their uniform, but
more by its uniformity, and the superior style of their equipments, in
haversacks, canteens, and knapsacks. This contrast between them
and Gen'l Bragg's motley, ragged troops was striking in the extreme.
If this command was a specimen of Lee's troops, they are certainly
superior to the troops of the Army of Tennessee, *in dress.*"[1]

The difference between the soldiery of the two armies was more
than cosmetic. Thomas L. Connelly asserts that the identities of the
Army of Tennessee and the Army of Northern Virginia have been
stereotyped—the former associated with the roughness of the Old

*Seventeen-year-old William Shores, drummer boy of the Sixth Arkansas,
was mortally struck in the Battle of Murfreesboro, with a gunshot wound
to the stomach. (Eleanor S. Brockenbrough Library, Museum of the
Confederacy, Richmond, Va.)*

Southwest and the latter as "an army of planter's sons." Connelly
continues, "For example, in the Virginia army, a man of the coarseness of Jubal Early was considered something of an oddity. In the
Tennessee army, a tobacco-chewing, cursing, hard-drinking general
such as Benjamin F. Cheatham was an accepted fact."[2]

In many respects, the coarseness of a Cheatham or a Nathan
Bedford Forrest represented the norm for the western army. The
genteel plantation living of the Virginia Tidewater was foreign to the
region. Henry Stanley estimated that one-fifth of his regiment, the

Sixth Arkansas, were educated gentlemen, but the balance were rough and untaught, knife-toting backwoodsmen. When an Alabamian first viewed Terry's Texas Rangers, he had to admit that they were "certainly a rough looking set." When one examines the postwar questionnaires of Tennessee troops who served in the Army of Tennessee, a composite profile quickly emerges. The typical enlistee was a nonslaveholding man in his early twenties, born in a small log cabin, with limited public education, who farmed for a living.[3]

In their various attitudes toward soldiering, the differences in the character of the westerners were more subtle. In relating comments about rations, drill, pastimes, and the like, their statements often mirrored those of their eastern counterparts. The western boys, however, had more rough edges, less self-discipline, and fewer of the gentler refinements. After Shiloh, Brigadier General Manigault stated that the army was excessively undisciplined. Although this laxness evaporated somewhat as the men were transformed into hardened veterans, it still remained a problem. As late as the Atlanta Campaign, Lieutenant Robert Gill of the Forty-first Mississippi conceded: "Their [William T. Sherman's] army is as well united as ours and better disciplined." For example, the venereal disease rate in the Army of Tennessee far surpassed that of its sister army in Virginia, a point to be discussed later but one that relates directly to army discipline and control. In one respect, this roughness worked to advantage for there was generally a less pronounced class distinction in the West, resulting in little evidence of strife between the refined and lower classes. Fully three-fourths of the Tennessee questionnaire respondents indicated virtually no awareness of class strife before the war. This, perhaps, may have made the transition to army life smoother than in the Army of Northern Virginia.[4]

A reporter for the *Richmond Dispatch*, who had previously viewed the troops of Virginia and the Carolinas, arrived in Corinth in the spring of 1862 after the Battle of Shiloh. He immediately noticed that the western soldiers lacked the discipline and military rigidity characteristic of those in the Army of Northern Virginia. The officers appeared to him simply to be the toughest men in each outfit. The troops from Louisiana were "small, wiry, quick as squirrels in their motions and thoroughly Gallic in their habits and associations. The men of Alabama and Mississippi are taller, [and] as a general thing less cosmopolized," he observed. The men from Tennessee, Kentucky, Arkansas, and Missouri exhibited a "Sort of don't-care-a-damativeness." The clothing of the troops was distinctive in its lack of uniformity. "Here you see the well dressed gentleman with nothing to mark the soldier but the cartridge box, body belt and shot gun. There is a group of Mississippi boatmen in their slouched hats, cowhide boots, coming up to the knee."[5]

Because of their less defined class structure, westerners viewed slavery somewhat differently than did soldiers from Virginia and South Carolina. The Tennessee questionnaires concluded that before the war, in the words of one, "slaves and all worked together white and black." There appears to have been a consensus among slaveholders and nonslaveholders that the institution was not a part of a social system that affected only the wealthier classes. Slavery existed within geographical pockets, and in those areas, according to several respondents, almost every family owned at least a few slaves. No letters or diaries gave the preservation of the institution as a motivation for enlisting. Westerners were much more likely to mention protection of their homes and social enthusiasm as reasons for joining.[6]

One historian has done a study of Yankee soldiers of the West who served in Sherman's March to the Sea. Although they exhibited a wide range of views on the subject of black contraband, the Federals were unquestionably more intrigued with blacks than were western Rebels. Perhaps reflective of their nonentity status, blacks were rarely mentioned in the communications of the latter. When they were discussed, it was usually in a paternalistic tone, portraying them as children. Wrote S. R. Simpson of the Thirtieth Tennessee on June 17, 1864: "The niggers are enjoying themselves finely dancing round big log fires and playing their home made flutes." Western Rebels, like Southerners generally, had little interaction with blacks. Those encountered within the context of army life were usually personal body servants or cooks, who adopted, if less than genuinely, the attitudes of whites. "Our Reg't. has had 60 negroes with it all through the war & none has run away. They have been taught to despise the Yankees and do so. You can't make one of our black boys madder than by calling him a 'fool abolitionist,'" remarked a Texas Ranger.[7]

Very few men in the ranks ever knew of Major General Cleburne's

1864 proposal to enlist slaves in the Confederate army. Captain
Thomas Key was one who did; he was told by Cleburne himself.
"The idea of abolishing the institution at first startles everyone, but
every person with whom I have conversed readily concurs that
liberty and peace are paramount questions and is willing to sacrifice
everything to obtain them. All, however, believe the institution a
wise one and sanctioned by God," he wrote. Even if there was a
consensus, as Key claimed, it appears to have been more an accep-
tance of the end of slavery than an embracing of the arming of
blacks.[8]

The intense racism that festered just beneath the surface emerged
late in the war, when westerners encountered black soldiers. The
first such instance was during the 1864 Tennessee Campaign, when
the Union garrison at Dalton, Georgia, was captured. "Some of the
soldiers were very anxious to kill them [black troops]. But as they
surrendered without fighting the men were not allowed to kill none
only those who attempted to get away were shot by guards. The
negroes had to obey the orders of the guards very strictly or they
were shot immediately," related a Georgian. When black troops
were encountered during the Battle of Nashville, the Confederates
reportedly went into a frenzy, yelling, "no quarter—to niggers."
Those Rebels captured by blacks acted as though they had been
particularly disgraced.[9]

It is impossible to determine the extent of illiteracy in the Army of
Tennessee, but a brief though illuminating piece in an Atlanta newspaper suggests that it may not have been as great as popularly
believed. The article revealed that the soldiers mailed 502,114 letters
at the Army of Tennessee Post Office in the quarter ending June 30,
1864. This number averaged to a surprising 5,517 letters a day
during a time when two out of three months were spent in active
combat. Surviving letters, however, are clear evidence that semi-
illiteracy, especially among privates and noncommissioned officers,
was widespread.[10]

Although a rough image represented the norm for westerners, this
view is one-sided, for the Army of Tennessee cannot be fully
understood without examining its components. As the Tennessee-
Arkansas core of regiments was expanded to include Brigadier Gen-

In early February 1862 Private Reuben McMichael of the Seventeenth Louisiana posed for the photographer at Camp Benjamin, Louisiana. He wrote his sister: "Sis, I sent you my ambrotype two or three days ago as you wrote me to send it to you. I don't believe that you will think it is my picture for I am so fat and ugly." Two months later, on April 6, 1862, McMichael was killed at Shiloh. (Gregg D. Gibbs Collection, Confederate Calendar Works, Austin, Tex.)

eral Daniel Ruggles's Louisiana regiments, Bragg's corps from the
Gulf, and two South Carolina regiments from the Atlantic coast, a dimension of sophistication and discipline was added that has often been overlooked. The Crescent Regiment of New Orleans, known as the Kid Glove regiment, was made up of bluebloods aged eighteen to thirty-five, some of whom brought their servants with them. Many parents, wives, and children followed the regiment to the railroad station in elegant carriages. Other outfits, such as the Orleans Guard Battalion and the Washington Artillery (Fifth Company) of New Orleans and the Twenty-first Alabama of Mobile, represented the flower of Southern society. Many of these outfits ended up in Jones Withers's division after the Shiloh reorganization. According to Brigadier General Manigault, it proved to be the exceptional division in an army that was otherwise lacking in order and discipline, and it exhibited a "complete absence of martial appearance amongst the troops."[11]

Unfortunately, the cultural differences between westerners and Gulf coast soldiers resulted in some friction. One of the more refined soldiers from New Orleans was frankly disgusted with the bulk of A. S. Johnston's army, considering them "unprincipled and very degraded men and officers." P. W. Watson, a member of the Forty-fifth Alabama (a midstate regiment), reciprocated. He noticed that several of the Louisiana regiments "are all dutch and irish & frinch the maddest people in the wirld I think tha stand mo [more] than we can tha have bin raised hard not a hardly anuf to eate in their lives the most of them are from new orleanes." Captain Robert Kennedy of the First Louisiana, a New Orleans regiment, admitted that on the retreat from Kentucky in the fall of 1862, his men suffered from lice as badly as other regiments. Yet they refused to strip their shirts and delouse on the march—"they [Louisianians] prefer to stand the *biting* than acknowledge they were lousy like the 'Yahoos.' " As late as January 1863 a meshing of troops had still not occurred, according to J. Morgan Smith of the Thirty-second Alabama, an outfit organized at Mobile. He openly confessed: "I hate the state [Tennessee], the institutions and the people and really feel as if I am fighting for the Yankee side when I raise my arm in defense of Tennessee soil." He also claimed that there was "an alienation between the troops of the Gulf and the Border States that may grow into something serious."[12]

Thus there was some intra-army conflict. There were differences between soldiers from, say, Mobile and the hill country of north Alabama and those from Memphis and east Tennessee. Still, if homogeneity is defined by states and nationality, the Army of Tennessee was much more analogous than was the Army of Northern Virginia. Approximately 75 percent of the regiments came from four states—Tennessee, Georgia, Alabama, and Mississippi. The Kentucky brigade had the lowest percentage of foreigners in the Confederacy—one-third of 1 percent. What aliens were present in the army were almost exclusively of one nationality—Irish.[13]

The army did not totally lack a cosmopolitan flavor. There were four regiments of ethnics—the Second Tennessee of Memphis, Tenth Tennessee of Nashville, Thirteenth Louisiana of New Orleans, and Twentieth Louisiana. The Second and Tenth Tennessee, both claiming the sobriquet "the Irish Regiment," were the Army of Tennessee's counterparts to the Sixty-ninth New York of the Army of the Potomac. Made up of 750 Catholics from the "Pinch" district of Memphis, the Second was known for its fighting prowess—and not just with the Yankees. It was said that the regimental chaplain, a Father Daly, served mass in the afternoon and settled drunken brawls at night. The regiment served appropriately in Pat Cleburne's division. Six companies of the Thirteenth Louisiana were originally called the Avengo Zouaves and included French, Spaniards, Germans, Italians, Chinese, and Irish. A lieutenant who was assigned to this "international" battalion was shocked to discover that, in addition to their colorful baggy uniforms, almost every member had a black eye, broken nose, or bandaged head. The Twentieth Louisiana had six companies of Irish and four of Germans.[14]

There was a pervasive prejudice against such foreigners. When the Thirteenth Louisiana camped next to his regiment at Corinth, Robert Patrick described them as "a hard looking set composed of Irish, Dutch, Negroes, Spaniards, Mexicans and Italians with few or no Americans, and it is the same with all the regiments collected in or about our towns and cities." Likewise, when several men from his regiment deserted one evening while at Corinth, Thomas Butler concluded: "Except the disgrace to the Regt. I do not care much

*Private John Rulle, a member of the Second Tennessee, was wounded at
Shiloh and later killed at Chattanooga. (Herb Peck)*

about their going for they were Dutchmen and Yankees and were of
very little use to us." After Shiloh, the Spanish and French Guards,
Companies G and K of the Twenty-first Alabama of Mobile, were
transferred to another regiment. "I am glad of it—they were more
trouble than all the rest of the regiment put together, and not worth a
continental shin-plaster for any duty or a fight—In the battle of
Shiloh they discharged their guns away up in the trees—with perfect
safety to the Yankees," testified a lieutenant in the regiment.[15]

The soldiers of the West were largely apolitical. On three occasions President Jefferson Davis visited the Army of Tennessee, and the comments evoked were those of spectators viewing a celebrity. An Alabama soldier at Murfreesboro declared, "we had a jenral revew yesterday and we wer revewed by our prezedent Jef Davis he is a good looken man." Reuben Searcy was thrilled that Davis "passed within ten steps of me and I got a good look at him." James Hall remarked that "you could not tell him from any other *old citizen*." At Chattanooga, a Texas cavalry trooper thought Davis a "fine looking old chap; he looks more like a farmer than a president." Regarding the president's policies or alleged favoritism toward the Virginia army, the letters and diaries were surprisingly silent.[16]

The possible exception was Davis's review of the army on September 25, 1864, at Palmetto, Georgia. By this time Johnston had been replaced, Atlanta had fallen, and troop morale was at a low ebb. Even so, antagonistic expressions toward the president were minimal. Three cheers and a Rebel yell were given as Davis stopped before each regiment. There were a few shouts of "Give us Johnston," indicating the men's desire for his return as commander. Two Florida regiments gave a flag salute but did not cheer, an action that noticeably shocked Davis, who quickly rode off. The Floridians later justified their silent demonstration as a protest against the government policy of not defending certain portions of their state. Still, most of the troops gave a polite, albeit reserved, reception, though one Georgian admitted that the cheering was "pretty weak."[17]

There was a prevailing feeling among westerners that they were up against a tougher breed of Yankee than the army in Virginia. This attitude was noticed by a foreign visitor, Lieutenant Colonel Arthur J. L. Fremantle of the Cold Stream Guards, in June 1863. "It is evident to me that a certain degree of jealous feeling exists between the Tennessee and Virginia armies," he observed. "This one claims to have harder fighting than the Virginia army, and to have opposed the best troops and the best generals in the North." One of Longstreet's soldiers similarly remarked: "Gen. Bragg's men say that the Western Yankees are harder to whip than Eastern Yankees," but he thought "this is all a mistake. All fight alike." Another of Longstreet's soldiers was perplexed at the western mentality: "The difference between this army and Lee's is very striking; when the men move in the army of Northern Virginia, they think they are doing the

proper thing, whether it is backward or forward, and if all the
success is not secured, at all events it is not Lee's fault. Down here the
men seem to feel the wrong thing is being done whatever it be and
when success is secured they attribute it to anybody else than to
Bragg."[18]

Perhaps the most significant question relates to the western spirit.
The army in Virginia had battlefield victories and an unshakable
belief in its commander to sustain it. The Army of Tennessee had
neither, yet it maintained its cohesiveness and returned to fight
again. What qualities enabled the soldiers to come back after the
humiliation of Missionary Ridge, the loss of Atlanta, and the slaughter of Franklin?

Connelly suggests that the answer lies in the intangible grass-roots
élan of the men. An esprit developed not so much on an army or
corps level but on a division or, even more evident, brigade and
regimental level. "Soldiers did not fight for army commanders such
as Braxton Bragg or even corps commanders. Instead they fought for
such outfits as Pat Cleburne's division or Ben Hill's regiment," he
contends. The army's "peculiar spirit" was also derived from the
way state regiments were organized.[19]

Tennessee state regiments, however, were not unique in their
organization. All companies throughout the South were raised on a
county basis or came from a local community and thus were the
objects of intense pride. Some commands, such as the Kentucky
brigade and Cleburne's division, undoubtedly did maintain high
morale. But does the grass-roots élan theory hold up consistently,
especially when by 1863 regiments were often consolidated and
brigades did not maintain organizational continuity? Also, does the
theory hold up as the Tennessee core of the army was expanded to
include other commands—Bragg's corps from the Gulf in 1862,
Stevenson's division after its prisoner exchange from Vicksburg in
1863, and Polk's Army of Mississippi in 1864? Did the men of Jones
Withers's division, George Maney's Tennessee brigade, and Bankhead's Tennessee Battery actually possess a higher esprit than, say,
the men of A. P. Hill's Light Division, the Stonewall Brigade, and the
Richmond Howitzers of the Virginia army? If so, substantive evidence is lacking in the letters and diaries of the western soldiers.

The glue that enabled the Army of Tennessee to maintain its

cohesiveness may not be so mystical and intangible. It was largely rooted in the deterrent value of punishments inflicted on deserters, in other words, coercion; a well-timed religious revival that stressed commitment, sacrifice, and the ability to take hardships patiently; an esprit developed through shared suffering of the soldiers; and the troops' often viewing battlefield losses from a different perspective than that of modern historians. More fundamentally, Connelly is correct when he asserts that the western spirit was derived from "the immense faith of the common soldiers in themselves."[20]

2

We Drill Seven Hours a Day

The Army of Tennessee lacked battlefield victories and confidence in leadership. Its unity was grass roots in nature. Two factors contributed to the development of an army-level esprit: protracted encampments and marathon troop movements. It was in these settings, coalescing on a division and corps level through drill maneuvers and the shared hardships of the march, that the army was imbued with a sense of cohesiveness, if not family. It was perhaps not coincidental that the soldiers ultimately used the imagery of the family when referring to their generals—Joseph E. Johnston became "Uncle Joe" and Benjamin F. Cheatham "Marse Frank," the patriarch of a plantation. It was this bonding at the lower ranks that, in part, sustained the army.[1]

Extensive training was, of course, not confined to the Army of Tennessee, but its development owed much to two protracted winter-spring encampments—at Tullahoma in 1863 and Dalton in 1864—during which the troops underwent a period of intensive refresher training and refinement of skills. Drills on the brigade, division, and corps levels, grand reviews, and sham battles served to harness the individualism of the western soldiers and coalesce them into a cohesive fighting force. These activities also helped restore the faith of the soldiers in themselves on the heels of the Murfreesboro and Missionary Ridge setbacks.

Competitiveness was one tool used in forming unit morale. While at Wartrace (near Tullahoma), Hardee's corps participated in a series of drill competitions. On March 23, 1863, a contest was held for the best-drilled regiment in Breckinridge's division, the prize being a highly coveted palm ornament to be attached on the regimental flag. Three regiments, one from each brigade, were in contention—the Eighteenth Tennessee, Thirteenth and Twentieth Louisiana, and First Florida. Initially the Tennesseans and Floridians were matched in competition, concluding with a bayonet charge across an open field. The men of the First were confident but were unaware that the troops of the Eighteenth had planned something spectacular. Explained a soldier: "They got half way across the field yelling as loud as they could when all at once the Drum rapped and they all dropped [as if to avoid a volley] like they were dead[;] even the Col. and his horse both came down. The horse lay as close [to] the ground as he could and the Col. right behind him. They all lay for several minutes before they got up. It beat everything I ever saw in my life and I never did hear such cheering [from spectators] in my life as was done when they dropped. They got the praise and well they deserve it for they beat anything drilling I ever saw."[2]

The corps competition ultimately came down to a match between the Thirteenth and Twentieth Louisiana and the Seventeenth Tennessee in Cleburne's division. An inspector noted that the Tennesseans were "remarkable for fine stature, manly bearing, and steadiness of movement," but the accuracy with which the Louisianians executed every movement on the double-quick "was unequalled."

The Tennesseans immediately demanded a rematch, bemoaning that they were embarrassed by newly received conscripts.[3]

In the meantime, Brigadier General Daniel Adams, commanding the army's Louisiana brigade, challenged the Kentucky brigade of Breckinridge's division to a contest. In regimental performance, the Sixteenth Louisiana would be matched with the Sixth Kentucky, the Thirteenth and Twentieth Louisiana with the Second Kentucky, the Nineteenth Louisiana with the Fourth Kentucky, and the Thirty-second Alabama with the Ninth Kentucky. In each of the first three contests the Kentuckians were declared the winners, and although active campaigning commenced before the conclusion, the men of the Orphan Brigade never doubted who were the champions.[4]

The artillery of Polk's corps had its own competition at nearby Shelbyville, the prize a beautiful banner. Eleven batteries entered the contest; Captain James Douglas, commander of a Texas battery, boasted to his fiancée: "My boys think that if they have a fair showing they will take the prize—all hands agree the contest will be between my battery and Scott's." On May 1 Douglas disgustedly wrote: "I rather think Scott will get the prize as he is a pet with Bragg's army." He was wrong, for Stanford's Mississippi Battery took the banner.[5]

Grand reviews were the order of the day. In early February 1863, J. P. McCown's division was paraded by General Joseph E. Johnston, then visiting the army at Shelbyville. "It was a grand sight to see so many troops moving at once & the glistening bayonetts, with all the pomp & circumstances of War," thought Lieutenant John Davidson. "It was quite an imposing scene the fine bands the heavy tramp of soldiers and rattling artillery just in our rear and all officers from Liuts to Genls was dressed in their best."[6]

English Lieutenant Colonel Fremantle happened to be in Bell Buckle, Tennessee, and witnessed the performance of Brigadier General St. John Liddell's Arkansas brigade. He noted that they "drilled tolerably well" and were "much better marchers than those I saw in Mississippi." They also advanced in line "remarkably good." He expressed the desire to see them form a square, a favorite British maneuver against cavalry charges, but was told it had not been taught, "as the country did not admit to cavalry charges, even if the Yankee cavalry had stomach to attempt it."[7]

Despite the spectacle they created, the time spent in reviews was frequently not viewed with pleasure by the men. When rain canceled a parade in mid-December 1862, it was rescheduled two days later. At that time a cannoneer in Thomas J. Stanford's battery grumbled: "Again prepare for the review, which takes place at 10 A.M. and requires only ten minutes to complete it, after having kept us two days with horses hitched and all the men at their posts. The men were disquieted with such official indifference to their comfort."[8]

At least the reviews had a tinge of glamour, which was decidedly more than most of the drill exercises provided. The men were exhausted in hours of marching and other fundamentals. "We are under the striked dissipling that I ever saw; we drill seven hours a day. General Claybourne [Cleburne] is our drill officer and the titest [tightest] one you ever saw," related a Texan. Recorded a Mississippian on April 17, 1863: "At 2:00 taken for brigade drill. Drilled hard for an hour rested a half hour and then drilled again to near sunset." A cannoneer revealed that his battery was drilled four to five hours a day in an open field. The men were "always glad when it is over in order to get a rest."[9]

There was also target practice. A soldier in the Thirteenth Tennessee noted in May 1863 that the two companies with which he practiced, E and I, did some fairly accurate shooting. The men hit the target seven times in thirty-one at three hundred yards, fifteen in thirty-four at four hundred yards, and sixteen in seventy at five hundred yards.[10]

At Dalton there was much of the same, although drilling had to be largely canceled throughout most of January 1864 because of extremely cold temperatures. Weather permitting, drills were conducted daily from 10:00 to 11:30 and 2:30 to 4:00, except on Sunday, when there was a 10:00 inspection. One Georgian indicated that by the time his regiment marched five miles to the parade ground, drilled, and returned to camp, "we have done a pretty good day's work." The infantry practiced at ranges up to five hundred yards. Each man was issued fifteen rounds over a period of several days, and the soldiers were required to recover all lead used in practice. Although most of the men considered the exercise a mere pastime, Brigadier General Manigault was convinced that "they learned much more of their weapons, their capability, and how to handle and direct them in those two weeks, than in the previous two and a half years."[11]

The artillery practiced at targets ten feet square at ranges of six hundred to a thousand yards. The results were mixed. On February 5, 1864, Tom Hotchkiss's battalion did some shooting on Tunnel Hill, but, according to one gunner, "three shots only struck." Garrity's Alabama Battery, by contrast, did some remarkable shooting with its four 10-pounder Parrott rifles, two of which were captured at Chickamauga. "I don't think that any of them will surpass it," boasted a lieutenant in the battery.[12]

Training in the cavalry consisted in part of charging an infantry line one hundred yards long composed of dummies dressed in old clothes. Sixty yards behind that line was a row of men on foot, who would shoot blanks as the charge began and then run. The troopers would then ride at full gallop, yelling and slashing at the dummies with their sabers. A disgusted captain concluded: "Very pretty sport to the generals but dangerous and fatiguing to the men doing the work. Day before yesterday several were unhorsed and severely bruised, one poor fellow catching a buckshot from a [supposedly] blank cartridge." He thought Wheeler's discipline "had some good effects, some bad."[13]

The February 4, 1864, grand review awed J. J. Davis of the Forty-sixth Tennessee. "I saw more than I ever saw at one time before. We were drawn up in three lines of troops in 4 ranks each line fully one mile long. General Johnston and his staff rode around each line stopping at each Brigade then dashing off again." To Lieutenant William H. Moore of the Twenty-fifth Alabama it was a "grand sight and sure never to be forgotten." John Jackman was embarrassed to write that the troops generally did not pass in review well: "Some commands came 'ganging' by, like flocks of sheep."[14]

Several sham battles were conducted on a corps level. The one of March 16 fell short of anticipation because of the miserably cold weather, but the one on March 31, featuring the divisions of Hardee's corps, was a grand spectacle. It was witnessed by several thousand women from Atlanta and the surrounding countryside. To add realism, "Dixie" and the "Bonnie Blue Flag" were played on one side and "Yankee Doodle" and "Hail Columbia" on the other. A Tennessee surgeon wrote: "Everything fixed like a real battle was to be fought. Only the cannon & small arms were loaded with paper instead of bullets, but the stir, noise & smoke, and everything looked like a real battle." One private had a different view: "I might have been forced to believe that there was some reality in it had there not been so many ladies, quartermasters, commissaries and their attachees present."[15]

Not all were pleased. Two men were injured, one losing an eye, and Captain Thomas Key was appalled at the waste of powder. One artilleryman, whose battery was chosen to be "captured," admitted that he could "see no fun nor sense in it." Lieutenant Andrew Neal, however, perhaps spoke for many when he commented that he preferred these battles "better than the other kind."[16]

The Army of Tennessee operated on a broad strategical front, and much of the soldiers' time was spent in lengthy travels, in contrast to the Army of Northern Virginia, which, with some exceptions, operated on a limited scale. The western army's bonding and survival mentality were molded in part during these lengthy and arduous trips.

The troops often traveled by rail, and accidents involving troop trains were not infrequent. About a month before Shiloh, a train carrying three companies of the Seventh Mississippi, bound for Corinth, collided with a lumber train, killing twenty soldiers and injuring a like number. In transporting troops to Kentucky in the summer of 1862, a rail accident occurred between Mobile and Montgomery, killing six and injuring thirty members of the Sixth Tennessee. The Twenty-seventh Tennessee had an accident on a trestle near the Alabama-Georgia line that violently threw off a number of men, killing and injuring several. The Fourth Florida was ordered to join Bragg at Chattanooga during that time, but there was a derailment between Pollard, Alabama, and Montgomery. The locomotive and a single car were thrown off, causing injury to eight soldiers. Before Chickamauga, a collision occurred with the "down" train three miles north of Marietta, Georgia. The Fiftieth Tennessee reportedly suffered losses of eighteen killed and seventy-five wounded.[17]

Typically, however, the men were involved in grindingly tiresome

marches. When the Louisiana Washington Artillery (Fifth Company) went overland from Grand Junction to Corinth in early 1862, one of its number related: "Some of the men did not ride any part of the way, desiring to test themselves, others only occasionally and a few walking but very little." After Shiloh, a Louisiana soldier wrote that he had had his "first experience in real campaign marching and I found it far more heavy and toilsome than I had supposed . . . the order constantly coming in our ears 'close up there—close up' or 'not so fast up front.'" Describing the withdrawal from Corinth, a lieutenant in the Twenty-first Alabama wrote that "the heat was like an oven, and we passed a fine little stream with only a ten minute's halt." A soldier of the Thirty-eighth Tennessee told of a similar experience: "By 12 M., our men are so exhausted they all begin to fall back and many are compelled to lay down on the roadside. Our suffering from [lack of] water is terrible. Many are falling down from attacks of congestion of the brain or sunstrokes. Our ambulances are all crowded with the poor sufferers."[18]

If any journey was viewed pleasantly by the men, it was the trek from Tupelo to Chattanooga in the summer of 1862. The infantry, some twenty-five thousand troops, went via rail from Tupelo to Mobile, Montgomery, Atlanta, and Chattanooga. The first soldier arrived on July 20, 1862, just six days after departure. Meanwhile, the wagon train, artillery, and cavalry went overland through central Alabama and northern Georgia by the ordinary dirt roads. They were accompanied by the First Louisiana as an infantry escort. The 430-mile trip required twenty-four days of travel.

In dozens of towns the troops were received royally by supportive citizens. One Tennessean humorously recalled that when his regiment, which had been reduced by sickness and casualties, marched through the streets of Mobile, many citizens laughed and asked why it was so small. Came the reply: "At Shiloh an Alabama regiment in front of us stampeded and killed half our number!" In LaGrange, Georgia, there were a "number of ladies looking for the 41st Georgia Regt. they having quite a number of friends and relatives in that Regt." One infantryman noted that all along the track groups of young girls threw Confederate flags, peaches, and apples, and at Marietta there was "an opera troup of young ladies [who] sang finely." In Atlanta hundreds of cheering women stood on the railroad platform with fruits and provisions for the soldiers as the trains rolled in. The overland column received similar treatment, with frequent picnics and dances along the route. A correspondent who accompanied the column reported that at every camp they were visited by civilians, especially women. Robert Bliss, who was with the wagons, remarked: "I call my trip my furlough from Tupelo to Chattanooga."[19]

The letters and diaries written during that time concentrated on two themes—geography and women. Floridian Washington Ives missed the moss on the trees, which disappeared north of Columbus, Georgia. George Winchester believed that Tuscaloosa was "a rather lonely, deserted place, with the relics of former pretension only." S. R. Simpson was impressed with Montgomery, although the crops in the surrounding countryside looked pitiful because of the recent drought. Atlanta, he thought, was "quite a city." Once in Chattanooga, some of the men hiked to the top of Lookout Mountain to enjoy the view. "Saw the names of some friends carved in the rocks," related one of Bragg's soldiers. Outside Chattanooga, the troops labored to get across Walden's Ridge, but one soldier thought the spectacular view was worth the trouble: "From the top of the mountain was one of the greatest views imaginable. Chattanooga lay way off in the distance, the smoke of the houses and manufactories circling up to the skies. The Tennessee River rolled along between the ranges of mountains for miles."[20]

More than the countryside caught the attention of the men. A Texas Ranger, stunned at the poverty he saw in northern Alabama, commented that he had seen "more big, fat, barefooted girls than I ever saw in my whole life." Cannoneer John Magee was thrilled at the "many pretty girls eager to see the cannon," although at Blue Mountain he believed that the women were "not very good looking." Another artilleryman confirmed the festive atmosphere and related that at an Alabama resort called Shelby Springs the men spent several hours "flirting with the girls," many of whom were refugees from New Orleans.[21]

As the army snaked through portions of east Tennessee and Kentucky, however, the troops were dismayed to discover a populace with staunch Union sentiment. "I have not seen a house fit to live in since we left Chattanooga, nor more than two or three honest

*Private Wright P. Sandige of the Seventeenth Tennessee was a participant
in the 1862 Kentucky Campaign. He was slightly wounded at Perryville.
(C. E. Avery)*

looking men, the women are still worse, such looking people as you would suppose traitors to be made of," commented artilleryman James Searcy. Witnessed Bolling Hall: "The people here [Cumberland Gap] are very hostile. They all openly confess their love for the Yankees. You find one in twenty who is true to the South." A Tennessean noticed a change in the social atmosphere as soon as he crossed the Cumberland River. "We were received with no demonstrations of joy; on the contrary, the people look sad and downcast, and I feel as if we were truly in the enemy's country," he explained.[22]

The veterans dispensed with many nonessentials on the march, resulting in a stripped-down, less polished, but more practical look. Explained a soldier in July 1863: "We got orders yesterday to throw away all our clothing but one suit[.] We aren't allowed to have but one pair of pants and have them on, one pair of drawers, two shirts, and one pair of socks."[23]

In June 1863 English Lieutenant Colonel Fremantle described Liddell's Arkansas brigade as being adequately clothed "but without any attempt at uniformity in color or cut; but nearly all were in gray or brown coats and felt hats. I was told that even if a regiment was clothed in proper uniform by the government, it would become parti-colored again in a week, as the soldiers preferred wearing the coarse homespun jackets and trousers made by their mothers and sisters at home. . . . Most of the officers were dressed in uniform which is neat and serviceable viz, a bluish gray frock coat of a color similar to Austrian yagers."[24]

Despite wear and tear, clothing supplies appear to have remained adequate throughout the Atlanta Campaign. A Georgian indicated that he had "clothes a plenty," and a Mississippian revealed that he could "draw all kinds of Clothing from the Government." Writing from Atlanta in August 1864, one Southerner admitted that some of the men were "in rags," but he wondered "why they cannot get clothing from home as I do?" Shortages were often the result of the men's carelessness. On the march, veterans were quick to toss away unwanted items. "There is a great many men in so large an army who neglect themselves and throw away their clothing. This necessarily looks shabby," observed a cavalryman. A Georgian remarked that "as to Co. G being naked that is not so all have got clothes that wouud carry them some threw their clothes but all have got clothes & shoes."[25]

Confederates captured at Missionary Ridge are shown at the Chattanooga rail depot awaiting transport. A Federal officer wrote that "they are a hard looking lot of men without overcoats" and with "dirty blankets marked generally 'U.S.'" The soldiers standing on the mound are Federal guards. (Library of Congress)

The men could do without excess clothing in summer, but on the march shoes were a necessity. Spot shortages occurred throughout the fall and winter of 1863. A captain in the Twentieth Alabama reported that fifty men in his battalion could not fight at Missionary Ridge because they were shoeless. Even though 4,200 pairs were received at Dalton in January 1864, General Joseph E. Johnston still counted 13,300 shoeless men in the infantry and artillery alone. He added: "The Fifth Regiment [Tennessee?] is unable to drill for want of shoes. The Eighth Regiment will soon be unfit for duty from the same cause; and indeed, when shoes are supplied, the men will be unable to wear them for a long while, such is the horrible condition of their feet from long exposure." Colonel Bolling Hall of the Fifty-ninth Alabama reported that he had 180 men with no shoes and another 150 who wore only pieces of leather that left the foot half exposed. Yet there is evidence to suggest that by the spring of 1864 the problem had been largely resolved. On March 7, for example, Stevenson's division of 6,631 men present listed only 137 as shoeless, down from 2,284 the previous December.[26]

A common complaint as the army moved toward Atlanta was the

lack of opportunity to bathe and change clothing. "At times we are the dirtiest and filthyest looking creatures you ever saw," confessed a lieutenant, while a cannoneer remarked that "I am as dirty as a hog—no clean clothes—all used up." William Stanley admitted to his wife in Alabama: "I have not changed my clothes in nearly five weeks. You may draw an idea what fix my clothes are in." Even on those rare occasions when there were opportunities to wash, there was little soap.[27]

For two weeks in June 1864 it rained almost incessantly, adding to the misery and bogging down both armies. A Georgian wrote his wife on the twenty-first: "I never was in so much rain it rains enciently our clothing & Blankets havent been dry in several days & the roads is all most so we can not travel atal." To a North Carolina lieutenant, the mud was "like batter & from 3 to 12 inches & no chance to shun it." A Mississippian informed his wife that she had "no idea how fast 60,000 or 70,000 men and horses with wagons will work up the mud when it is raining." Attempting to extricate his cannon from the mud during a night march, remarked a member of Cowan's Mississippi Battery, was "all together . . . the worst night march I ever experienced in the army."[28]

Unlike the 1862 march to Kentucky, Hood's 1864 trek to Tennessee was a depressing and sobering affair, creating a mood that was reflected in the letters and diaries. There were no cheering throngs along the route. Indeed, a Texan observed, "All the citizens have run off." On October 18, J. W. Ward of the Twenty-fourth Mississippi thought that he was in Cherokee County, Alabama, but he was uncertain because the soldiers had not "seen any citizens in some time to tell us." All they observed were scenes of destruction and decline. "This country [Tennessee Valley] is level and you can have an open view as far as your eyes will let you see," noted William Berryhill. "But their is little of it in cultivation now. The Yankees have destroyed every thing but the Negro cabins and I do not recollect seeing a dwelling house left standing on the road from Courtland [Alabama] to this place [Tuscumbia]." Captain Key saw nothing in the Tennessee Valley "except wrecks of palaces and devestated plantations." The business section of Tuscumbia, he noted, was "burned and all streets looking weather-worn and delapidated." Captain Samuel T. Foster thought that Waynesboro, Tennessee, was "a very nice little town, but nearly ruined by the war," and Wash-

Twenty-one-year-old Private N. H. Martin of the Twenty-second
Tennessee wears the slouch hat that was so popular in the Army of
Tennessee, as opposed to the kepi. (Margaret Harrison Collection,
Confederate Calendar Works, Austin, Tex.)

ington Ives described the surrounding countryside as "very poor."
Captain E. M. Graham of the Twelfth Louisiana thought that Wayne
County was a desolate place. "The roads are very rough today this
place is quite a wilderness country. The people are all Union, with
very few exceptions," he wrote.[29]

Thomas Roane, surgeon of the Fifty-first Tennessee, was impressed with the speed with which the column moved. "We are doing the finest marching I ever saw from 15 to 20 miles a day with ease on rough roads although many of the men are barefoot & their feet raw & blistered," he wrote on October 21, 1864. "We have a large train of Supply Wagons to haul meal & bacon & drive our beeves along ahead of us. We have here [Gadsden] 7000 beef cattle & Eat from 250 to 300 a day. We have also a Pontoon train of 80 boats which are fitted as wagons like the body of a wagon. . . . So you see we are well prepared for traveling."[30]

So long was the march that the troops apathetically gave up on any attempt to second-guess their destination. A participant conceded that he had "no idea where we will go before we are done. If you will notice in my other letters I have ventured several times to say where we are going but have missed so often that I have quit saying what I think." A Texan, writing the same month, remarked that it "has got to be a matter of indifference as to where we are going. There are but few men who make any inquiries or seem to care anything about it."[31]

Crossing a creek often meant taking a plunge, despite the weather. It was a cold day in October 1864 when S. D. Lee's (Polk's old) corps waded through a waist-deep creek. The men stripped to their drawers and tied their clothes, haversacks, and knapsacks around their necks and, according to one hardy soul who took the jump, went "up to their armpits, singing and hollooing at the top of their voices. Only think of 8,000 *nude* soldiers wading a creek under these circumstances."[32]

Perhaps the most notable event on the journey was the crossing of the Tennessee River at Florence, Alabama, on November 13–15, 1864. Fifty pontoons, each holding twenty men, were initially crossed over to secure the opposite bank. The bridge, when completed, was a thousand yards in length. Each brigade crossed by fours, with the band playing at the head of the column. One Southerner observed that it was the "longest Pontoon bridge I have ever seen," and at a distance it appeared as though "the men were walking on water." All did not go entirely as planned. Several pontoons sank when a herd of cattle was crossed on the thirteenth, dumping two mules and forty-five steers into the river.[33]

During the Tennessee Campaign, issues of winter clothing and

shoes, which by then were in great demand, were made at Gadsden,
Tuscumbia, and Florence, Alabama. Shoes, however, remained in
short supply. B. P. Weaver of the Forty-second Georgia wrote on
November 3: "This march has nearly worn out my shoes. Do not
know what I will do if I get barefooted for I could not march at all
then." Another Georgian was even more desperate: "Father, I am
plom barefooted. I haint got a sine [sign] of a shoe on my foot nor I
dont no when I will hav." The men were ordered to sew shoes of beef
hide, putting the hair next to the foot. This makeshift arrangement
apparently worked well but caused a terrible odor after the first day
or two. Clothing picked up on the Franklin battlefield proved adequate to get the army through most of December. "I cant scarcle see
a man but what has a good Yankee blanket," observed G. W. Athey.
James Lanning of the Eighteenth Alabama noted that after Franklin
he gave away much clothing because he could not carry it all. "I
could have gathered a thousand Dollars worth of clothing etc," he
boasted. Yet by December 9 he was writing, "Many a poor soldier is
suffering for want of shoes & other clothing."34

Colonel Elliston Capers of the Twenty-fourth South Carolina kept
an accurate account of the clothing his unit received during the
campaign. At Gadsden his 285 men, 20 of whom were barefoot,
received 21 blankets, 112 pairs of pants, 74 pairs of shoes, 44
jackets, 82 pairs of socks, 37 shirts, and 46 pairs of drawers. "This
issue by no means supplied our necessities, but relieved the most
needy," he reported. By the time his regiment arrived at Tuscumbia,
23 men were shoeless. At that place 64 jackets, 16 pairs of pants, 38
pairs of socks, 24 blankets, and 28 pairs of shoes were received,
which the colonel believed to be "a very inadequate supply." At
Florence another 45 pairs of pants, 50 pairs of socks, 26 shirts, 34
pairs of drawers, and 16 pairs of shoes were received.35

Major General Bate reported that his division was well shod when
it departed Florence. "I pressed [confiscated] every pair of shoes
which could be found for them, which partially supplied the command," he related. Yet before the division reached Nashville, he
estimated that one-fourth of his men were shoeless, "many with
bleeding feet," in the sleet and snow.36

Following the Nashville disaster, the army retreated to Tupelo.
From there the infantry took railroad cars to North Carolina via

Mobile, Montgomery, Columbus, and Augusta. "Our Brig [Hiram B. Granbury's] behaved shamefully all the way around from Tupelo Miss to Raleigh, N.C.," admitted a Texan. "The Boys had not been paid off for ten months they would not issue tobacco and that made the boys angry They would break open stores, get the Tobacco and Lichors. I was not in the game." A reporter at Augusta was stunned when he saw the depleted ranks and tattered condition of Cheatham's division, and another correspondent testified that there had been large-scale straggling all along the route.[37]

The extensive drilling at the Tullahoma and Dalton encampments, coupled with the common suffering encountered during extensive campaign marching, helped shape the personality of the Army of Tennessee. Such experiences molded the esprit of the army and coalesced the men into a cohesive unit. The training was also of significant value because far fewer of the men in the ranks of the Army of Tennessee had the experience or previous training enjoyed by those who served in the Army of Northern Virginia.

3

We Have Drew the Finest Arms

In the first year of the war, the most serious shortage confronting Albert Sidney Johnston's fledgling army was the dearth of small arms. The state of Tennessee possessed only 8,000 antiquated muskets, half of which were unserviceable, 185 percussion muskets, and 350 Hall's carbines, all seriously damaged. Some of these arms were farmed out to various contractors to be altered to percussion. In September 1861, Brigadier General William H. Carroll, in east Tennessee, seized more than 2,000 country rifles and had them sent to Memphis, Nashville, and Murfreesboro for alteration. By mid-December he had received back only 400 shotguns and flintlocks from Memphis, and these he described as "almost worthless."[1]

The volunteers' reaction to obsolete muskets was decidedly negative. In June 1861 Enoch Hancock of the Third Tennessee, at Camp Cheatham, informed his daughter: "We are not verry well prepared for fighting at present as we have nothing but the old fashioned muskets to fight with. We had them boxed up once and sent to Nashville expecting to get improved arms but failed in getting them which came as a great dissatisfaction among the troops." James T. Mackey of the Forty-eighth Tennessee had a similar experience. He related: "Received our guns to-day; they are better suited for squirrel hunting than military purposes. They all needed repairs and were taken to a shop in the city for that purpose."[2]

Throughout the fall of 1861, fully one-fourth of the corps at Bowling Green were unarmed. Indeed, Johnston considered disbanding some of his unarmed regiments. Some assistance was received when John Breckinridge was able to acquire a thousand smoothbore percussion muskets from his old political friend Governor John Letcher of Virginia. Major General Mansfield Lovell, commanding at New Orleans, also forwarded five hundred shotguns. The countryside was scoured for anything that would shoot, but it was estimated that one-fourth of these weapons were worthless, even after repair.[3]

Some outfits arrived with their own weapons, but there was usually such a conglomerate that it created chaos in supplying ammunition. Terry's Texas Rangers reported at Bowling Green in October 1861 with no fewer than twenty varieties and calibers of weapons, mostly six-shooters and shotguns. The next month the Seventh Texas, 750 strong, detrained at Clarksville, Tennessee. Although these troops reportedly were well armed, Colonel John Gregg noted that the entire regiment actually had only 377 weapons—123 shotguns (25 in disrepair), 150 mixed rifles (48 in poor condition), and 104 percussion muskets, supplied by the state of Louisiana as the regiment passed through.[4]

The situation remained bleak throughout the winter. The Tenth Tennessee at Fort Henry, described as the "best equipped regiment of the command," was armed with Tower of London muskets used by the militia in the War of 1812. The Fifty-second Tennessee, at Henderson Station, reported having only one hundred arms, all shotguns, for its 760 troops. The east Tennessee wing of the army was probably the worst off. There were four regiments at Chattanooga and Knoxville with 3,400 troops, only 1,750 of whom were armed, and most of them with flintlocks and muskets. This defi-

*Private A. H. Smith of the Fifty-first Tennessee enlisted in March 1862,
and this tintype was probably taken about that time. He holds an 1816
flintlock musket and bowie knife. (Herb Peck)*

ciency played a major role in the subsequent defeat of Johnston's
right wing at Mill Springs in January 1862. When the Seventeenth
Tennessee fired its flintlocks at a range of two hundred yards, the
balls fell harmlessly short. Further complicating the issue was the
rain, which made the flints useless. Some of the soldiers of the

Twentieth Tennessee, after half a dozen futile attempts to discharge their weapons, smashed them against trees and fence posts in frustration.[5]

As late as the Battle of Shiloh in April 1862, many of Johnston's regiments, such as the Sixth and Seventh Arkansas, were improperly equipped with sporting rifles, nondescript muskets, and flintlocks. When the Seventeenth Tennessee received some better arms, the colonel offered his old flintlocks to the Thirty-seventh Tennessee. They were an improvement on nothing and were accepted. It was estimated that not one-third of the cavalry had arms, and those who did had a "medley of pistols, carbines, and shotguns, chiefly the latter." Some weeks after Shiloh, nearly 53 percent of A. P. Stewart's division still shouldered old smoothbore percussion muskets, and 103 had flintlocks. The Forty-seventh Tennessee had ten different calibers in use.[6]

Johnston eagerly sought imports through the blockade, but the Confederate government controlled distribution of arms. The arm specifically desired was the highly efficient English-made .577 Enfield rifle, a weapon renowned for its accuracy and range. In September 1861 Johnston pleaded with the secretary of war for 30,000 Enfields that were rumored to have come on the steamer *Bermuda*. In truth, only 3,500 had arrived and of that number only 1,000 were sent to Nashville. On November 14, the general was gratified to learn of another shipment destined for his army—3,760 Enfields from the cargo of the *Fingal* at Savannah. "You see you are not forgotten," noted the secretary of war. The weapons were soon being passed out among the troops. The Second Arkansas and First Arkansas Battalion were two of the first units to receive Enfields. "Our new weapons were handed out to camp this evening, and it has put the men in excellent humor," reported Captain Elliott Fletcher of the latter.[7]

The popular Enfields continued to come in through the blockade. In February 1862 the War Department ordered 3,600 arms to the West, including 2,000 Enfields from the steamer *Kate*. The Ninth Mississippi at Corinth was issued 800 of these, and the balance went primarily to regiments in Breckinridge's Reserve Corps, such as the Fifth Kentucky, Seventeenth Tennessee, and Twentieth Tennessee. A member of the Sixth Mississippi wrote: "We have received a large number of Enfield rifles, Co. B & A have to take these as they are the wings of the Regt." Likewise, a proud sergeant in the First Tennessee wrote on March 29, 1862: "We have Drew the finest Arms in the Confederate states they were made last year they are Enfield rifles." In March 700 more Enfields brought in by the *Florida* were sent to Johnston, but they did not arrive in time to be used at Shiloh. In February rumors circulated that a shipment of 15,000 Enfields had come aboard the *Victoria* at New Orleans, and Johnston promptly requested the entire shipment. Once again the rumors were false; the *Victoria* carried mostly powder and only 150 arms.[8]

The Confederates at Shiloh had perhaps 6,500 Enfields. On April 1, 1862, Hardee reported that Hindman's and Cleburne's brigades possessed 1,060 Enfields. These arms were also available through other sources than England. Cook & Brother of New Orleans manufactured rifles on the Enfield pattern, and some, such as those issued to the Twenty-seventh Mississippi, ended up in Johnston's army. The Forty-seventh Tennessee arrived at the end of the first day's battle at Shiloh. Although unarmed, the troops picked up enough Enfields on the battlefield that night to equip the regiment.[9]

Although not as widely used in the Army of Tennessee as its English counterpart, the U.S. .58 Springfield rifle was also available. In range and accuracy it was comparable to the Enfield but could be obtained only through capture from the Union army. After Shiloh, the Thirteenth Tennessee reported that it was armed with 429 Springfields, making it one of the first Confederate regiments, if not the first in the West, that was fully equipped with this weapon.[10]

The most lucrative source of small arms throughout the last half of 1862 was capture from the Federals. The Kentucky Campaign netted the Confederates 15,000 arms and 2 million cartridges. After the capture of a Federal division at Richmond, Kentucky, some 800 percussion muskets in Cleburne's division were exchanged for Springfield rifles. The Fourth Tennessee fully supplied itself with Enfields picked up on the Perryville battlefield. In late October 1862, a member of the Texas Rangers boasted: "This Regt. has captured over 1000 breech-loading guns & six shooters since the battle of Shiloh & is finely armed." An additional 6,000 arms were bagged at Murfreesboro.[11]

Throughout 1863–64 the primary ordnance problem confronting

*The revolver in the belt of Private W. F. Henry of the Sixth Tennessee was
most likely a prop furnished by the photographer. (Herb Peck)*

the Army of Tennessee was not quantity, as it had been earlier in the
war (by the spring of 1863 there were 4,200 arms in storage at the
Chattanooga and Tullahoma depots), but modernizing the armament. Specifically, this meant a concerted effort to phase out all
smoothbores in favor of rifles, a task the Federals had completed
before the Battle of Murfreesboro. The standard smoothbore percussion musket had a range of about 100 yards. By contrast, the
rifled musket was not only more accurate but also had an effective

*Armed with carbines and revolvers are Privates John W. Montjoy and
Jarret Montjoy of the Third Kentucky Cavalry of Wheeler's Corps.
(Robert H. Ahlstrom Collection, Confederate Calendar Works, Austin,
Tex.)*

range of 400 yards and could kill up to 1,000 yards. In May 1863
Hezekiah Rabb of the Thirty-third Alabama informed his wife that
"our Regt & the 16th Ala Regt are all armed with the very best
guns. . . . We have Spring Field and Enfield Rifles. The guns shoot
from 150 to 900 yards they are marked to shoot with accuracy 900
yards & we have tried them at a target of 550 yards they shoot
Elegantly." Improved firepower became an increasingly important
issue for the Army of Tennessee.[12]

An April 1863 report revealed that 44 percent—16,570 of

37,232—of the arms in Bragg's infantry were short-range smooth-bores. Fortunately, at least for the sake of ammunition supply, all were .69 percussion smoothbores—the old mainstay of the Army of Tennessee. Another 37 percent were Enfields and 14 percent were Springfields, the balance being miscellaneous calibers. Included in the latter were 450 .70 Belgian rifles, a notoriously inferior weapon. The cavalry was supplied with a hodgepodge of weapons, including 1,155 smoothbores, 1,796 Enfields, 473 Belgian rifles, 545 Springfields, 1,483 carbines of various calibers, 546 shotguns, 841 miscellaneous rifles, and 663 Austrian rifles, a weapon not as sought after as the Enfield but still effective. In addition, there were 2,114 revolvers.[13]

Complicating the modernizing process was the soldiers' wasteful but appallingly commonplace habit of tossing guns away on the march. Some 4,000 were lost in that manner on the retreat from Murfreesboro and another 4,320 (2,241 from John A. Wharton's and William T. Martin's cavalry brigades alone) when Bragg withdrew from Tullahoma in the summer of 1863. "The stoppage of payments on muster rolls is no means to correct this evil, and unless stringent orders be enacted making commanders of companies directly responsible for this negligence, the evil cannot be corrected," summarized the army chief of ordnance, Colonel Hypolite Oladowski.[14]

During August 1863, Bragg received 1,660 rifles (model unspecified) through Charleston, 1,000 from the cargo of the Harpeth. The Confederate victory at Chickamauga in September netted an additional 8,008 rifles (about 60 percent Springfields and the balance Enfields). There was also a sprinkling of other weapons—70 Spencer rifles, 350 carbines, 22 revolving rifles, and 410 revolvers. Some troops exchanged their smoothbores on the spot. Brigadier General Bate reported that his brigade "went into the fight with [smoothbore] muskets in the hands of one-third of my men, but after the first charge Saturday evening every man was supplied with a good Enfield and ammunition to suit." The Fifth Tennessee of O. F. Strahl's brigade exchanged all its old Belgian rifles for captured Springfields. Thousands of these muskets were damaged and in need of repair, thus requiring weeks of work at the Atlanta and Selma arsenals. In the meantime, the loss of 6,175 arms at Missionary Ridge, mostly

Enfields, largely offset the previous gains. By mid-December, there was a shortage of 4,135 arms.[15]

The problem of uniformity also continued to plague many outfits. In March 1863 the regiments of Brigadier General Lucius Polk's brigade were armed as follows: the Second Tennessee and Fifth Tennessee with Springfields, the First Arkansas and Forty-eighth Tennessee with Enfields, and the Fifth Confederate with .69 smoothbores. There were mixed calibers within some regiments. The Tenth South Carolina, of Manigault's brigade, had one company with Enfields, one with Harpers Ferry rifles, one with Mississippi rifles, and the balance with smoothbores. It was not until after the Battle of Franklin in November 1864 that the regiment was uniformly equipped with Enfields.[16]

On December 20, 1863, Oladowski reported that he was still short 2,603 arms in the infantry, despite the recent shipment of 1,200 repaired arms from the Atlanta Arsenal. A week later he claimed that the number of unarmed men had risen to three thousand because large numbers of men were returning from hospitals in the rear. He urgently requested that 4,000 repaired arms from the Selma Arsenal (apparently part of the Chickamauga lot) be sent him, rather than to the projected trans-Mississippi theater. He was partially successful—1,000 were sent. On March 18, 1864, Captain Marcus Wright promised that his shops could deliver 2,300 repaired arms by April 17.[17]

By the time of the Atlanta Campaign, most of the troops of the Army of Tennessee were well armed. Some 55 percent of the one cavalry and three infantry corps carried Springfield and Enfield rifles, while 32 percent shouldered Austrian rifles. Still, 11 percent were armed with smoothbores and 2 percent (mostly in the cavalry) with a hodgepodge of odd-caliber rifles. Some 359 men still had no weapons.[18]

The soldier in the field also needed basic accoutrements, which were often difficult to obtain. The situation of the Fifth Tennessee was representative. There were 992 men in the regiment in March 1862, but the equipment on hand included only 785 muskets, 781 cartridge boxes, 870 cap boxes, 764 bayonets, 734 bayonet scabbards,

TABLE 1

Supplies Held by the Second Brigade of A. P. Stewart's Division, June 1862

Regiment	Total arms	Cartridge boxes	Knap-sacks	Haver-sacks	Can-teens
5th Tenn.	261	261	141	N/A	326
13th Ark.	215	N/A	187	220	236
31st Tenn.	305	305	223	287	304
33d Tenn.	239	N/A	143	238	220
4th Tenn.	236	278	235	226	253

514 knapsacks, 152 haversacks, and 188 canteens. The figures in Table 1, taken from the June 21, 1862, reports of the Second Brigade of A. P. Stewart's division, reveal that the troops were basically well supplied.[19]

While at Tullahoma, the infantry reported a dearth of bayonets; only half of the troops were supplied with them. Lieutenant Colonel Fremantle noted the shortage but remarked that many of the men had thrown theirs away, "as they assert that have never met any Yankees who could wait for that weapon." The cavalry was also short of sabers; there were only 656 in Wheeler's corps in April 1863. Fremantle remarked that the Fifty-first Alabama Cavalry had both rifles and revolvers but no sabers. There was also a need of cartridge boxes, a condition often caused by the troops themselves. On the Tullahoma retreat, the troops tossed 2,307 cartridge boxes along the roadside.[20]

There seems to have been no shortage of ammunition. By March 1863 the troops had 140 rounds each—40 in the cartridge boxes and 100 in the ordnance wagons. Although well short of the prescribed 200 rounds per man, the supply apparently was adequate. Cheatham's division at Perryville, more actively engaged than any other, expended only 35 rounds per man, and Hardee's corps at Murfreesboro, engaged from early morning until sunset on the first day's battle, expended 40 rounds per man. At Chickamauga, Polk's corps, which was heavily engaged, averaged only 26 rounds per man.[21]

The main supplier of equipment for the Army of Tennessee was
the Atlanta Arsenal. By January 1864 Captain Wright had his shops working at full capacity. He estimated his monthly output to be 100 single sets of artillery harness, 100 sets of cavalry accoutrements, and 500 sets of infantry accoutrements. In April Oladowski insisted that there were 16,941 effectives in Hardee's corps, but the equipment on hand tallied 19,417 cartridge boxes, 18,001 haversacks, 16,888 canteens, and 12,610 knapsacks. There was an average of 83 rounds per man. Yet this information appears inconclusive. Only a couple of weeks earlier, Hood's corps was reporting shortages in all areas. On March 7, 1864, there were on hand 8,828 bayonets (short 6,753), 15,486 cartridge boxes (short 1,110), 15,245 cap boxes (short 1,357), 13,608 knapsacks (short 4,134), and 15,454 haversacks (short 2,546).[22]

Most of the cannon in the long arm of the Army of Tennessee during the first two years of the war were 6-pounder and 12-pounder howitzers cast by local foundries. This is demonstrated by the types of guns that Oladowski turned in to the Atlanta Arsenal between August 1863 and June 1864: two 6-pounders made by Quinby & Robinson of Memphis, one 12-pounder howitzer and three 6-pounders by A. B. Reading & Brother of Vicksburg, one 12-pounder howitzer and four 6-pounders (all iron) by T. M. Brennan & Company of Nashville, nine 12-pounder howitzers and one 3-inch rifle by Tredegar of Richmond, one 12-pounder howitzer by John Clark of New Orleans, two 6-pounders, two 12-pounder howitzers, and six 3-inch rifles by Noble Brothers & Company of Rome, Georgia, one 6-pounder and two 6-pounder rifles by Leeds & Company of New Orleans, and one 12-pounder howitzer by W. J. Hubbard of Richmond.[23]

Captured guns also provided a lucrative source during the latter part of 1862. The Kentucky Campaign and the Battle of Murfreesboro netted the army seventy-seven field guns. A few of these were placed into service, such as two 12-pounder Napoleon guns in Melancthon Smith's Mississippi Battery, trophies from Perryville. Also, seven 6-pounder rifles and two Wiard rifles, taken at Murfreesboro, were used for a time by Bragg's artillery. Four guns bagged at Richmond, Kentucky, were claimed by a new battery organized at that time. Many, however, were shipped throughout the West—ten to east Tennessee and six to north Georgia—to guard railroad trestles and bridges. Also, sixteen were sent to General J. E. Johnston in Mississippi to replace guns lost in the Battle of Jackson.[24]

The army's largest artillery cache of the war was won at Chickamauga. Included in the spoils were thirty-nine fieldpieces, twenty limbers, thirty caissons, and one battery wagon. Some of these guns were issued to Stevenson's division to reequip his three batteries after their prisoner exchange from Vicksburg. These gains were soon offset by the loss of thirty-nine cannon at Missionary Ridge.[25]

The main supplier of cannon to the Army of Tennessee was the Augusta Arsenal, supplemented by guns cast at the Macon and Columbus arsenals. These foundries produced 12-pounder Napoleons, which became the favorite of the western Rebel artillery. By the spring of 1864, all 6-pounders in the army had been phased out and replaced with Napoleons, as well as a sprinkling of Parrott rifles. Most of the latter were cast at Tredegar and the Macon Arsenal, and a few were captured from the Yankees. At Nashville Hood lost sixty-four guns, forty-five of which were of Southern manufacture (mostly government-made 12-pounder Napoleons), and the balance of U.S. make.[26]

The story is told of the Forty-fourth Mississippi at the Battle of Murfreesboro, which arose to attack a battery but had no arms; the men were brandishing only sticks.[27] Such anecdotal stories shroud the truth. Although never as efficiently armed as the Federal troops in the West, the soldiers of the Army of Tennessee had a more sophisticated armament than has been generally appreciated. One thing seems clear. The troops never lost a battle because of a scarcity of arms.

I Am Hearty as a Pig on Half Rations

The western soldier fared well in the way of rations during the early months of the war. A captain stationed at Union City, Tennessee, instructed his parents not to bother mailing any provisions from home, save butter. "We have fried ham, biscuit, and coffee for breakfast, dinner and supper. Sometimes we get peas, beans, onions, and potatoes for dinner." An Alabama diarist acknowledged that many in his regiment, stationed at Knoxville, were better fed in the army than they were at home. When the Eleventh Louisiana reached Columbus in September 1861, its provisions had not yet arrived so for several days the men had to forage. "We can live well enough here if we chose to pay for it," concluded a member.[1]

Before Shiloh, Sergeant B. H. Green of the Washington Artillery, camped at Grand Junction, boasted to his father: "At dinner today we had soup, pork, beans, rice and molasses, in as great quantities as we could eat, besides one big pilot biscuit a-piece." Following the battle, a Texas Ranger admitted, "We live very well in camp, we have plenty of coffee, which was taken from the Yankeys, sugar, meal, flour, bacon and beef, and we can always get chickens and eggs, and butter some times." Samuel Shelton complained that the government ration consisted of "nothing but meat and clamy biscuit with a little coffee." Yet he freely conceded that this was supplemented by purchases from local farmers and packages from home. He concluded that "we do not suffer for anything" in the way of vegetables, chicken, cakes, and butter.[2]

General P. G. T. Beauregard, who briefly commanded the army after Albert Sidney Johnston's death, conducted frequent and sharp exchanges with Commissary General L. B. Northrop in Richmond. He was convinced that the "false view of administration—to say the least—of Colonel Northrop will starve out this army unless I make other arrangements, which I have done." Agents were dispatched to northern Texas and Arkansas, where large herds of cattle were purchased. Part of this supply was later used by Confederate authorities to feed other armies.[3]

There was a temporary shortage of beef following Shiloh. Some eighteen thousand head of cattle from Louisiana, which were supposed to have gone to Beauregard's army, were unavailable following the fall of New Orleans. Regulations called for one pound of beef rations five days out of seven, but the actual issue was only once per week. In lieu of the beef, each man was allowed one-quarter pint of molasses per day and eight ounces of lard every five days. Additionally, there was a higher than regulation issue of both rice and sugar. When the army withdrew from Corinth to Tupelo, the supply of beef increased, the greater portion of the cattle coming from the local vicinity. In June 1862 Lieutenant James Searcy wrote his mother: "For food now we get bacon two pounds to each man a week one pound of fresh beef a day. Yesterday we got pickled beef, the best I have ever had since I left home . . . molasses & salt. So you can see I am not starving." A couple of weeks later, however, another soldier observed that "we get plenty of bread but not plenty of meat, we get plenty of molasses—and plenty of sugar."[4]

Complaints cropped up early regarding the supply of coffee. At Columbus the ration was cut from ten to three pounds per hundred men, which, according to one infantryman, "is just no coffee at all." Yet a complaint to Northrop brought an angry response. He pointed out that on April 17, 1862, Beauregard's army had 1.3 million half rations of coffee and was presently being issued rations larger than the regulations allowed and better than the army in Virginia received. He insisted "that the whole army [Beauregard's] enjoyed this luxury long after the bulk of our people, and there is still a reserve for the sick."5

It was typically the quality, rather than the quantity, of food that was denounced by the men during the early months of the war. A recruit of the Twelfth Tennessee at Columbus said, "Our beef is so tough that we have to boil it nearly all day." Writing from Fort Donelson, Martin Busk complained that "wee don't draw anything but bad beef," and the bread, he claimed, "had but little salt and water and that don't do good." Part of the problem was related to the preservation process. Beef was commonly packed in a strong brine pickled with salt from Avery Island in Louisiana, which, being stronger than the ordinary article, burned the meat. Writing in June 1862, an Alabamian explained: "Sometimes we get pickled beef, but it is so salty we can hardly eat it. We may put it on and boil it half a day and then it will be so tough that we can't chew it."6

Another problem was the shortage of cooking utensils. Cornmeal frequently had to be issued in the men's hats, and cooking was done in old skillets and battered pans. At Fort Donelson General Simon Buckner reported that there was "scarcely any means of cooking." The men thus learned to make do, which led to some ingenious improvisations. A soldier in the 154th Tennessee testified that boards and bark were used as skillets and beef was cooked on sticks. Lacking utensils in his company, Lieutenant William P. Davis, camped in Kentucky in 1861, described how his men twisted biscuit dough on oilcloth and then wrapped it around musket ramrods to cook. Beef was roasted in the ashes.7

The troops cooked in messes of six to nine men. A veteran of the Sixth Tennessee recalled that early in the war nearly every mess in his regiment had a Negro cook. This luxury soon disappeared, and each man took his turn at cooking except in some messes that paid a single man to perform this function. A July 1862 report concluded that the men "mess in small squads and cook badly" but that they had "improved somewhat by the lessons of experience." An attempt to establish large brigade bake ovens while the army was at Tupelo met with mixed results, the quality of the bread often depending on the competence of the bakers. Some companies used small dutch ovens.[8]

Despite some spot shortages, the first sustained period of privation did not occur until the retreat from Kentucky in the fall of 1862. The amount of captured stores the army took with it has been exaggerated. Bragg claimed that a herd of about five thousand cattle was brought back into Tennessee, although other reports place the number closer to two thousand. Even so, the withdrawal was so precipitous that there was little stopping to slaughter steers. Also, Bragg's policy was to issue three days' rations at a time, thereby keeping the commissary wagons far to the rear. This practice often led to shortages, forcing the men to forage.[9]

The troops bore testimony to the suffering. A sergeant in the Second Tennessee declared in September: "Last night our commissary issued 3 days rations to the troops; he gave us full rations of meat, but only one pound of flour to the man for three days. Some of the men have eat it up already—they will have to live on parched corn, wall-nuts & acorns for the next two days—rather hard living." Hungry Rebels were frequently seen filtering through the dirt where a horse had earlier eaten in an attempt to salvage leftover grains of corn. A lieutenant in the Sixth Florida indicated that his men received meat and bread for only one meal per day and otherwise subsisted on parched corn. "It is a wonder they all didn't die," he concluded. An Alabamian confided to his wife: "We spent 3 day A time or two Without any provision only what poorched corn We could get which was a small Amount." A scant one or two biscuits per day was typical fare for most of the men, although there were reports that some went as long as three days with no rations.[10]

When the Kentucky Campaign was completed, the supply of food once again stabilized. A young Mississippian at Murfreesboro wondered why so many of his comrades scrubbed around daily in the woods for nuts and berries when, in his view, the government ration was entirely adequate. An artillery officer notified his sister in November 1862: "Our bill of fare this morn was biscuits, batter cakes, fried bacon and corn meal with no sugar. We have plenty to eat now

such as it is. The boys are now drawing fresh beef." John Hill
concurred: "We are getting plenty to eat," he recorded on December 8, 1862.[11]

Historians have long recognized that Robert E. Lee's army in
Virginia drew heavily on food supplies from Bragg's department. By
March 1863 the Atlanta commissary warehouses held some 8 million pounds of salt meat and four thousand steers in pasture, most of
which came from middle and northern Tennessee. The bulk of this
meat was being shipped to Lee at the rate of five hundred thousand
pounds per week, prompting Bragg to make the caustic comment:
"But for my much abused campaign in Kentucky and Tennessee we
should now all be in a starving condition."[12]

This government supply policy meant that the Army of Tennessee
had to disperse over a seventy-mile front to forage. By March 1863
the army was consuming on a daily basis 35,000 pounds of bacon,
87,500 pounds of meal, 3,500 pounds of rice, 1,400 pounds of soap,
350 gallons of vinegar, 522 gallons of molasses, and 44 bushels of
salt. It was estimated that by foraging the army could supply itself
with all the meal, vinegar, and soap and half the meat required. Of
course, foraging in lengthy forays wore down the mules and wagons.[13]

The policy of logistical inequity prevented Bragg's army from
concentrating and thus adversely affected operations. Yet several
factors were involved which modern writers have not fully appreciated. Northrop's objections aside, the Army of Tennessee did continue to draw on the reserve meat supply in Atlanta to the detriment
of the Army of Northern Virginia. Additionally, even though Bragg's
army was placed on one-half-pound pork rations, that was still
twice the amount issued to Lee's army at that time.[14]

It does seem certain that drawing supplies from Tennessee to send
to Virginia did not impose hardships on Bragg's soldiers. When
Colonel William Preston Johnston inspected the army in March
1863, he conceded that it led a "hand to mouth" existence with
meat, but he also reported that he "heard no grumbling about the
rations." His claim is substantiated in the letters and diaries. One
soldier stated that "we are doing pretty well in the way of rations
now, we get enough to make out on," while a less restrained infantryman commented that "we are farrying very well here about

something to eat we get plenty of meat and bread." In late May a private in the Thirty-third Alabama candidly told his wife, "wee are getting a long tolerabul well yeat some of the boys complain a bought not having a nuf to eat but I never sufered for something to eat."[15]

Complaints from the men dealt not with shortages but with the quality and monotony of the rations. "I should feel very well if we had anything to eat but our chance is bread without grease and beef that can climb a tree," Fayette McDonald of the Twenty-fifth Tennessee grumbled. A sergeant's concern was the never-changing menu: "I never was as tired of corn bread and bacon in my life. We have had no flour for several weeks." Another of Bragg's soldiers, camped at Wartrace, made it clear that the primary problem was the relentlessly unchanging menu: "We get plenty [to eat] here, such as it is, but I am tired of one thing all of the time." The complaint of an artillery officer was that the corncob was often crushed up with the meal, resulting in sickness and bowel disorders. "Our army here [Shelbyville] is eating corn bread and it is making them sick—unless they could sift it and have it ground finer it will make them sick," he observed.[16]

One way of breaking the monotony was by hunting. Writing from Wartrace, William Rogers of the First Florida told his parents: "The boys have been amusing themselves all the morning catching squirrels. They have caught 16 this morning." Because ammunition was not allowed for such pursuits, there developed some ingenious methods of trapping. A large robin roost in a cedar brake near Shelbyville proved to be a tempting target for some men of the Twenty-fourth Alabama. At night several privates, including J. H. Puckett, climbed a nearby tree. When all was ready, men on the ground lit torches and thrashed wildly through the brakes. Puckett wrote that "it beats all they came into the tree so fast and thick that they would [perch] in our faces, on our heads feet hands and sometimes you can catch them with your mouth . . . [we caught] . . . in all about 50." That night the men sat down to robin stew. Perhaps the most successful hunt occurred in April 1863, when scores of men in Liddell's brigade surrounded a huge field. Working toward the center while beating on sticks, the men corralled and bludgeoned some 130 rabbits and 11 partridges.[17]

Despite substantial evidence that the men were well fed through-
out the spring of 1863, Bragg continued to insist that there was a severe shortage of meat and that four hundred thousand rations would be required "to carry us to March 31." One official countered that if there was any truth to the alleged dearth, it was because of lack of energy on the part of commissary agents. In Lincoln County, Tennessee, alone there was an estimated 1 million pounds of salt meat and half that amount in nearby Giles County. The problem was partly of Bragg's own making for not supplying sufficient wag- ons to bring the meat out. General Joseph E. Johnston, western theater commander at the time, urged that cattle be driven overland to Bragg's army rather than slaughtered and salted. "Meat salted cannot be saved. Our troops have not the means of boiling meat, and therefore throw away the greater portion of this, except when pressed by hunger," he concluded. Sometimes the problem was related to inefficient commissaries. When the Twenty-fifth Tennessee suffered ration shortages, it was discovered that the commissary sergeant was not properly weighing the food issues.[18]

Food did become in shorter supply in the late summer of 1863 when the army withdrew to Chattanooga, thus eliminating middle Tennessee as a source. When Bragg railed to the War Department that the lack of subsistence was hurting morale and causing deser- tions, however, he evoked an angry response from Northrop that was reminiscent of earlier exchanges with Beauregard. "General Bragg has fallen into a delusion," Northrop insisted, and with im- plied sarcasm suggested that a successful army would not be demor- alized on even less rations.[19]

Major Giles Hillyer, army chief of subsistence, reported on Au- gust 25, 1863, that adequate supplies were available until the end of the month. There was no difficulty in securing sufficient amounts of rice, peas, soap, salt, and vinegar. Nor was there a serious concern over breadstuffs because flour was being supplied from the Co- lumbus, Georgia, depot. Regarding the supply of meat, however, the prospects were "not merely uncertain, but gloomy indeed." During a five-week period in late July and August 1863, Bragg received fifteen hundred to two thousand head of cattle from the depot at Madison, Florida, but this supply had now largely evaporated. Since Major Alfred Cummings in Atlanta was still shipping meat to Lee at the rate of fifty thousand pounds per day, he could supply the Army of Tennessee only through September 20. A five-day supply of beef and bacon could be procured from east Tennessee, as well as six to seven hundred beef cattle from north Alabama, a three-day supply. By October 1, however, all of these sources would be depleted.[20]

The letters and diaries reflect the serious shortages that were experienced. Writing in August, a private testified that "evy thing in the shape of provision is getting scears we ar onely getting half rashins now and I am afraid they wount hold out long at that." Several weeks later a sergeant said, "Entire weeks have passed without getting as much as I could eat even in a day." A young Texan related to his mother, "We only get a little corn bread and beef and the perest beefe you ever saw, and only one quarter of a pound per day and a part of the time no beefe a tail." To wash down their meager rations, the soldiers depended on homemade coffee, generally brewed from cornmeal, and sassafras tea. While at Chattanooga, G. W. Athey remarked: "We make sactfract teea and meeal brand coffee and sweeten it with the shuger."[21]

Even after Chickamauga the situation did not measurably improve because poor weather and washed-out bridges bogged down wagon transportation. While Bragg besieged the Federals at Chattanooga, eventually reducing them to quarter rations, his own men suffered nearly as much. Lieutenant Robert Watson noted in his diary on October 19 that he had nothing to eat "except a little sour cornbread." A few days later he recorded: "Drew 1 days rations of cornbread and bacon, just enough for one meal and we eat it up immediately although it is for tomorrow." A private agreed with this assessment, stating that "we are living very harde we are barely getting half rashions."[22]

The situation remained serious throughout November. Daniel Weaver, a member of the Forty-fifth Alabama, disclosed to his father: "We have not received any bacon since I have been in the fight [Chickamauga] we do not get beef ever day 3 days out of 10 we have not got any beef They give us rice & sugar in place of beef." A soldier in Z. C. Deas's brigade echoed those words: "I learn that we aire not a going to get any meat only beeaf every seven dayes and bacon every ten dayes . . . that is pretty haird liveing we [have] not had aney meat in too dayes now when we don't get any meat we get too ounces and a half of shuger a day to the man." Actually, the situation would have been much worse but for the efforts of three Georgia counties along the Western & Atlantic Railroad. Answering a government appeal, Coweta, Troup, and Campbell counties shipped 2,800 head of cattle to the Army of Tennessee during November.[23]

In December, following the Missionary Ridge disaster, Lieutenant General William Hardee, temporarily in command, informed Richmond that the army was rebuilding and that "the ration is now full and uniform." The troops told a different story. "We air here [Dalton] abot half starved to death we have to live on quarter rashen we draw nothing but corn bread and knott a nuff of that this morning we draw a little pees," complained a Georgia infantryman. A similar statement came from a cannoneer: "We have had no bacon or lard since we left Missionary Ridge, and still unable to get any." A Texan who had not had "but one pound of beef in seven days" told his mother that he was "nearly starved on cornbread." Meat was rarely available more than three times a week, and sweet potatoes often served as a substitute.[24]

When Joseph E. Johnston assumed command in January 1864, commissary shipments once again became regular because steers were butchered in Atlanta rather than being shipped on the hoof in boxcars to Dalton, thus transporting in two cars what before required five. The daily ration was again cut, this time to one-third of a pound of bacon and one and one-quarter pounds of meal. Except on the march, flour was largely discontinued. Complaints, not surprisingly, were quickly forthcoming. A soldier in the Thirty-third Alabama notified his wife: "We eat the beef we drawed for breakfast and some of the boys said they could eat as much more." Yet such statements must be balanced by the comments of others. A surgeon wrote that "I am very well & hearty as a pig on half rations of corn meal & 1/3 rations of bacon and poor beef sometimes." Stated another soldier: "We would have starved on this in the commencement of the war. But we have learned to live on little and are much healthyer than we were then."[25]

One thing seems certain—rank was not royalty in the Army of Tennessee. When Captain Samuel McKittrick of the Nineteenth South Carolina went to dine one evening in late April 1864 with his brother-in-law Major Adam Stennis and a colonel, the fare consisted of a glass of water and a piece of corn bread. "The colonel made some apology, but said it was the best he could do. Officers live as hard as privates," concluded McKittrick.[26]

Two rather ugly, but noteworthy, events occurred at Dalton in the winter of 1864: a train filled with provisions was ransacked by a mob of soldiers as it rolled into the depot, and an unruly throng of two hundred attempted to storm a commissary warehouse but was detained long enough by a single guard until a provost detachment arrived and dispersed the men. These events must be regarded as aberrations, however.[27]

Johnston did attempt to introduce some variety into the daily fare, as evidenced by the comment of an appreciative Reb: "He ordered tobacco and whiskey to be issued twice a week. He ordered sugar and coffee and flour to be issued instead of meal. He ordered cured bacon and ham instead of blue beef." The commissary sergeant of the Sixty-fifth Georgia, who kept an accurate diary, revealed that between January 14 and March 11, 1864, his regiment on average received grits, rice or peas, salt, and soap every other day and vinegar and sugar once a week. Supplements also continued to be received from the home folks. Some items, such as gingerbread and peanuts, were "temptingly displayed at many cabin doors for sale."[28]

An effort was made to resolve the chronic deficiency of fruits and vegetables. Several boxcar loads of tomatoes were shipped up from Florida and southern Alabama, but issues remained sparse. Donations of vegetables were requested from the populace with some success. A member of the Thirty-third Mississippi told his wife, "We are getting green apples occasionally. . . . We are getting plenty of corn bread & Bacon and sometimes a few vegetables and coffee. The soldiers are nearly starved for Vegetables." Several days later a Texan in Cleburne's division observed: "We drew Irish potatoes, blue Collards, and Tomatoes, besides our regular rations of beef and corn bread." The Thirtieth Tennessee drew its first vegetable ration on June 25, 1864, consisting of onions, cabbages, potatoes, beets, turnips, and squash.[29]

Despite these efforts, complaints still abounded. "We get tolerable plenty of meat & bread now but we want something in the way of

vegetables," declared a Georgian. Another Southerner, near Marietta, wrote, "I am nearly parished for vegetables, nothing to eat but
boiled meat and bread." Even when issues were made, the individual
soldier received only a pittance. The Army of Tennessee's 1864
allowance of one pound of potatoes per man existed on paper only.
A Tennessee captain remembered that his entire company once drew
only two beets and half a dozen potatoes. At Dalton the Marion
Light Artillery received a paltry, if not laughable, three peas per
man. The next issue came at Kennesaw Mountain and was little
better. The ninety-four men received one peck of potatoes, half a
dozen cabbage heads, two squash, and four or five beets. Lamented
one Southerner: "When they [vegetables] have to be divided among
so many they amount to little." The men believed that the best fruits
and vegetables were taken by clerks, teamsters, and quartermasters
in the rear. Substitutes were tried with some success. In a letter to his
wife, a Tennessee surgeon expounded: "We get a kind of small
vegetable that grows in the water like clover & use it for salad it is
fine as good as turnip salad."[30]

If the fare was not particularly palatable, it was apparently filling.
Johnston's men offered few complaints about suffering from hunger
during the Atlanta Campaign. "We get plenty of meat and corn to
eat," remarked a soldier of the Twenty-fourth Tennessee. Writing
from the trenches north of the Chattahoochee, an infantryman of
the Ninth Tennessee assured his children: "Doing well in the way of
rations. Have plenty of bread, meat, a little coffee, and occasionally
a few vegetables." A Mississippian assured his wife that there was
"no complaint among the men on the score of provisions." Captain
James P. Douglas wrote on June 10, 1864, "Our army is well supplied with good rations. I have plenty of coffee now."[31]

A new system of preparing rations during active campaigning was
devised before the Battle of Chickamauga. A permanent detail of
cooks was detached at the ratio of one per twenty men. Cooks were
usually convalescent or barefoot soldiers unfit for regular duty. The
system was highly unpopular with the troops. The bread was always
cold by the time it was issued, the ownership of utensils became
confused, and there was a general feeling that the rations were
poorly prepared. During the Atlanta Campaign, the rations were
cooked and brought to the trenches at night to avoid enemy fire.

Although the bread was precooked, the bacon continued to be issued raw.[32]

Rations could always be supplemented by purchases from local farmers, prompting some soldiers to make pitiful pleas for those at home to send money. "I am again reduced to the necessity of writing for money, send me twenty dollars in as small bills as [soon as] possible you must remember that I have never drawn a cent of pay since I came into service that . . . [it] is often in my power to buy chickens and such like when we are marching through the country."[33]

Hood's Tennessee Campaign produced the greatest suffering for the troops. On September 11, 1864, a diarist recorded: "We are in camp eating beef and corn bread once more but short [reduced] rations." In early October a Texan wryly commented: "Our rations are very short. I have had neither meat nor bread since yesterday 12 o'clock, and then I had nothing but a beef rib with not enough meat on it to feed a cat." Also that month, an Alabama private wrote that on the march from Palmetto, Georgia, to Tuscumbia, Alabama, he and his comrades lived for three days exclusively on parched corn. A Georgian added: "Cut rations short quite short. Cornbread & jorked Beef is all we get except as we forage in the country. We can get a goat or mutton occasionally." The colonel of the Twenty-fourth South Carolina reported that in late November his regiment subsisted for two days on two biscuits per man.[34]

In a lengthy letter, written in diary format, Washington Ives entered on November 24: "Marched 19 miles and drew 2 small biscuits for the days rations and was very happy (a biscuit anytime during the campaign readily sold for $1)." Two days later he noted: "Our rations are very short but the boys don't complain. We gather corn out of the fields and boil it in camp kettles (which we carry in our hands on every march) until it is soft enough to grate and every man carried a little tin grate and by patiently grating it a man can get enough meal from one ear of corn to make him a mess of mush and although it is a tidious process yet is far better than going hungry."[35]

As the army passed through Alabama and Georgia en route to North Carolina in early 1865, rations somewhat stabilized. On January 8 Captain Key took pleasure in recording: "We fared sumptuously last night, having a bushel of sweet potatoes and a gallon of sorghum. . . . For months our fare had been simply bread and meat, and you cannot imagine . . . how soldiers relish such a change of diet." Following the surrender of the army in April, the Federals issued a generous supply of rations for the soldiers' trip home.[36]

One historian has concluded that when the Confederate government divided up its limited resources, "the Army of Tennessee did not get its fair share." Policies aside, however, the soldiers of the Army of Tennessee never ate less than those of the Army of Northern Virginia, and at times they enjoyed considerably more.[37]

5

The Aire Is a Right Smart of Sickness

As in other Civil War commands, the western army was hit with an onslaught of disease early in the conflict. During the winter of 1861–62, the new recruits fell easy victim to typhoid fever, pneumonia, mumps, and diarrhea, but the most disabling disease was measles. The few urban regiments, such as the Thirteenth Louisiana of New Orleans, were barely affected, but the numerous rural outfits were devastated. The Third Tennessee, at Camp Cheatham, had 650 of 1,100 stricken within six months.[1]

The divisions in central Kentucky were particularly hard hit. By early December 1861, of the 18,000 men on the rolls of Hardee's corps at Bowling Green, 3,600 were in Nashville hospitals and another 1,400 were sick at Clarksville and other towns. Writing from Bowling Green, the surgeon of the Fourth Tennessee observed:

"The most obstinate form of diarrhea and dysentery is prevalent and in some cases fatal. The cases are lingering and some of them seem

to defy all treatment. The worse cases are those following measles." When the Seventh Texas arrived at Bowling Green, the colonel reported that there were "more coughs and colds than I ever
saw among the same number of men." By January 1862, half of
Thomas C. Hindman's brigade at Bell Station were so sick with
measles and diarrhea that they were unable to walk. Three of Lloyd
Tilghman's regiments went from 2,199 effectives to 1,421, primarily
because of measles. One of Johnston's infantrymen remarked: "I
have had the mumps and Pneuralgia Prety Bad. The aire is a Right
Smart of Sickness Sutch as mumps and yellow Jandice and winter
fever."[2]

Some illness was the result of negligence. When Company A of
the Forty-fourth Tennessee arrived at Bowling Green in December
1861, the inexperienced captain ordered a bivouac on low ground
outside of town. The area was quickly washed out and one-third of
the men taken ill with chills. The sick were placed on drafty freight
cars and sent to Nashville, where they were unloaded at the depot in
the midst of a sleet storm. Some died before they got to the hospital.
Once there, they were practically starved on one cracker, two tea-
spoons of chicken broth, and a gill of coffee twice a day. A friend
smuggled sweet potatoes to them, which had to be eaten secretly for
fear the nurses would confiscate them. The entire experience proved
nothing short of a nightmare.[3]

Initially the sick were sent to makeshift hospitals. The Green River
Tavern in Bowling Green was converted to accommodate one hundred patients. At Hopkinsville, a large tobacco stemmery and the
homes vacated by refugees were taken over as infirmaries. When the
sick continued to pour in, medical officials made arrangements to
have all convalescents and chronically ill sent to Nashville. The State
Hospital and the Nashville Blind Asylum, as well as the Clarksville
Female Academy, were set aside for use. The sick of Polk's corps at
Columbus, including the wounded from the Battle of Belmont, were
sent to Memphis. By the end of 1861, that city had more than a
thousand hospital beds in use.[4]

The fall of Fort Donelson and Johnston's winter retreat to Nashville added to the distress. There were only 500 sick at Bowling
Green when the army withdrew, but by the time it reached the

Tennessee capital some 5,400 of 14,000 men had been placed on the sick roll. David Yandell, army chief surgeon, admitted that the troops were "unable to undertake a walk." A panic ensued when the city was evacuated, causing patients at the Gordon Hospital needlessly to abandon their beds and go streaming down the Murfreesboro Road.[5]

About 1,200 of the Nashville sick were removed to Chattanooga, where three large buildings were quickly converted for hospital use by slaves and women. Contracts were made with two local bakeries for bread, coffee, and sugar. The first train arrived with 300 patients and was soon followed by two other trains. For some, the journey required eighteen hours. The patients were not accompanied by attendants, surgeons, or supplies, and the men were in a pitiful state. Three were found dead on the cars, one died at the depot before being removed, and yet another died on the way to the hospital.[6]

Confusion reigned on the Shiloh battlefield. On the second day of the battle, Chaplain Jeremiah Collom of the Twenty-fourth Tennessee assisted medical personnel in a house that had been improvised as a hospital. "I carried out my arms full of [amputated] legs and arms," he wrote. He noticed one poor fellow who had been shot in the head and whose brains were oozing out, yet he was still conscious and pleading for water. There was none to be given, however, for the old well out back had been emptied.[7]

A brigade hospital was established at the Mickey house, and tents were erected in the front yard to shelter the wounded. The rain poured on the night of April 7, drenching hundreds of patients who had no shelter. One Mississippi cavalryman noted that on the retreat from the battlefield, "numbers of wounded begged to get up behind us [on the horses], it went hard to refuse I assure you."[8]

The grim harvest of Shiloh dumped thousands of wounded into Corinth virtually overnight. All available space was converted for hospital use, and doctors from as far away as Mobile and New Orleans rushed to assist. The Sisters of Charity, run by a Mother Superior and a dozen nuns, operated one hospital. One soldier observed, "The Railroad platform is almost covered with coffins and wounded soldiers—every train brings some anxious parent looking after their sons." A nurse remarked that at the Tishimingo Hotel everywhere were "the mangled forms of dying and dead soldiers."[9]

Captain Pleasant G. Swor of the Fifth Tennessee is shown armed with revolver, knife, and sword. He was slightly wounded at Shiloh. (Herb Peck)

Although regiments varied, records reveal that generally about one-half of the wounds were not serious. The Thirteenth Tennessee, for example, listed 108 wounded—10 mortally, 45 seriously, and 53 slightly. The First Arkansas had 184 wounded—14 mortally, 24 dangerously, 61 severely, and 85 slightly. There were exceptions. Nearly two-thirds of the 130 wounded of the Third Kentucky were

*Privates William H. Landis and J. A. Landis served in the Twenty-third
Tennessee. William lost an arm during Cleburne's assault on the first day
at Shiloh.* (Confederate Veteran)

of a serious, dangerous, or mortal nature. In the First Louisiana
some 13 percent of the casualties were head wounds, while 43
percent were arm, hand, leg, or foot wounds. Casualties from artillery fire were minimal. Only 5 of 195 killed and wounded of the
Nineteenth Alabama were from artillery shots; the Crescent Regiment had only 7 of 103 killed and wounded; the Sixteenth Louisiana, 3 of 51. The notable exception was the Thirteenth Louisiana,
in which nearly 20 percent of the casualties were inflicted by ar-

tillery. Almost every regiment had a couple of accidental casualties. Some of these men shot themselves; others were hit by falling limbs or run over by wagons. The Crescent Regiment listed 6 of its wounded as accidental, the First Louisiana, 3. The Twenty-first Alabama had its regimental hospital captured, losing 25 patients and 17 in the ambulance squad.[10]

The wounds of many of the men had long been subjected to exposure and were gangrenous when they reached Corinth, necessitating some amputations. A Louisiana soldier passed a church that was jammed with wounded and saw a grisly sight—a large box "filled with feet and arms & hands. It was so full that 2 horrible & bloody feet protruded out of the top." Nurse Kate Cummings passed the amputating room at the hospital where she worked and witnessed "a stream of blood [that] ran from the table into a tub in which was the arm. It had been taken off at the socket, and the hand . . . was hanging over the edge of the tub, a lifeless thing." Yet the records reveal that the actual number of amputations may have been small. There were 79 wounded each in the Thirteenth Louisiana and Crescent Regiment, yet there were only three amputations in the former and two in the latter. Of the 191 wounded of the First Louisiana, only 3 received amputations.[11]

The wounded from Shiloh were farmed out to hospitals in Tennessee, Mississippi, and Alabama. Some 300 were sent to Overton and Irving hospitals in Memphis. By April 23, some 123 had been received at the Marine Hospital in Natchez, Mississippi. A train carrying wounded to Memphis was derailed about fifteen miles from Grand Junction, leaving dead and injured all along the track. "I shall never forget the jumble of wretches screaming and cursing in our car, as we were tossed up in a heap," recalled a victim.[12]

The typical wounded soldier was out of action for about a month. The more slightly injured were often given a furlough and allowed to recuperate at home. Of the fifty-seven wounded of the First Louisiana who required a leave for longer than a month, thirty-three were in a general hospital, sixteen on furlough, and eight in camp unfit for duty. Unfortunately, eight of that regiment's wounded died in hospitals, most within a month, and another twenty-four were so seriously injured that they were permanently discharged.[13]

Even after the wounded had been dispersed, disease persisted on an appalling scale. Exposure, bad rations, lack of proper latrines, and neglect of police duty were all to blame. John A. Harris of the Nineteenth Louisiana blamed the sudden change of climate of the Upper South for much of the sickness in his outfit. "We have lost 50 men since we got here [Corinth]. Pneumony is the worst disease we have to contend with." The chief culprit in causing the disease, however, was the drinking water. A lack of rain in May 1862 caused the soldiers to depend on shallow holes dug around camp, but what came up was a foul-odored, milky-colored water, contaminated by magnesia and limestone. One soldier recalled that these holes quickly became infested with "wiggletails." Attempts to dig artesian wells eight to ten feet deep met with failure.[14]

The men were thus left with water that smelled so offensive that they had to hold their noses while drinking it. Indeed, the horses and mules often refused to drink it. The result was diarrhea and typhoid fever that disabled thousands. "All of us suffering from Diarrhea," remarked an Alabama soldier. On May 18, 1862, eighty-two men in Lumsden's Alabama Battery were in various hospitals, leaving only forty-two in camp—"just barely enough to man the pieces," commented a member. The general hospitals were filled with wounded so the sick were typically confined to regimental facilities—simply a tent. "It is heart sickening to see the poor soldiers in a cold tent on the cold ground without one comfort," lamented a member of S. A. M. Wood's brigade. The surgeon of the Eleventh Louisiana informed his wife: "I sent four of our men to the hospital this evening and there are several others who ought to be there, but there is no room for them, although we have two hospitals for our Regiment alone."[15]

The situation was indeed serious, but it must be remembered that people were witnessing suffering on an unprecedented scale. One soldier admitted, "There is considerable sickness here [Corinth], but not as much as is represented by some who leave here." Statistics bear out this observation. There were 32,889 cases of disease treated in the army during April and May 1862, which was not disproportionate to that occurring in ensuing months. Indeed, during June, when the army was at Tupelo, 41,244 cases were treated. Further, the disease mortality rate was a moderately low 4 percent (1,432 deaths). The two prominent disablers, diarrhea and dysentery, accounted for 6,983 cases in April but only 12 deaths.[16]

The health debacle at Corinth continued when that place was evacuated at the end of May 1862. So precipitous was the departure of the last train to leave town, which was jammed with sick and wounded, that seven men sitting atop freight cars fell off and had to be left. Worse yet was the capture of five hundred convalescents south of Corinth.[17]

Large-scale evacuation of the wounded remained a serious problem. After the Battle of Perryville, Bragg was forced to abandon some nine hundred patients at Perryville, seventeen hundred at Harrodsburg, and four hundred at Danville, a total of three thousand. In Ringgold, Georgia, all the hospitals were filled to capacity, but officials were told to prepare for a train bringing two hundred sick and wounded from Kentucky. Against the wishes of a local congregation, medical personnel ordered that a church be commandeered. Straw was spread over the floor and headrests were made by tearing off the backs of pews and nailing them slantwise to the baseboard so that knapsacks could be used as pillows. When the train finally arrived, "there poured through the doors of that little church a train of human misery such as I never saw before," witnessed Fannie Beers. She observed that not one in twenty soldiers had a haversack, and many did not possess coats or jackets, despite the bitter cold weather.[18]

J. A. Bruce, a Tennessean, was wounded at Perryville. While recuperating in a hospital, he wrote his brother about the details: "I was not in the fight very long, only fired five rounds before I was shot down. We had nearly reached a battery we were charging at the time. A ball struck my clothes lightly, one went through my coat sleeve, one through my coat pocket, one took off my cartridge box, one went through my haversack, and the next one brought me down while in the act of loading. It struck me in the thigh and I dropped my gun and walked about twenty yards and then commenced to crawl."[19]

Following the Battle of Murfreesboro, the problem of evacuating patients once again cropped up. Bragg deliberated whether to postpone his withdrawal twenty-four hours so as to evacuate all the wounded. Waiting proved impossible, however, and in a wrenching decision, he abandoned seventeen hundred men (twelve hundred wounded, three hundred sick, and two hundred surgeons and attendants) to the enemy. Most of the Murfreesboro wounded were

Andrew Jackson Vawter of the Twelfth Tennessee was wounded in the groin at Shiloh and in the leg at Murfreesboro. (Robert Vawter)

transported by rail to Chattanooga and south into Georgia. One train filled with sick and wounded was derailed two miles east of Stevenson, Alabama, killing seven.[20]

During the winter and spring of 1863 the army remained in and around Tullahoma. Camp hygiene was strictly enforced. In February an inspector uncovered certain laxness in John C. Brown's brigade.

He reported that the "camps of the 45th Tennessee have not been
ditched as . . . directed and the drainage of the other camps, except
that of the 32d Tennessee, which did not require ditching, is imper-
fect. Moses's battery is not provided with sinks [latrines] at all, and
the Regiments of the brigade, except the 26th Tennessee, have no
guards posted to confine the men to the use of sinks and they
consequently frequent the slopes of the hill leading to the creek,
which has already become offensive."[21]

Despite these efforts, sickness remained a serious threat. Hardee
remarked that his divisions had clean camps and good water and
that he was "at a loss to account for the very large sick list, which is
increasing daily." His only recommendation was that vegetables be
issued. "We have twice the amount of sickness here in Tennessee that
we had at any time at Mobile," William D. Cole of the Thirty-eighth
Alabama informed his wife. So deathly ill was one Mississippian at
Tullahoma that he confessed that "if I thought we would have a fight
soon, I would rush to the front and end all this." Once again, two
bowel disorders, diarrhea and dysentery, were the chief problem.
They accounted for 35,683 cases between January and May 1863,
or 29 percent of all entries. Typical was the comment of a soldier in
the Twenty-ninth Georgia in April: "I thought I was getting a loung
very well until a bout 3 days ago it turn Louse on me and my
Bowealls has bin Runing of very bad."[22]

Next to bowel disorders, the leading cause of illness was what
was generically termed "fever." Surprisingly, the incidence remained
fairly constant during the five-month period, indicating that weather
was not necessarily a contributing factor. Indeed, twice as many
were hospitalized in this category in May than January, primarily
because of an increasing number of remittent fever cases—from 491
in January to 1,498 in May. Winter exposure may have been a root
factor, however, because these were repeat cases. Some fevers, such
as typhoid, were totally unrelated to weather and remained fairly
constant. It accounted for only 1.6 percent of all entries, indicating
that no serious threat was posed.

Two closely related categories were scurvy and debilitis, or a
wasting away. Indeed, the latter may have been a subclinical case of
scurvy. There were 7,385 cases reported, or 6 percent of the total.
The experience of the Sixth and Ninth Tennessee at Tullahoma was

*Disease, not a Yankee bullet, claimed the life of Robert Patterson of the
Twelfth Tennessee in May 1863. (Library of Congress)*

unique, if not comical. When several cases of scurvy cropped up in
the regiment, Dr. John S. Fenner ordered the regiment into the
woods and instructed the men to eat grass and selected green things.
This process was continued until the commissary could furnish
vegetables.[23]

There were only 167 cases of smallpox (variola). Still, a fear of the
disease exhibited an influence far beyond its numbers. When a few
cases of smallpox appeared in the Thirteenth Tennessee in late No-

vember 1862, the regiment was quickly isolated. Desertions began occurring when additional cases developed, and the roll had to be called three times a day to keep others from leaving.[24]

Between December 1862 and January 1863, a staggering 60,552 patients were treated in the Army of Tennessee, only 18 percent of them for battle wounds. Many of these soldiers recuperated in Chattanooga hospitals. The Gilmer Hospital was expanded by building five two-story pavilion wards, each with a capacity of 50 patients, and the Academy Hospital was enlarged by the addition of a dozen one-story wards. At Cherokee Springs, near Ringgold, Georgia, a showcase tent city was erected that covered thirty acres and had accommodations for 500. By October 1863 there were thirty-seven hospitals in northern and central Georgia and extreme eastern Alabama, with 8,818 beds, 7,665 of which were then occupied. Medical and support personnel included 142 surgeons, 41 stewards, 73 ward masters, 111 matrons, 836 nurses, 258 cooks, and 262 laundresses. Indeed, the Army of Tennessee's medical system was far more sophisticated than has been generally appreciated.[25]

To expedite the removal of wounded from the battlefield, Medical Director Edward Flewellyn requested additional ambulances. In early 1863, contracts were made for one hundred new spring ambulances for Bragg's army and, although deliveries were hampered by a shortage of steel for the springs, most had been delivered and placed in service by April. The bulk of the army's ambulance pool consisted of ordinary wagons without springs, drawn by two mules, and covered with a heavy cotton duck cloth. Every now and then a fully equipped Federal ambulance was captured (twenty-eight were taken in the Battle of Murfreesboro and seventeen at Chickamauga), in which case it was an easy matter to paint a "C" over the "U," leaving the "S" and "A."[26]

Despite all these efforts, the Battle of Chickamauga, with its deluge of fifteen thousand Southern wounded and more than eighteen hundred captured Northern wounded, clearly overwhelmed the medical department. Captain William P. Howell of the Twenty-fifth Alabama remembered how the Confederates built fires among the rows of wounded to provide some measure of comfort. Groups of women searched the field with lanterns looking for loved ones.[27]

*Private Ancel Sawyer of the Tenth Mississippi served as a hospital
steward. (Jack Robinson and David Conwill)*

Manigault's brigade was typical of field operations to care for
wounded. The command went into action with 2,025 men present,
of which 609 were killed or wounded. The casualties were removed
by the brigade's 105 litter bearers to a field hospital, which consisted
simply of tents set up around a barn and some sheds. "They [sur-
geons] were out in the rain nearly all morning, trying to make
some patients comfortable as possible," commented Kate Cummings, who visited the site. "They said the rain was pouring down

on them [wounded], but it could not be avoided. They informed me that what they had heard of many of the brigade hospitals, the men were in worse plight than theirs." She also toured Cheatham's division hospital, where the chief surgeon, a Dr. Rice, "took us into a 'fly' about one hundred feet long, and every man in it had a limb amputated." Surgeons later told her "that many a time they have had nothing but old tent cloth to bind up wounds."[28]

The biggest task remained—removing the wounded to the rear. For several days a train of 150 ambulances and a number of commissary wagons hauled the wounded to the Wood Station, south of the burned railroad bridge on the Western & Atlantic, nine miles from the battlefield. Some five hundred of the worst cases remained in field hospitals three weeks later. The journey to the railroad was, according to one surgeon, "exceedingly hot and dusty." Once at the station, thousands of wounded were dumped without food or shelter. Fortunately, the sky remained clear and the temperature pleasant.[29]

Much of the suffering was clearly the result of inefficiency. It was only by strenuous efforts that cars could be obtained to transport the wounded. Frenzied efforts were made to move up ammunition, and the trains were not detained long enough to load the wounded for the return trip. As late as September 26 there were still enough patients at the Wood Station to fill forty cars. The trains frequently lacked water kegs, warming stoves, and medical personnel, and several surgeons complained that some of the cars "had just been unloaded with beef cattle."[30]

With a total department capacity of only seventy-five hundred beds, most of which were already filled with sick, the new patient load could not be absorbed. Many of the wounded were, therefore, sent out of the department (to Montgomery, Columbus, and Augusta) or placed in private homes. Patients not requiring surgery were granted thirty-day furloughs and allowed to go home. Some nine hundred of the more slightly wounded were sent to Augusta, where the hospitals quickly became swamped. Gangrene cases soon appeared in all the hospitals, claiming several fatalities. The epidemic was attributed to the dirty freight cars in which the troops were transported and probably was spread by attendants who went from patient to patient using the same sponge.[31]

An additional twenty-two hundred wounded were channeled into the hospital system following the Battle of Missionary Ridge. Although painfully injured, Captain James Cooper of the Twentieth Tennessee made his way to Chickamauga Station, only to learn that the trains were not running north to that place. Accompanied by many other wounded, he walked all the way to Dalton, where he got on a freight car in the midst of a cold rain and was transported to Marietta.[32]

While at Dalton, many of the troops, though remaining at their posts, suffered from sickness. "We are without tents and a great many of the boys have very bad coughs and colds and there is some pneumonia in the company. I have a very bad cough," remarked an Alabamian. Georgian W. R. Hurst related that he was enjoying good health, "with the exception of the bowel complaint. I have been affected in my bowels for two or three days though not very bad off. This complaint is very common in the company." By the end of March 1864, the hospitals in Atlanta, LaGrange, Newman, Rome, and Cassville, Georgia, had a capacity of 12,513 beds, of which 7,434 were occupied.[33]

The Atlanta Campaign presented the Army of Tennessee's medical corps with its biggest challenge. Not only were there enormous numbers of casualties during July and August 1864, but a bout of summer sickness swelled the patient load to unprecedented numbers. Some 79,709 men were treated during this time—37 percent wounded and 63 percent sick. One historian has calculated that one of every two men in Johnston's army was incapacitated each month.[34]

The leading diseases, as always, were diarrhea and dysentery— some 8,353 cases, or nearly 17 percent of the sick. "I have been affected with Diarrhea, Itch and piles and part of the time lousey," confessed one of Johnston's soldiers. Typhoid and malarial fevers represented 5,516 cases, or 11 percent of the sick. There were only 481 cases of pneumonia, but nearly 10 percent of those stricken died. A. Q. Porter, a musician in the Thirty-third Mississippi on hospital duty, observed: "The ditches [trenches] are full of mud and water and they are compelled to stay in them or to be exposed to the bullets of the enemy. . . . They are coming in constantly, dripping wet and cold from the ditches." Another soldier thought it "surprising that we do not have more sick than we do as the men have to stay in the ditches all the time."[35]

Another major sickness was scurvy and debilitis, of which there were 2,780 cases, or 5.5 percent of the total. The surgeon of the Twentieth Tennessee remarked in July: "Several of the soldiers are here prostrated from scurvy. Nothing to eat but corn bread & old bacon. . . . Will give the oldest man in the world scurvy." The outbreak of measles remained consistent with 1863 statistics. There were 1,406 cases reported, with 58 deaths, probably the result of conscript-age youths coming into the army.[36]

Hood's frontal attacks in the struggle for Atlanta resulted in 17,260 wounded Southerners being hospitalized during July and August. The mortality rate was a surprisingly low 4.7 percent, however, down from 10 percent at Murfreesboro and 16 percent at Shiloh. A total of 1,593 Confederates died in general hospitals, both from wounds and disease, and 823 patients deserted.[37]

Behind the statistics were stories of human suffering. John Davis, a Georgian wounded in the Battle of Peachtree Creek on July 20, told of his plight in a letter to his wife. He remained on the battlefield for several hours before being removed. Once he reached a field hospital, a surgeon examined his wound and bluntly told him that nothing could be done because the bullet was too close to the spine. For two days efforts were made to remove him to a general hospital, but he fainted when he was picked up. He was finally removed to Griffin, Georgia. By this time his wound was covered with maggots. He was cleaned up, fed, and eventually surgery was performed. By August 1, barely two weeks after the battle, he was able to report to his wife that he was "mending fast."[38]

Another Rebel was wounded at Peachtree Creek by a ball that passed diagonally through his head, taking off sections of both ears as it entered and exited. He laid on the battlefield for two days and then only a slight dressing was applied to the wound before he was removed to the rear. By the time he arrived at Newman, Georgia, his head was so swollen that his eyes were shut and he barely resembled a human being. He could not speak but only groaned faintly. Cold packing (the process of continual applications of thick wet bandages and salve) was placed on his head but nothing more was done, and within four weeks the patient was up and walking about.[39]

Not all were so fortunate. John J. Davis of the Forty-sixth Tennessee was wounded while on picket duty on July 26, 1864, by a ball that entered his right arm between the elbow and shoulder. A surgeon removed the bullet, and the wound was not considered dangerous. He was transferred to Flewellyn Hospital in Barnesville, Georgia, to recuperate. Phlebitis, an inflammatory condition of the veins, set in, and on August 18 he expired. Such was the fate of many.[40]

Some patients remembered their time in the hospital as pleasant and preferable to life in the trenches, but most complained of receiving little attention or medicine. William Norrell, an old man in the Sixty-third Georgia, had a decidedly poor opinion of Confederate doctors. They stole articles from the sick, he claimed, and their "ignorance and indifference to the needs of the sick . . . their airs of pomposity, and the coarse jests, while examining the sick is disgusting in the extreme. . . . This is at the division Infirmary. It is somewhat different at the Reg't."[41]

Hood began his Tennessee Campaign with an adequate number of physicians. On September 20, 1864, for example, S. D. Lee's corps, with 12,061 present for duty, counted 5 medical directors, 35 regimental surgeons, and 47 assistant surgeons. Even discounting the directors, this left an average of 1 doctor per 147 men.[42]

Returning sick were forwarded to the army as quickly as possible. By mid-October 1864, some 4,500 had arrived at Gadsden, Alabama. A soldier in the Thirty-fourth Alabama commented that he was glad to be back because "I get more to eat here than I did their [hospital]." Writing from a hospital in Alabama, an infantryman of the Twenty-ninth Georgia remarked to his parents that he would soon request to be returned to the ranks because "I can quit [get] more toete at camp."[43]

The Battle of Franklin, with its 7,000 Southern casualties, including 4,500 wounded, wrecked the Army of Tennessee. Homes and buildings were soon filled with the injured, and the town was converted into one mass ward. Dr. D. J. Roberts was assigned two surgeons, a steward, and a detail of soldiers and instructed to go into town and prepare a hospital for Bate's division. An old two-story wagon shop, an unoccupied two-story brick store, and the courthouse were commandeered. The buildings were swept clean, the floors covered with straw twelve inches thick, and rough bunks

*Private Columbus Tullos of the Eighth Mississippi was wounded May 27,
1864, at Dallas, Georgia, and again on July 20, 1864, at the Battle of
Atlanta. He was later killed at the Battle of Franklin. (Eugene C. Tullos)*

constructed for the most seriously wounded. Within hours all was in
readiness. Dr. Henry Holmes, an assistant surgeon in the Florida
brigade of Bate's division, noted that the Franklin wounded were
also sent to Columbia and placed in numerous homes along the road
to Nashville as the army advanced.[44]

In a skirmish on December 13, Captain Samuel Brown was

wounded in the right leg, about six inches above the knee, the bullet passing through without touching the bone. He wrote in his diary that he was taken to a little house, where his pants were ripped open. The surgeon then "put the fore finger of one hand in one hole; and the fore finger of the other hand in the other, and then he jabs them in and out, and the woman of the house looked at the operation until she had to run out of the house to keep from fainting." The wound was then dressed, and he was sent to the brigade hospital, which was a kitchen in an old farmer's house. The room was about sixteen feet square and filled with wounded. "We lay in tiers or rows and the hardest floor imaginable—they gave me a dose of morphine, and I go to sleep," he wrote. The next day he was placed in an ambulance with three others for an agonizing trip back to Franklin.[45]

Following the Battle of Nashville, some of the Southern wounded were transported by ambulance back into Mississippi with the returning army. Many wounded were unable to ford Shoal Creek and would have been captured but for cavalrymen riding them across. On December 24 a large number of wounded were ferried across the Tennessee River in pontoons near Florence, Alabama. W. B. Crumpton, wounded at Nashville, was furloughed and sent to Alabama. On April 15, 1865, he reported for duty at Montgomery. There he was joined by five hundred other returning soldiers who were to be sent to the Army of Tennessee, then in North Carolina.[46]

On the whole, the medical personnel of the Army of Tennessee performed an admirable job. They labored under constant disruptions and lack of supplies. Yet the mortality rate from battle casualties consistently dropped throughout the war, and though the disease mortality rate remained fairly constant, it rarely exceeded 2 percent. Under the circumstances, an enviable record was established.

I Will Have My Fun

Battle represented the ultimate experience for an army, but it accounted for only a fraction of the time. Far more days were spent in camp than either on the march or in battle. This was especially true of the Army of Tennessee between January 1863 and April 1864, during which nearly eleven of sixteen months were spent virtually dormant.

There was a pervasive boyish excitement about army life during the early months of the war. Writing from a camp of instruction during the summer of 1861, a sergeant of the First Tennessee concluded: "I am at this time injoying the pleasures of a Soldiers lif." James Hall of the Ninth Tennessee, encamped at Union City in June 1861, was of a like mind: "I think camp life will agree with me. . . . We have a delightful encampment in a shady grove." A Tennessee surgeon at Camp Trousdale observed that though some were anxious to go home, most seemed to enjoy themselves.[1]

Camp visitors were a common occurrence that first summer. "We shall expect you soon," James Hall informed his wife. "The camp [Camp Brown at Union City] is crowded with visitors from all parts of the district. We are making arrangements to have a tent made for the accommodation of our friends." Two days later he wrote his daughters: "We see ladies and little girls here reminds me of my little girls at home." According to another Tennessean, it was the same at Camp Trousdale, where dances were a nightly event. The various generals soon clamped down on such activity, despite the protests of the soldiers. As late as March 1862, however, a member of the Washington Artillery reported that his camp was filled with visitors from nearby LaGrange, Tennessee. His only regret was that the women "cannot compare to our New Orleans girls as to looks."[2]

Between March and May 1862 an especially imposing sense of grandeur pervaded the Corinth encampment. Never had there been a gathering on such a scale in the West. "We are part of a grand army whose tents are pitched on the ridges all about us as far as we can see through the woods: at reveilee we hear bands of music in every direction: some so far off as to be almost inaudible," observed an Alabama officer. An impressed officer of the Nineteenth Alabama wrote: "There is so many men camped about here that the camps look like a large Town of White Houses." A member of the Forty-seventh Tennessee described the scene to his wife: "Imagine you are on the streets of New York or not quite so much crowded & you have a pretty good notion of the amount of soldiers about here, carts mules horses but instead of pavement mud about ankle deep."[3]

Soon the excitement and spectacle wore off, and most of the soldiers discovered that army life was different than they had anticipated. It turned into a routine that was tiring, dirty, and grindingly monotonous. The reaction of the troops was decidedly negative. "I am tired of camp life," insisted a soldier of the Thirty-third Alabama at Tupelo in June 1862. "There is a great deal of sickness in our company and it makes the duty very hard on the rest. What time we are not on guard nor on detail to work we have to drill. We have just now come off a battalion drill and I am very tired. We have to carry our cartridge box with forty rounds of ammunition and a very heavy gun." Lieutenant James Williams concurred: "Soldiering is no child's play here [Corinth], we are experiencing hardships we never thought of before we left Mobile for Tennessee."[4]

Camp of the Fourth Kentucky at Corinth, Mississippi, in 1862.
(Library of Congress)

Camp vermin were a curse that afflicted officers and privates alike. Body lice, commonly referred to as "graybacks," were the most troublesome. An Alabamian, whose family was considering visiting him, discouraged them: "If you was here [Shelbyville] the Boddy lice would eat Booth of the children in one knight in spite of all we could doo; you don't have any idea what sort of animal they are." Writing from Chattanooga, a Mississippian candidly admitted to his mother: "I don't make any more of sitting down in a crowd and pulling off my shirt and picking the lice off me than I would to sit down at a good meal at home. I have caught as many as 40 to 50 at one time and others more but we never write such things home." During the reenlisting fervor at Dalton in early 1864, one wag was prompted to say that he had seen a large grayback with the letters "I.W." on his rear, indicating that he was "in for the war."[5]

There were other pests of a more serious nature. When the troopers of the Seventh Tennessee Cavalry were clearing an area at Randolph, Tennessee, they found it infested with yellow jackets. It took several days to make the place habitable. There were also occasional references to rattlesnakes. Johnny Green of the Kentucky brigade awoke one morning to find a large rattler on top of his blanket. One

Members of the Ninth Mississippi encamped at Pensacola in 1861. Just before Shiloh, a Confederate noted of the Army: "Some wore uniforms, some half uniforms, some no uniforms at all." (Library of Congress)

man captured it alive and jokingly chased almost everyone out of camp until his captain made him kill it. General Cleburne barely escaped serious injury one night when a large rattlesnake crawled in bed with him. He did not realize it was there until the next morning when he shook out his blanket.[6]

Dangers occasionally occurred even while the men enjoyed the relative ease of camp life. R. P. Boswell barely got out of his tent one evening at Bowling Green before it went up in flames. "I jumped up and holowed at the other boys and then Ran." Everyone got out safely, but many of their personal items "got burnt pretty bad." While walking through camp one day while at Corinth, A. H. Mecklin suddenly heard a bullet zip over his head. "It is a matter of surprise that the casualties among our own men from random bullets are no greater. Thousands of guns are fired off almost every day," he noted. A tree at Corinth came crashing into a tent one day, but fortunately no one was injured. A similar incident at Dalton had less fortunate results. A lieutenant, a corporal, and four privates were killed instantly. At Tullahoma a tornado roared through the camp of the First Tennessee, killing one and injuring others.[7]

Rain and mud added to the overall misery of camp life. "A camp
will bear a shower very well, and look none the worse for it; but these soaking rains play the deuce with it," concluded an officer at Corinth. "The ground is saturated, and the floors get wet; and all around the water lies in pools; blankets and clothing are saturated with damp air, even in trunks and knapsacks." A jokester at Columbus asserted that he had calculated that the place contained precisely 78 billion cubic feet of mud and suggested that some of the missing army mules were "either halfway down or at the bottom." Captain Todd Carter of the Twentieth Tennessee remarked that Tullahoma was "as chill inspiring as the swamps about Corinth." A story commonly shared at Tullahoma was that the name of the town came from two Greek words—"tulla" meaning "mud" and "homa" meaning "more mud."[8]

The rain, of course, confined the soldiers to their tents, which exacerbated the boredom. The entries of a diarist at Shelbyville in February told of his confinement:

February 15: Rained
February 17: Still raining which keeps us in our tents.
February 18: The same routine. No drill, no mails, idleness.
February 20: Confined to tent all day by rain and bad weather. Read and study. Can't think much. So hard to concentrate in camp.
February 21: Raining. Still confined to tent.[9]

When the troops first settled in camp, they frequently had to go without shelter. The summer of 1861 was humid, and the uniqueness of the camping experience meant that there were few complaints. By early fall, however, the weather was becoming increasingly cold, and the shivering soldiers discovered that their tents, if indeed they had any, would be insufficient. Work soon began on winter quarters. The lumber was supplied by the government, but there was never enough to go around. There was also some complaint that the Tennessee troops were given partiality and were able to construct their cabins with plank flooring and even build stables for mules before some men received any lumber. As late as December 1861, Israel Gibbons of the Eleventh Louisiana was reporting that "there are still thousands who have no shelter than their flimsy tents, all waiting patiently for lumber."[10]

There were several varieties of quarters. Some tents were boarded up on either end and a chimney added of mud, bricks, boards, or barrels. Sergeant Albert Fall wintered at Bowling Green in 1861–62. He constructed a brick fireplace after his chimney barrel caught fire and nearly destroyed his tent. Most built conventional log cabins with a capacity of six to eight men. Brigadier General John Bowen's brigade wintered at Feleciana, Kentucky, during 1861–62. Each company had about 14 cabins for the privates. An entire regiment averaged 175 cabins, which included those for privates, officers, hospital, and guardhouse. About fifteen days were required to construct the entire camp.[11]

The Tullahoma encampment was similar in appearance. Most of the men winterized their tents by boarding them up and attaching chimneys. A Reb near Shelbyville wrote of the variety of quarters: "You wanted to know if we have tents," wrote Thomas Warrick. "We have got tents and some durt houses and some bordy shelters and so we all mak out the best we can." At the evacuation of Tullahoma, a Federal officer was surprised to see that the Confederates had "left about 1,500 good wall tents, all standing just as if the troops had marched out for dress parade." Shortly thereafter, a lieutenant in the Thirteenth Tennessee jotted: "All our tents being worthless & condemned were burnt at Tullahoma. A blanket stretched is a poor substitute for a tent, though it does very well."[12]

Winter quarters at Dalton consisted of rows of one-room log huts "chinked" with red clay. To one soldier, Dalton took on the appearance of a shantytown, while another thought it similar to "a western town—built in a day." One Georgian admitted that his shanty was not much but still considered himself more fortunate "than half our men [who] have no cabins yet. They are taking the weather as it comes." Concerning his hut, Thacher Owens of the Thirty-fourth Alabama concluded simply: "I reckon it is better than staying outdoors."[13]

Men of the First Alabama strike a relaxed pose in their Pensacola camp in April 1861. The regiment participated in the Atlanta and Tennessee campaigns. (Florida State Archives)

Drills, camp routines, and constructing quarters consumed much of the soldier's time. An Alabama cannoneer at Dalton wanted his cousin to know that he had little time to spare, "in proof of which I will state that having just finished my days cooking for the mess consisting of eight, I am now penning these lines to you by candle light, the rest having retired." Yet most soldiers made it clear that they spent many hours with nothing to do. Thus the sheer monotony was unquestionably the most universal complaint. Griped a cannoneer at Tullahoma: "Camp is dull nothing but Eat sleep and drill with an occasional review by some General that wishes to show himself in his military glory." Likewise, a Razorback in the Fifteenth Arkansas was candid about his agenda at Dalton: "We are doing what all others of this army are doing at this time—lounging around camp and nothing to employ our spare moments or divert our minds. It is dull, insufficiently dull."[14]

Mail call was the most popular moment of the day, yet the mail ran very irregularly during active campaigning. The experience of several Southerners during the Atlanta Campaign was exemplary. "We have no mail only by chance," lamented J. N. Davis on May 29, 1864. On July 14 Lieutenant Berryhill informed his wife, "There is such an immense amount of mail matter sent out from Atlanta that it gets badly mixed up and there are many letters that never get through." On August 1 he noted that no mail had been received for two weeks because of a break in the railroad. A Mississippian, also writing during this time, believed that outgoing mail was being detained in Atlanta. On July 22 W. A. Stephens explained to his wife: "I have heard that General Hood have stoped the mails I dont no that to be the cais though we have had no mail for 6 or 7 day." On September 7 Captain S. H. Dent remarked: "The army PO was destroyed at Atlanta with the mails and no arrangements have been made for distributing the army mail."[15]

Vendors sometimes provided needed supplies and a break from the monotony. During the Atlanta Campaign, a Texan remarked, "Our camp has been invaded by peddlers selling pies ground peas—paper—envelopes pins needles buttons &c. &c." Writing about the same time, a Georgian noted that he "went back toward midday to meet the Sutlers Wagon and found one and bought a little paper, bread, and cakes."[16]

Social contact with civilians, although limited by 1863, was occasionally made. "I know a good many girls here [Shelbyville] & go to see them frequently," Captain Robert Kennedy informed his sister. "I have an engagement to go to church with one tomorrow—Most of them are rather of the cornbread order, but there is one occasionally that possesses some attractions. We are going to have a picnic Thursday just below our camp. I am on the committee of arrangements & will go out this evening to engage the baking of some cakes."[17]

The troops enjoyed a variety of sports, "some of which are harder than any work I ever saw," observed a Louisiana soldier at Columbus. Among them were footraces, several kinds of ball, wrestling, climbing trees, and a herculean game in which a cannonball was hurled into one of nine holes in the ground. On Christmas Day 1862 the officers of Manigault's brigade had a footrace, and afterward the colonels "chose sides from among their officers and men to play base[ball]." At Dalton the men played ball "just like school

boys." Related one: "The 6th Fla. challenged the 1st & 4th [Florida] 91
for a game of Town Ball and the 4th accepted it and beat the 6th two   *I Will*
games on the 3rd [May] and one on the 4th [May]. the 7th Fla.   *Have My*
played and made a tie game of 66 rounds 25 men to each side."[18]   *Fun*

One of the more soothing diversions was listening to music. "We have the best kind of martial music every morning and evening," wrote a Southerner from Corinth. "Bands and drums of the best kind. One is discoursing the 'Bonnie Blue Flag' exquisitely now over the hill near by. In one brigade two or three regiments have bands. They tend to enliven camp life." Washington Ives was camped only one hundred yards from the band of the Thirty-seventh Georgia at Dalton and enjoyed such songs as "Let Me Kiss Him for His Mother," "The Lone Rock by the Sea," "Kelly May," and the "Village Quick Step." Records indicate that few regiments had large bands. In A. P. Stewart's division in May 1862 only one of nine regiments boasted a sizable band—the Fourth Tennessee's band with fourteen members. The Thirteenth Tennessee listed eight musicians and the Fifth Tennessee six, but all others had between one and four. The bands were eventually grouped together at the brigade level. At Dalton Lucius Polk's brigade band consisted of one cornet, one brass horn, two violins, two flutes, and one guitar. In September 1864 S. D. Lee's corps of over 12,000 troops had only 138 musicians.[19]

Sometimes the melodious strains filtered into the enemy camps and vice versa. Indeed, during the siege of Chattanooga, there was a battle of the bands, with "Dixie" and "Yankee Doodle" being batted between the lines. In the trench warfare of the Atlanta Campaign, the cornet player of the First Georgia Battalion Sharpshooters would come up after supper and take requests shouted from the Federals.[20]

Banjo players and fiddlers enjoyed tremendous popularity in camp. Lieutenant Frank Rowlett of the Twenty-fourth Tennessee always attracted a large crowd when he played his fiddle, and his loss after Shiloh, from ill health, was sorely felt. When Henry Semple's Alabama Battery joined the army during the Kentucky Campaign, a soldier thought they were "gay boys—some of them right good musicians. Several played tunes on a fiddle and banjo."[21]

Theatrics were also in the list of entertainments. In early 1863 the Kentucky brigade was encamped at Manchester, Tennessee. A play

This 1861 photograph shows troops of the Fifth Georgia in camp. The regiment served in the Army of Tennessee from Murfreesboro to Atlanta. (United States Military History Institute)

was performed one evening before two hundred townspeople. It was a farce in which a few of the Kentuckians dressed up in women's clothes, which had been borrowed from some of the local belles. Two artillery companies formed themselves into acting troupes while at Dalton. One evening "Turner's Battery Amateurs" presented "two pantomines and one burlesque tragedy—'The Pirates of the Aegean Sea.' A good hit and well performed," evaluated one soldier-critic. Fenner's Louisiana Battery possessed unusual dramatic talent. It performed the opera *Zimluco,* accompanied by a band and a choir composed of Kentuckians. During the 1864 Tennessee Campaign, the same troupe presented a play at a college in Florence, Alabama.[22]

Practical jokes were frequently the order of the day. A cannoneer with A. S. Johnston's army noted that writing letters was always done with great difficulty, "for as soon as it is commenced every body makes all the noise they can on purpose to interrupt the person so engaged." All kinds of "great sport" were played on April Fools

Day. According to a Georgian at Dalton, the boys often attempted to
see who could "ruffle the other's hair the most." While at Columbus,
it was the officers who had the fun one evening, when a colonel,
adjutant, two majors, and several captains and lieutenants extempo-
rized an "orchestra," consisting in part of a cracked drum, a wheezy
clarinet, a trumpet, and a banjo. They then proceeded to the quarters
of Colonel J. B. G. Kennedy of the Twenty-first Louisiana and
awakened him with their infernal racket. It was Kennedy who got
the last laugh, however, when he offered them a bottle of whiskey in
appreciation for their serenade. The bottle was passed around and
quickly emptied before they discovered that the good colonel had
actually given them ipecac. Most of them spent the night vomiting
and reported for duty the next morning with pale faces and vowing
revenge.[23]

There were at least two outfits at Fort Donelson that had mascots
to help pass the time more enjoyably. Sergeant Jerome McCanless of
Company H, Third Tennessee, kept a rooster named "Jake Donelson," which was captured, along with its owner, at the surrender
of the fort. Also seized was "Frank," the dog mascot of Company B,
Second Kentucky. Frank was later "exchanged," along with the
regiment. He was wounded several times during the war but served
until the Atlanta Campaign, when he was reported missing. He ate
dog rations carried in a haversack strapped on his back and eagerly
took part in maneuvers, although it was said that he disliked dress
parade.[24]

Books and newspapers were eagerly sought but often difficult to
obtain. At Murfreesboro some enterprising soldiers published their
own paper, the *Daily Rebel Banner,* which, at ten cents a copy, ran
lost and found items, rewards for deserters, and advertisements for
recruits.[25]

Other camp diversions included vocalizing around the camp fire,
choirs (the Kentucky brigade had a glee club specializing in classical
music), chess, checkers, debating clubs, and making wooden or corn
pipes. At Dalton gander pullings were a favorite with the cavalry. A
greased gander would be tied by its feet to a tree, and a trooper
would come riding at full speed and attempt to grab its jerking,
slender neck.[26]

If there was any single activity that stood out in the memories of the men, it was the Dalton snowball fight. On March 22, 1864, a late winter storm dumped five inches of snow, a novelty to many of the boys from the lower South. Several impromptu scraps soon elevated to a regimental level. Otis Baker described a fray between the Tenth and Forty-fourth Mississippi and the Forty-first Mississippi, reinforced by the Seventh and Ninth Mississippi. "In the afternoon they again advanced upon our camp in three columns, having previously made an insolent demand for the unconditional surrender of the army of the East, as we were called, allowing us but ten minutes in which to decide," Baker wrote. "The demand being refused a hot attack was made and after an engagement of a half or three quarters of an hour terminated in their repulse. Their losses were their commdr in chief, besides several other officers of rank, and two or three stands of colors."[27]

The spectacular event of the day, however, was a massive snow battle between the divisions of Cheatham and Walker. An estimated five to six thousand men participated, and the air became thick with thousands of snowballs. Colonel George W. Gordon of the Eleventh Tennessee electrified the Tennesseans when he rode out waving an improvised flag—an old bandanna. This action earned him the sobriquet "the Snowball Colonel." Walker's Georgians were eventually routed through their camps and into the woods. One of Walker's colonels cried foul, claiming that half of the men in his regiment had never before been in a snowball fight.[28]

The day was one of great frolic for the army, but it was far from child's play. Charges were later made that a few rocks were chucked amid the snowballs. "Every thing was taken in good fun but it was rough play. The ground was speckled with blood from bruised noses," recorded a Florida artilleryman. Casualties among the Fifth Company Washington Artillery included the captain (two teeth knocked out), a lieutenant (a black eye), and five privates (bloody noses). There was even one report that two men were accidentally killed.[29]

There were, of course, other ways to escape the tedium of camp and the dread of battle, and these included a diversity of sins and moral lapses. The most prevalent vice in the army was swearing. Although to the modern observer this may seem a harmless enough transgression within the overall dynamics of war, to many nineteenth-century Southerners it ran deeper. One historian has observed that in the mid-1800s public profanity was viewed largely as a class sin, displayed by the "common" and "ill-bred." Joseph Lyman, a blueblood from New Orleans, was appalled at the cursing in his outfit, "from the major to the drummer." "I don't think I will ever assimilate myself to low and dissolute men by using any of their favorite vocabulary." Yet it is clear that most of the western soldiers comfortably engaged in the practice. Lieutenant Robert Watson was one such who had no intention of giving it up, despite pressure from his prudish company commander. "Several of us were drilled today for swearing. I was one of this number," he wrote from Chattanooga in October 1863. "I told him [captain] that when I joined the Confederate Army that I did not intend to become a Methodist preacher and if he thought he could make me a preacher or hypocrite of me by punishment that he was mistaken."[30]

A more disruptive vice was excessive drinking. The problem cropped up early in the war and was frequently prompted by accessibility to cities and towns as the troops moved about. In July 1861 the Sixteenth Tennessee left Camp Trousdale and passed through Nashville. While at that place, many of the troops became blatantly drunk and troublesome. Despite strict martial law in Memphis, a number of the men of the Fourth Tennessee became inebriated when that regiment passed through. Similarly, when the Twentieth Tennessee had an hour to wait at the Chattanooga depot, it proved enough time for many to become intoxicated with mountain apple brandy. The guilty were arrested and confined to a mule pen until sober. At Fort Donelson, Colonel Adolphus Heiman had all skiffs destroyed to stop his troops from frequenting Lady Peggy's, a saloon and dance hall across the Cumberland River. The liquor trafficking was not stopped, however; the soldiers simply swam the river. In March 1862, a private in the Fifteenth Mississippi noted that some men in his regiment went into nearby Fayetteville, Tennessee, and "got drunk and as a result . . . we had several quarrels—some fights, two of which were rather sanguinary."[31]

The problem persisted throughout the early stages of the 1862 Kentucky Campaign as the army journeyed through dozens of towns. The Thirteenth Tennessee, en route via Mobile, made a fifteen-minute stop at Tupelo. The men piled off the boxcars and hurriedly began buying gin, brandy, and whiskey from local vendors. When the engine whistle blew, those who had not yet been served snatched all they could grab and jumped back into the cars. As Stanford's battery passed through one town, a member remarked that several artillerymen "got tight and wanted to fight."[32]

Whiskey, issued to the troops on holidays, frequently caused problems. A sergeant in the First Tennessee thought that Christmas Day 1861 at Bowling Green was "very dull," although some of the men "got drunk and cut up generally and was put under guard." There were similar problems at Murfreesboro the following Christmas. A member of the 154th Tennessee remarked: "Eggnog was fashionable and Captains, Lieutenants, and Privates was drunk and very troublesome." The officers of the Twentieth Tennessee bought a barrel of whiskey for their men, which resulted in many brawls. Christmas 1863, at Dalton, was little different according to a sergeant: "Whiskey issued to the troops. Some of the boys got on a spree."[33]

Irregular issues of whiskey were made for the purpose of raising morale and during cold weather, apportioned at the ratio of two gallons per hundred men. Borrowing from nondrinkers, some of the men were able to secure enough that they got more than a little high. Indeed, a shocked officer noted at the beginning of the Atlanta Campaign, after a whiskey issue had been made, that some of the men could hardly march and had to be helped along. The quality of the drink was not always guaranteed. When government whiskey, made of sorghum seed, was issued to the Thirty-ninth North Carolina at Lost Mountain, north of Atlanta, the vile concoction caused scores to vomit.[34]

Despite the best efforts of the provost, whiskey was also available through illegal sources. The ways to smuggle it were as ingenious as they were innumerable, including hiding it in watermelons and pouring it down the muzzle of a musket, the latter attempted by an Irishman in the Second Tennessee. Some ways were more public, as reported by a news correspondent at Dalton: "On the railroad . . . a drinking saloon is sometimes open in the shape of a man with several canteens around his neck. . . . There is generally a crowd around this 'saloon,' which seems to do a thriving business in a small way."[35]

Another pervasive, if somewhat less destructive, vice was gambling. As was true with drinking, some soldiers shunned gambling as sin. "Much of my time in camp is spent doing nothing," admitted a Mississippian at Corinth, yet he was committed to "not fall into the habit of many others in camp, who spend their leisure time playing cards." A Texas Ranger, also at that place, admitted, "There is a great deal of gambling in camp, and I have seen enough to disgust me with it, and I have sworn never to touch a card again while I live." An Alabamian at Murfreesboro was likewise appalled at the "panful [painful] spell of Rafalin here at this time. But I don't take no hand in non of it. Some makes money at it But some Loose all that they have got."[36]

Despite moral objections and the prohibitive efforts of some officers, many did partake in gambling. Perhaps the most notorious gambling hole was Chattanooga's "Hell's Half Acre," three-fourths of a mile in front of the city, just behind the picket line, in the center of the Rebel line. Here some three to five hundred gamblers daily collected and indulged in faro, draw poker, seven up, down to thumble ring, dice, and three-card monte. The participants were reported to show up with bags of gold, silver, U.S. greenbacks, and Confederate money.[37]

In the cavalry there were horse races, despite restrictions to the contrary. Such races were forbidden, not for moral reasons but for the welfare of the animals. In the infantry footraces were in vogue. "This morning there was a foot race of which there were over 1000$ bet on it. The soldiers are very frequently at such games as this," scribbled a Mississippian at Tullahoma. Cockfighting was the mania of others. James Hall remembered that there were five or six men in his Tennessee regiment who participated but all were killed at Shiloh. Thereafter, the sport was not rekindled in his regiment. William S. Dillon of the Fourth Tennessee, camped at Shelbyville, remarked: "Cock fighting is now a great amusement among the men but they have not suceeded in getting me to join in this sport." It was said that Taylor McCoy of the Fourth Kentucky maintained the largest stable of cocks in the army, and whenever he was found eating chicken soup it was assumed that another of his birds had lost.[38]

A moral lapse less talked about but also present was illicit sex. A

TABLE 2

Incidence of Venereal Disease in Selected Regiments of the
Army of Northern Virginia, July 1861–March 1862

Month	Mean strength	New cases	Average
July 1861	11,452	248	1 per 46
August 1861	27,042	254	1 per 106
September 1861	33,284	218	1 per 152
December 1861	34,865	76	1 per 458
March 1862	19,942	24	1 per 830

soldier-correspondent with Albert Sidney Johnston's army in Kentucky during the winter of 1861–62 described the three classes of women in camp. The first consisted of officers' wives, the second of "rough cooks and washers, who have their husbands along." The third and lowest class "is happily the smallest," he reported. "Here and there a female of elegant appearance and unextionable manners; truly wife-like in their tented seclusion, but lacking the great and only voucher of respectability for females in camp—the marriage tie."[39]

Evidence indicates that some lewd women frequented army camps throughout the spring of 1863. John Harris of the Nineteenth Louisiana deploringly informed his wife: "The army is all the time surrounded by debased women—and I believe they are the cause of so much wickedness. I am disgusted with them.... Suffice it to say that there is no place for a decent woman—I have heard many good men say no decent woman would come the second time, and I respectfully beg you not to come the first time."[40]

Bell Wiley has studied the subject of venereal disease as it relates to sundry regiments in the Army of Northern Virginia from July 1861 to March 1862. His data, shown in Table 2, lead him to conclude that venereal disease was "not widely prevalent" and that, with minor temporary exceptions, it declined as the war progressed because of "tightening of discipline and ... active campaigning took the bulk of the army away from Richmond."[41]

An examination of medical records for the Army of Tennessee reveals a different conclusion. There were only 220 reported cases of

TABLE 3
Incidence of Venereal Disease in the Army of Tennessee,
January–May 1863

Month	Mean strength	New cases	Average
January	50,604	258	1 per 196
February	63,494	280	1 per 226
March	61,226	384	1 per 159
April	64,441	455	1 per 141
May	55,121	418	1 per 131

syphilis in the army between June and November 1862, averaging only slightly more than one new case per day during the period. There were no statistics on gonorrhea cases. During the Tullahoma encampment there was a dramatic increase in the incidence of venereal disease. Between January and May 1863 there were a total of 991 cases of gonorrhea and 804 cases of syphilis, or an average of twelve new cases per day. The army was not involved in active campaigning, nor was it encamped near a large city because Nashville was occupied. From January to March 1863, Bragg's army averaged one case of venereal disease per 183 mean strength (Table 3), as compared with one in 330 in John C. Pemberton's Army of Vicksburg. Thus in the Army of Tennessee, the instance of venereal disease did not decrease as the war progressed. Indeed, it remained considerably higher than in Lee's army and higher yet than in the other main Confederate army in the West.[42]

At Dalton Captain Key confided that "rumor says that almost half of the women in the vicinity of the army, married and unmarried, are lost to all virtue." A staff officer told the post commander at that place: "Complaints are daily made to me of the number of lewd women in this town [Dalton], and on the outskirts of the army. They are said to be impregnating this whole command, and the commissariat has been frequently robbed, with a view of supporting these disreputable characters." General Johnston responded by issuing an order that all women in the vicinity who could not give proof of respectability and livelihood be transported to other parts.[43]

Even during active campaigning around Atlanta, the incidence of venereal disease remained consistent with that of the Tullahoma encampment. During July and August 1864 there were 561 new reported cases, or an average of 9 per day. The ratio of cases per effective strength was somewhat higher in the Army of Tennessee than in the Union army opposing Johnston at that time: in July the Confederate forces averaged 1 case for every 203 soldiers, as compared to the Union troops' average of 1 for every 241 soldiers, and in August the Confederate rate was 1 per 150, while that for the Union was 1 per 256.[44]

Camp life thus presented widely diverse experiences for the western Confederate soldier. Although pastimes were similar to those in Lee's army, the stark variance in the venereal disease rate was perhaps a social comment on the people and climate of the region. Wrote one soldier at Dalton to his mother: "I never play cards for money, nor gambel any; some times I play a little for fun. I hardly ever drink any whiskey and dont swear any, though [I] will have my fun if there is any to be had."[45]

I Saw 14 Men Tied to Postes and Shot

As in all Civil War armies, discipline in the Army of Tennessee could be harsh. Some men were tough cases and clearly deserved their fate, while others were mere boys whose transgressions evoked the sympathy of the troops. There were a variety of degrading punishments, several of which bordered on the cruel and many of which were publicly administered. Unquestionably the deterrent value of punishments and the consequences of disobedience helped maintain the army's cohesiveness despite battlefield losses. Wrote a Tennessean after the war: "So far now as patriotism was concerned, we had forgotten all about that, and we did not now so much love our country, as we feared Bragg."[1]

In examining the disturbances that took place in the army, it is easy to lose sight of the fact that the norm was one of strict discipline. In September 1861, a soldier-correspondent dispelled a rumor that a riot had occurred at Camp Brown in Union City with several soldiers being killed. "Nothing took place," he insisted, and he further noted that breaches of discipline "are extremely few and far between."[2]

When offenses did occur, they were usually the result of comparatively minor moral lapses—drunkenness led the list. Most culprits were simply placed in confinement. Indeed, during November 1861, the Kentucky brigade averaged nineteen soldiers per day in the guardhouse. There were, of course, more punishing ways to keep drunks in line. During the Kentucky Campaign, a staff officer witnessed the "buck and gagging" of thirteen men, all from the same company of the Thirteenth Louisiana, for being intoxicated. All had their hands tied behind their knees, with a stick between the arms and knees and a bayonet affixed lengthwise in their mouths. For being drunk while on guard duty, Private Henry Jones, while at Tullahoma, was required to stand on a barrel with a whiskey bottle hanging around his neck for two hours a day for a month.[3]

Not all incidents avoided bloodshed. While at Columbus, twenty-six-year-old Private Thomas Miller of the Eleventh Louisiana became drunk and attempted to forge a pass and sneak out of camp. The sentinel was not fooled and ordered him back. When he refused to go, the officer of the day, Captain J. E. Austin, was called, but Miller simply cursed him. The captain placed him under arrest, but when he took him by the shoulder Miller jerked loose. By this time a large crowd had gathered and the situation was growing tense. Austin drew a revolver, and when this brought more oaths, shot Miller in the arm. The drunken man then lunged forward, at which time he was shot in the head and killed. Austin immediately reported the incident and requested an inquiry, but there were so many witnesses that none was held. Several weeks later a similar incident occurred involving a drunk Tennessean. When the sentinel refused to let the drunken man pass, he went to his tent in a rage and returned with his musket. As he charged forward, he was shot and killed.[4]

Drunkenness led to other altercations that turned violent. One such fight resulted in the death of a soldier at Bowling Green in November 1861. The next month a soldier was stabbed to death by a drunk Tennessean at Columbus. During the march to Kentucky, a fight broke out between two drunken cannoneers, one in the Washington Artillery and the other the Jefferson Artillery, which led to the latter's death.[5]

Whiskey was issued to the troops at Dalton on Christmas Day 1863, perhaps a needed morale booster under the circumstances, but one that resulted in a great deal of trouble. Discipline completely broke down in many camps, and guns were discharged in every direction. It was rumored that no fewer than five men were killed by indiscriminate shots. Fights also broke out. So appalled was John Farris, surgeon of the Forty-first Tennessee, that he was convinced that a malaise had gripped the army. In his brigade, many officers, including some colonels, had become "beastly drunk," along with the troops and some guards. The officers who attempted to restore order "were cursed and abused by drunken officers & privates alike. No regard was paid to any law or regulation whatever."[6]

Alcohol was usually the root cause of much insubordination. A drunk sergeant drew a dagger on an artillery captain at Columbus, causing the latter to draw his sword and gash the attacker's hand. At Tullahoma a drunk cannoneer called his dark complexioned, slant-eyed captain, Felix Robertson, "half 'Injin," and for this he was strung up by his thumbs with his feet barely touching the ground.[7]

The conviction for insubordination of Private Patrick McDonald of the Twenty-first Tennessee, while at Tupelo, was apparently unrelated to alcohol. He simply refused to go on drill, and when his lieutenant came into his tent McDonald ordered him out and threatened to strike him. For this action he was given twenty days of extra fatigue duty and fined three months' pay.[8]

Thievery was another common offense. Early in the war a distinction was made between stealing from citizens and from one's comrades, but this fine line evaporated as the war progressed. During the Atlanta Campaign a Georgian admitted: "These old soldiers will steal anything they can get their hands on. A great many will do it." A soldier at Shelbyville related: "It is now a common thing to see men wearing before their respective Regiments boards with thief written thereon." Only a few nights earlier, he had witnessed half a dozen convicted thieves yoked together between two rails, with only twelve inches separating each from the back of the person in front.[9]

At Murfreesboro in December 1862, most of the men of the

Forty-fifth Tennessee received a holiday furlough because the outfit came from that vicinity. They returned to camp with pies, cakes, and cookies, which promptly raised both the attention and hunger of the nearby Twentieth Tennessee. The latter thus devised a plan that resulted in challenging the Forty-fifth to a snowball fight. While the soldiers were thus engaged, a raiding party from the Twentieth made off with food, cooking utensils, and even some muskets. What disciplinary action was taken, if any, is not known.[10]

There is apparently no record of anyone in the Army of Tennessee having been shot for sleeping while on duty, although at times the possibility seemed real. Writing from Columbus, Dr. Charles Johnson, surgeon of the Eleventh Louisiana, advised: "One of our men, LaVergne, from Cat Island, went to sleep last night at his post and was caught. I have been in a pack of trouble to save his life, finally, by a deal of begging, coaxing, etc. he has been excused from the severist punishment." At Dalton, Oliver Strickland reluctantly told his mother: "I reckon that you want to hear the truth about me. I am under guard for going to sleep on my post last night before last. I don't know what they will do with me, that I don't know. . . . They may shoot me."[11]

Comparatively lenient sentences were given out for those absent without leave, a category distinct from desertion. The difference was apparently based on intent: the destination of the soldier, length of departure, and whether he turned himself in. In 1862 the Army of Tennessee's predecessor, the Army of the Mississippi, administered to a defendant absent two weeks who turned himself in a sentence of two months in the guardhouse. For another soldier who took a four-day unauthorized trip to Memphis, the punishment was thirty days' stable cleaning, wearing a ball and chain for ten days, and forfeiture of four months' pay. A similar conviction at Shelbyville required a man to wear a barrel shirt (arms and legs protruding out of a barrel) with a sign "Absent Without Leave" for three days, plus seven days' hard labor.[12]

Cowardice in the face of the enemy was a more serious infraction. Two privates in the Nineteenth Alabama were tried and convicted at Tupelo for "misbehavior before the enemy." Both deserted during a skirmish at the Tuscumbia River on May 3, 1862, but subsequently turned themselves in. They were sentenced to have their heads shaved, to be drummed out of the service, and to serve one year of hard labor in a local jail. The punishments for cowardice frequently involved some form of public humiliation. "I was aroused from sleep by a drum and fife passing through the quarters, escorting a fellow carrying a board on which was in large letters 'cowardice' for shirking in battle," noted Captain Samuel Kelly at Dalton.[13]

Officers found guilty of cowardice were usually cashiered. Such was the fate of Lieutenant B. F. Arnett of the Ninth Kentucky, who left his company during the Battle of Shiloh. Lieutenant John W. Davidson of the Twenty-fifth Tennessee was drummed out for his actions in the Battle of Murfreesboro; he hid behind a tree rather than advance with his men. Lieutenant I. W. Butler of the Ninth Mississippi suffered a similar punishment for his conduct at Mur-freesboro. He took a shovel into battle, and every time the regiment was halted, he began digging his own personal earthen protection. In February 1863 a first lieutenant in the Second Arkansas was shot for cowardice, but the circumstances are unclear.[14]

The punishments meted out varied depending on the discretion of individual commanders. Cleburne did not permit buck and gagging and once had an officer "busted" for administering it. He preferred extra guard duty, cleaning guns and equipment, or withdrawal of leave privileges. General Hindman had an aversion to putting men on extra guard duty, which he considered "the most honorable duty of a soldier, except fighting, and must not be degraded." Cheatham made those who recklessly discharged their weapons mark time from midnight till dawn.[15]

Some lower-grade officers acted as tyrants and went overboard in their strictness. According to an infantryman in the Nineteenth Louisiana, his colonel "issued orders this week that if any Soldier While on drill Should break ranks for the call of Nature, and Should Stay longer than [the] usual time, he will be punished by being tied up by the thumbs for fifteen minutes or until he faints. A great many men have Diorhear and they have to suffer—Some do their business occasionally in their clothes." B. L. Wyman of Semple's Alabama Battery missed a roll call at Tullahoma one day because someone had stolen his shoes and he did not want to stand in the mud in his socks. For this he was given extra guard duty. "This was done by order of his majesty, H. E. Semple, and a meaner Captain cannot be found in the Confederate army," he insisted. So cruel was Captain Felix Robertson that it was rumored that he might be killed by his own men.[16]

Some generals came to the assistance of their men. When a Kentuckian refused to sweep out his lieutenant's tent, he was thrown into the guardhouse. Upon hearing of this, Breckinridge rode at a gallop to the lieutenant's quarters and gave him a thorough tongue-lashing. "I want you to understand that when a private refuses to voluntarily sweep out my tent I will do it myself. They are not menials in [this] brigade. They are all gentlemen, and you have no right to command one of them to do menial service. Now you go to the guardhouse and apologize to the soldier you have insulted and sweep about your tent, or you will take his place," he demanded.[17]

When Cleburne's division was camped on the Spring Road in the spring of 1864, the inspector general, a Major J. C. Dickson, inspected the picket guard daily, ordering the men to shoulder arms. If there was any movement whatever they were given extra guard duty. It became such a show that as many as four to five hundred troops would assemble to watch Dickson's performance. One day Cleburne happened by and observed what was taking place. He shouted: "Major Dickson, bring your men to order arms while you give those instructions not in a book." A hearty Rebel yell went up from the troops. For a long time following, each time the major passed, an anonymous yell was heard: "Who gave those instructions not in a book?" Came the reply: "Major Dickson."[18]

A commission was established at Corinth to deal with crimes of a civil nature such as murder and rape. Such incidents were apparently rare but not unheard-of. In July 1863 a deserter from Ben Hill's regiment was turned in by his wife. He was caught but soon deserted again and returned to murder her. The wife's brother subsequently saw the man at Tyner's Station and shot him to death.[19]

A military police force was required to carry out court-martial judgments, inflict punishments, and arrest the disorderly. These responsibilities fell to the provost guard. At Columbus a company of the First Louisiana Cavalry was nightly ordered into town to arrest drunken soldiers and whiskey sellers. In combat, they were placed behind the battle line to prevent shirking and were in charge of prisoners. Bate's brigade carried 1,055 men into action at Chick-

amauga and had a provost detail of 30. The provost of Marcellus A.
Stovall's brigade was placed as skirmishers at Chickamauga to re-
lieve weary soldiers at night. The provost detail eventually evolved
into a permanently assigned detachment. In Manigault's brigade, for
example, the squad consisted of 2 officers and 30 soldiers. After the
Battle of Atlanta, Hood directed that each division should have a
provost detail of 60 men.[20]

The provost guards were not regarded kindly by the troops, who
never lost an opportunity to jeer at them. Brigadier General Manigault recalled an incident when the provost squad was passing by.
"Look out, boys. Anybody with a pocketbook or a plug of tobacco
in his pocket, put his hand over it, for here comes the Provost
Guard!" shouted a jokester. Several men promptly pretended to hide
such items, although none existed. There was hearty laughter by all
except the provost guards, who kept silent but gave a scornful
glance.[21]

Desertions occurred with embarrassing regularity in the Army of
Tennessee, and severe measures had to be taken to deal with the
problem. Yet there was a troubling lack of consistency. In June 1862
Privates J. F. Roach and Charles Markham of the Seventh Arkansas
stole mules and deserted, only to be captured and returned. They
were sentenced to three months' hard labor and forfeiture of pay for
a similar time. Meanwhile, Privates William McIntyre and William
Fagan of the Twenty-first Tennessee were given six months' hard
labor and fines for a similar offense. Surprising leniency was shown
toward two privates in the Thirteenth Tennessee who deserted after
Shiloh. Owing to their youth and former good record, the court
sentenced them to wear a barrel shirt for two hours and forfeit three
months' pay. Bragg was enraged at the "totally inadequate" sentence
and warned the court that in the future he would not "approve of
such a trivial punishment." Yet other convicted men were let off with
head shavings, fines, and one month in the guardhouse with ball and
chain. As late as April 1863, a deserter in the 154th Tennessee,
described only by the last name Fitzgerald, was sentenced to only six
hours of hard labor a day for six days.[22]

Most deserters did not get off so easily. A soldier-correspondent happened to witness the administration of a punishment in December 1861 in Kentucky. Three men of the First Missouri who had deserted had their heads shaved, were branded with the letter "D" on the left hip, lashed fifty times, and drummed out of the service in front of their brigade to the tune of the "Rogue's March."[23]

This punishment, with some variations, remained standard in the Army of Tennessee. The lashing could be particularly brutal. One incident at Tupelo stood out in the mind of Sam Watkins. Two men of the Twenty-third Tennessee—Dave Brewer, about sixty years old, and Rube Franklin, about forty-five—were strung up by their hands to a tree, after having had their heads shaved and shirts stripped. Franklin was whipped 39 times with a piece of leather cut into three strips, thus making 117 welts, thoroughly blistering the man and causing much screaming. Brewer was whipped much more lightly for fear that at his age the punishment would prove fatal. On May 27, 1862, William Dillon of the Fourth Tennessee noted that he witnessed the punishment of a man by the name of Reddon of the Twenty-fourth Mississippi. "He went home last October and was brought back a few days ago. He received 30 lashes, was branded on the left hip with the letter D and had his head shaved and was then drummed out of the service." Rufus Daniel described the lashing of two deserters of the Seventh Arkansas as follows: "They were tied to a wagon wheel and struck 38 lashes with a cat of nine tails upon their naked backs, one of them fainted while whipping him."[24]

Lashing seems to have been phased out (the last documented one took place at Tupelo in July 1862) and replaced with other punishments. At Dalton, Johnston had men placed in a pillory for four hours a day for sixty days. Though seemingly less painful than a lashing, it proved to be so physically punishing that it raised the ire of the troops and proved to be one of the rare behaviors that detracted from Johnston's popularity. In lieu of the pillory, four men of the Fortieth Alabama were made to wear barrel shirts for ten days. A Georgian at Dalton was prompted to write: "We have got the titest [tightest] Jenral now." He saw some convicted men "on a wooden horse—some one way some a nother. Some a hanging by the thumbs. It is bad to see such." Washington Ives opposed all such treatment, reasoning that "every man in the 4th Fla. Reg't except one who has been bucked or had to wear a barrel or do anything else disgraceful have deserted." The head shaving and drumming out

were punishments that were retained. Indeed, one soldier who was sheared subsequently caught pneumonia and died.[25]

Executions were initially reserved for deserters who took the Oath to the Union and actually joined the enemy ranks. Doubtless scores did so, but several were unfortunate enough to be captured and recognized. For them justice was as swift as it was consistent. A private in the Fifty-fourth Tennessee who had previously donned a blue uniform was taken at Shiloh. He was tried as both a spy and a deserter and shot. Lieutenant Colonel Fremantle observed a similar execution at Wartrace in June 1863.[26]

One of the more noted cases was that of a man known only as Rowland, who served in the Twenty-third Tennessee, then crossed the line and volunteered in the Union army. He was captured at Shiloh and condemned by a court to die. Rowland was hauled to the site in a wagon, sitting atop an old gun crate, which was soon to serve as his casket. His last request was for a bucket of water because, he said, he had heard that water was scarce in hell. Defiant to the end, he proceeded to curse Bragg, Davis, and the Confederacy and exclaimed that he would show the Rebels how a Union man would die. The order to fire was given, and Rowland tumbled to his death.[27]

In sharp contrast was the story of Henry Roberts of the Twenty-sixth Tennessee. He deserted while at Tullahoma and was not seen again until after the Battle of Chickamauga, where he was captured in the Union ranks and recognized. At his execution he quietly knelt by his coffin, while an aged minister offered a final prayer. According to a Floridian, "It was a very solemn affair." The next month, a Texas regiment claimed an unusual capture—one of its own men who had previously deserted and was now in the enemy ranks. They "took him out of camp and shot him. They has glad to get him," observed a Georgian. B. F. Elkin, who deserted from the Eighteenth Tennessee, was captured in the enemy ranks near Lookout Mountain on October 27, 1863. He was sentenced to be hanged in December.[28]

When Bragg assumed command, he initiated an increased level of strict discipline, which, wrote Captain George T. Blakemore, was much more rigid than the army had previously experienced. At

Tupelo he evoked capital punishment for those who deserted to go home—a first in the Army of Tennessee. It was extremely unpopular with the troops. John Magee wrote in his diary: "Gen'l Bragg is trying to get the army under strict discipline—he is not much liked by the boys on account of having several men shot for being absent without leave and desertion." Two men of the Twenty-first Tennessee—Melville Baillie of Raleigh and Polk Childress of Hickory Wythe—were sentenced to die. Both had deserted because they claimed they felt no obligation to remain under the new conscript law. Bragg determined to make an example of them. On June 30, 1862, they were taken out to a field and executed. A soldier of the Seventh Arkansas was also shot at Tupelo. "He refused to do duty of any kind in defiance to military power," according to a diarist. Sam Watkins actually saw only two men shot while at Tupelo—"they were mere beardless boys," he claimed, but he did not know to what regiment they belonged.[29]

In evaluating Bragg's punishments it must be remembered, first, that capital punishment was imposed with extreme reluctance and was usually reserved for those caught in a second offense. In August 1863 Bragg granted a rare twenty-day amnesty for all deserters, even those guilty of a second offense. Additionally, all offenders were tried and sentenced by a military court—not by the commander of the army. Second, the stories about Bragg were sometimes exaggerated. A rumor spread throughout the army at Tupelo that the general had a man shot for killing a chicken. Actually, an order had been issued forbidding the firing of muskets in camp. In disobedience, a soldier fired at a stray chicken (some reports say a pig) and accidentally killed a man. It was for that crime that he was executed. Finally, some of the troops wholeheartedly endorsed Bragg's heavy-handed approach. Alabamian Tom Hall believed that men were being shot "for just causes now."[30]

These executions were public affairs and were designed as much to provide object lessons for the troops as punishment for the guilty. Sam Watkins remembered such an execution at Tullahoma, and although writing eighteen years later, he still vividly recalled the scene. The condemned was a seventeen- or eighteen-year-old boy by the name of Wright, belonging to the brigade of Brigadier General Marcus Wright. The boy was hauled to the site in a wagon sitting atop his coffin. For two hours he watched as men prepared his grave.

Many soldiers went up to talk to him. "He had his hat pulled down over his eyes, and was busily picking at the ends of his fingers," recalled Watkins. When Cheatham's division was assembled, the chaplain of his regiment read some Scripture, sang a song, and offered a prayer. The order to fire was given, and Wright's body, tied to a stake, immediately went limp.[31]

On at least one occasion, in late 1862, a firing squad bungled an execution. The squad consisted of twenty men, half with blank cartridges and half with loaded guns (so that the men would not know who fired the fatal shot), positioned only twelve paces from the condemned. Yet when the volley was discharged, the man was barely wounded. Four men held in reserve for such a contingency took their turn, but the prisoner was still not killed. All twenty-four men were then ordered to reload and fire, this time completing the grisly task.[32]

In a well-documented incident, a soldier received a reprieve as a result of a dramatic incident. Forty-seven-year-old Nathaniel Pruitt of the Nineteenth Tennessee was found guilty of desertion and on June 10, 1863, was taken to a field beside his regimental camp, his coffin placed beside an open grave. A minister cut a lock of hair to give to Pruitt's wife. The firing squad was positioned and ordered to take aim, but just then an officer came galloping up with a special order to suspend the sentence. The prisoner began crying. "I was truly glad [of the reprieve], but must say some of the boys were disappointed," a Mississippi diarist noted. Incredibly, the very next day, Pruitt again deserted and was never heard from again.[33]

A similar incident about the same time involved a soldier of the Twenty-fourth Tennessee. He had been given an extension of leave before the Battle of Shiloh but could not prove it, for, he claimed, his colonel was not presently with the army. After the Battle of Murfreesboro, he was court-martialed and, much to the surprise of all, found guilty. The troops of the Twenty-fourth seriously considered protesting. The soldier was taken before a firing squad and placed on his coffin, then granted a last-minute reprieve.[34]

Such scenes were rare, however, and most executions went on as scheduled. On December 26, 1862, at Murfreesboro, four soldiers were shot for desertion. Two were from William Preston's brigade, one of them a member of the Sixtieth North Carolina. A Louisiana soldier was shot at Wartrace and another deserter at Shelbyville. Despite the petitions and pleas of many, three soldiers at Shelbyville were condemned to die. They were handcuffed in an ambulance and taken out the Fairfield Pike to a field, where they were shot, all three falling on the first discharge.[35]

One case resulted in considerable animosity on the part of the Kentucky troops. Asa Lewis of the Sixth Kentucky was captured in December 1862 by a bounty hunter. Lewis explained at his trial that he had originally enlisted for twelve months and did not feel bound to stay under the reorganization law. Additionally, his father was now dead and his mother needed him to get in a crop to feed the three children at home. He had requested a furlough, and when it was denied he left anyway, fully intending to return. It came out at his trial, however, that when he was denied a furlough he had requested, and was granted, an audience with Bragg. When the general also refused, Lewis became abusive and insubordinate and was arrested. Two days later he escaped. The court found him guilty and sentenced him to death. The officers and men of the Orphan Brigade immediately began a campaign to get the sentence commuted, but, despite even a personal plea from Major General Breckinridge, Bragg refused to relent. On December 26, 1862, the sentence was carried out, thus creating a permanent rift between Bragg and the Kentuckians.[36]

At Dalton, under Johnston, a new round of executions was initiated. Indeed, despite modern perceptions to the contrary, "Old Joe" was every bit as strict as Bragg.[37] On January 2, 1864, a Georgian wrote: "We are compelled to witness another painful sight yesterday. A man belonging to this regiment [Sixty-sixth Georgia] was shot for deserting. I never want to see another such sight." Later that month, a man by the name of Doggett of the Nineteenth Alabama was executed. In February a twenty-four-year-old member of the Third Florida was shot. This was his second desertion, the first having been from a Georgia regiment, and he openly told a friend that he intended to run away again. On March 22 a deserter of the First Arkansas was placed before the firing squad. "The contrast between the gloomy man, white, whirling snow, and black coffin was striking," observed a veteran. On March 25 a soldier by the

name of Keen of the Second Florida fell before the firing squad. In
April five men of the Twenty-eighth Alabama were sentenced to be shot, but the executions were apparently postponed because of a petition on their behalf. An Atlanta newspaper later reported, however, that the penalty was carried out. Eight men were shot in Deas's brigade, four each on two days. It took three rounds to kill one man of the Thirty-ninth Alabama.[38]

Robert Owens remembered the execution at Dalton of a soldier in Hardee's corps. The division was formed in a square, with the fourth side open. The deserter, surrounded by guards, was made to march around the square, then led to the open side. "The poor wretch appeared to have some false hope as the officer at the last minute adjusted the bandage," recalled Owens. The order to fire was given, and the top of his head was blown away. The division was then marched by in double file to view the ghastly sight.[39]

Despite the frequent blasts of the firing squad at Dalton, what happened on May 4 clearly stunned the army. Fourteen men were scheduled for execution at noon that day—two from Stewart's division, eight from Stevenson's (mostly of the Fifty-eighth North Carolina), and four from other infantry and cavalry commands. In preparation, fourteen poles were placed and a like number of graves dug. Many of the condemned had received tearful visits from their relatives the night before, and some had cut off locks as parting mementos. Four men appealed to Johnston for the life of their brother, and he was spared. A young Georgian was also excused at the last moment because his father was able to convince Johnston that the boy was a half-wit. The remaining dozen were not so fortunate. At the appointed time the troops were formed. A Georgian wrote to his wife: "Susan, I wit nest the oflest sen [scene] last wednesday that I ever did in my life I saw 14 [sic] men tied to postes and shot. Tha war North caroliner men Thare were 19 shot that day, although I never saw five of them shot. I hear some of them bushed whacked while at home." A prayer was offered, and at noon the order to fire was given. Three of the prisoners, though wounded, did not fall. A second volley, this time within ten paces, finished the work. "Most of them died manfully," remarked the attending chaplain. They were buried without further ceremony.[40]

As the war dragged on a growing despondency and defeatism led many to desert. To combat this serious problem, both Bragg and Johnston turned increasingly to capital punishment as a tool of control. Yet one must wonder if the desired goals were achieved. As the number of executions increased throughout the war, so, proportionately, did the number of desertions. Clearly, however, the situation would have been much worse had it not been for the executions. Although the effect of the punishments cannot be precisely measured, their frequent mention in the letters and diaries reveals that many soldiers were, indeed, intimidated. Thus punishments served as yet another glue to hold the army together, despite poor leadership and battlefield losses.

8

The Army of Tennessee Is
the Army of the Lord

The pervasiveness of religion in the Army of Tennessee has never been fully appreciated. Its influence transcended the ranks, extending from the commanding general to the lowest private. The cohesiveness of the army cannot be fully understood without considering its evolutionary religious pilgrimage.

During the early months of the war, in large part because of the festive atmosphere in camp, a general religious indifference permeated the army. In July 1861, a private in the 154th Tennessee attended a worship service at which about one hundred of the one thousand men in the regiment were present. "Such is the proportion of God fearing men in the camp," he concluded. That November President Davis declared a day of fasting and prayer, but a lieutenant at Bowling Green noted wryly: "There was very little of it done in our Reg. as well as others." In December, S. R. Simpson of the Thirtieth Tennessee expressed the fear that "religion and the worship of God is on the retrograde." Writing from Corinth, a soldier admitted to his brother that he would have totally forgotten that it was the Sabbath had he not looked at the calendar. A Louisiana private, also at Corinth, was disgusted at the business-as-usual atmosphere that prevailed on Sunday—"No bell, no better dressing, no church, no difference in hours, no praying, no bible, no psalm, no rest."[1]

Disheartened by the lack of spiritual awareness, many chaplains quit in frustration. While at Columbus, a member of the Eleventh Louisiana admitted: "Our chaplain is going to leave us. He is well nigh crazy, poor fellow, and is duly accredited for it by the whole Regiment." During the winter of 1862–63, the chaplains of Bragg's army considered resigning en masse and returning to their homes.[2]

The example of the Eighth Tennessee reveals the irreverence that was demonstrated in many outfits. Lige Hester applied for the position of chaplain, but the colonel insisted that a vote must be taken by the regiment, a decision he would later regret. Mark Luna, a jokester, also began campaigning for the position. He mounted a stump or a woodpile and gave mock sample sermons. Then a ridiculous text would be announced, such as "Whar de hen scratch dar be bug also." He would conclude his "sermon" by announcing: "Now, if you don't believe I am a better preacher than Lige Hester, vote for him, darn you." The majority voted for Luna, but the colonel overturned the election and threatened to throw the wag in the guardhouse if he did not behave. For a while, at least, nothing else was said about a chaplain.[3]

In the spring of 1863 revivalism began in the Army of Tennessee. This phenomenon later occurred in the Army of Northern Virginia but not to a similar extent in Federal armies. Bell Wiley has suggested that it was fueled by aggressive denominational activity, the preexistence of revivalism in the Southern culture, and growing national and personal insecurity in the form of military reversals and fear of death. Yet with the exception of sustained military reversals, these conditions, to a greater or lesser extent, also existed in Northern armies. Perhaps a more plausible explanation is that of Drew

Gilpin Faust, who argues that there was greater homogeneity in
Southern religious outlook and Rebel soldiers endured more pro-
found stresses because they received fewer furloughs and suffered
greater physical deprivation.[4]

At Tullahoma in 1863 there was a genuine desire for religion,
demonstrated by the overflow crowds in worship areas several hours
before services began. When Bishop Elliott, the Methodist Episcopal
leader of Georgia, preached one Sunday afternoon at Shelbyville, an
estimated thousand worshipers formed a vast circle. Two brigades in
McCown's division, M. D. Ector's and R. B. Vance's, held worship in
a rough glade of cedars with a thousand present. Some 140 conversions were reported in two regiments alone. Reverend John B. Mc-
Ferrin, one of the more active chaplains, preached in five brigades
during a six-day period in May, and each time he recorded that there
was a significant response.[5]

The soldiers testified to the religious activity. William Estes of the
Forty-eighth Tennessee recorded in his diary on May 19: "A revival
of religion is in our brigade and in two other brigades in our division,
many souls have been converted." A lieutenant joyfully told his wife
that many in his brigade had "professed faith in Jesus Christ," while
another Reb was thrilled that there was "a grand revival going on in
the 12th [Tennessee]."[6]

The revivals might have had an even greater influence but for
two deterring factors—the poor weather that persisted throughout
much of the winter and spring of 1863 and prevented outdoor
assemblies and the scarcity of chaplains. Technically, a chaplain was
assigned to each regiment, but in reality, a shortage existed. At
Tullahoma there were four or five brigades without a single chaplain, and the army barely averaged one per brigade. One of Bragg's
soldiers estimated that a good preacher in his brigade could easily
average a thousand in attendance each Sunday, but to his dismay
there was not a single chaplain in all five regiments. On April 25,
1863, a Mississippian stated: "In the afternoon there was preaching
in the Reg't but it was a very short sermon. The soldiers seemed very
anxious to hear it, for it had been a good while since they had heard
preaching, as it is very seldom that such is done in the Reg't we not
having a chaplain."[7]

The cavalry regiments, which were scattered on outpost duty, did not have the opportunity to participate in much of the religious activity. In July 1863, however, a Presbyterian minister arrived in the camp of the Texas Rangers and held nightly meetings for a month. Thirty troopers were received by profession of faith and another 130 were said to have come under the influence.[8]

Although many experienced conversions that spring of 1863, there was one whom Dr. Charles Quintard, chaplain of the First Tennessee, thought was unapproachable—Braxton Bragg. No one ever heard of his being connected with any church, and he never attended communion. Because of his abrasive nature and reputation for sarcasm, many were afraid to approach him, but Quintard decided to go where angels feared to tread. He went to Bragg's tent one day but was met by a sentry, who said: "You cannot see him. He is very busy, and he has given positive orders not to be disturbed except for a matter of life or death." His enthusiasm cooled, Quintard retired to his tent. The next day he returned, only to be met by the same sentry with the same message. This time, however, Quintard replied: "It *is* a matter of life or death." The sentry went inside and returned saying, "You can see the General now but I advise you to be brief. He is not in a good humor." On that chilling note, the chaplain entered and found Bragg dictating to two secretaries. "Well, Dr. Quintard, what can I do for you? I am quite busy as you can see." Stammering, he asked if he could speak to the general alone, but Bragg snapped that it was impossible. Quintard persisted, however, which prompted Bragg's stern remark: "Your business must be of grave importance, sir." Once they were alone, Quintard began to speak to Bragg of Jesus Christ and the responsibility of discipleship. He then asked him to be confirmed. With tears in his eyes, Bragg took Quintard's hands and replied: "I have been waiting for twenty years to have someone say this to me, and I thank you from my heart. Certainly I shall be confirmed if you will give me the necessary instruction." Following subsequent interviews, the general was baptized and confirmed at Shelbyville.[9]

Most chaplains were dedicated servants who incarnated the hardships of the common soldier with their ministry of presence both in camp and on the battlefield. Besides preaching, they assisted the medical staff in caring for the sick and wounded. Serving in the dual role of clergy-physician came naturally to Quintard, who had previously relinquished a professorship at the Memphis Medical College to be ordained. Chaplains in the Army of Tennessee wore a Maltese cross as their distinctive badge. Although most served in totally noncombative roles, some were killed during the war, seven during the Atlanta Campaign alone. The Seventeenth Alabama referred to Reverend I. T. Tichenor as the "fighting chaplain" after he rallied the regiment at Shiloh, killing six Federals in full view of everyone, before he himself was wounded.[10]

Unfortunately, not all of the troops were enamored of their chaplains. A diarist in the Thirteenth Tennessee attended worship one day only to record that it was "the most ignorant sermon I have ever heard in my life." A sergeant in the Thirty-eighth Alabama thought that his chaplain was "one of those cold men who never shows any life in preaching." A North Carolinian concluded that many chaplains were so old they were of little use. There were also complaints about the imbalance in the amount of time chaplains spent between camp and the hospital. One soldier informed his mother that his regiment had a chaplain but that he was "generally off at the hospitals, waiting on the sick and scarcely ever preaches." A similar complaint was heard from a Georgian: "We have had no religious services of any kind since we left camp. . . . Our chaplain spends his time with the sick, wounded and dying, and we seldom see him. . . . If only he could join us for singing and prayer once or twice per week, it would help us." During the Atlanta Campaign, a Rebel denounced chaplains who, during combat, skulked in the rear with noncombatants.[11]

Military operations in the summer of 1863 temporarily interrupted revival activity, but services soon continued when dozens of civilian preachers, acting as missionaries, made their way to the army. In the fall of 1863 meetings were reported at Missionary Ridge, Chickamauga Station, and Tyner Station. Writing to a friend from the vicinity of Chattanooga, Daniel Kelly related: "I am going to tell you there is a revival of religion going on protracted meetings are now being held threw the entire Army so fare as I notice and souls are being converted to God everywhere."[12]

The spiritual outpouring reached a crescendo during the Dalton encampment of 1863–64. Soldiers gave frequent testimony in their letters to the heartfelt experiences that were seizing the army. A captain wrote: "We have [a] warm meeting going on in our brigade. Several have joined the church and are to be baptized into different denominations. In one meeting ninety persons joined. There is quite a serious feeling in our brigade and in other brigades." Jasper James of the Twentieth Alabama informed his parents: "Until late hours or [our] congregations in many places can be heard singing and praising the great Jehovah. When the Companies, or at least some, I am told, assemble on their parade ground for roll call, turn it into a prayer meeting."[13]

In John C. Brown's brigade, a chapel twenty-five feet square was built by volunteers of the Twenty-sixth Tennessee. It soon became evident that this limited space would be insufficient so one wall was knocked out and a brush arbor constructed to expand the facility to a capacity of one thousand. Services were begun at 6:30 P.M., immediately after dress parade, and the soldiers literally ran from their quarters, many not waiting for their supper, to get a seat. Singing lasted for about an hour, and services sometimes extended past midnight. Even then singing and shouting could be heard from some cabins.[14]

Reverend T. J. Stokes, chaplain of the Tenth Texas, was astonished by the fervor that swept the army. "I have never seen such a spirit as there is now in the army. Religion is the theme. Everywhere you hear around the campfires the sweet songs of Zion," he informed his sister. He estimated that on April 17 upward of 200 converts were baptized in a nearby creek. Over several days in early May, 154 were baptized and 40 more requested the sacrament, but their outfits were called out before it could be administered. Stokes was convinced that "should we remain three weeks longer, the glad tidings may go forth that the Army of Tennessee is the army of the Lord."[15]

Virtually no brigade was untouched by the religious activity. After only several weeks there were more than one hundred conversions and ninety joined the church in W. K. Tucker's Mississippi brigade. The Florida brigade reported one hundred conversions and a like number joining the church. Sixty joined the church within a week in S. R. Gist's brigade. On May 1 alone, more than three hundred baptisms and five hundred professions of faith were counted in the army. On May 4, one of the last nights in Dalton, over a thousand in Alfred Cummings's Georgia brigade assembled to hear preaching.

Youthful but determined, a group from the Fifth Company of the Louisiana Washington Artillery was photographed in early 1862. The grim realities of war caused many men in the Army of Tennessee to turn to religion as their solace. (United States Military History Institute)

Since half of the batteries were at Kingston grazing their animals, Reverend McFerrin journeyed there for twenty days, during which time he preached nineteen sermons. There were sixty conversions, including three sons of ministers.[16]

There were two separate calls at each service, one for church membership and the other for profession of faith, the latter always receiving the greater number of respondents. An ecumenical spirit prevailed, with the exception of the Catholics. The previous spring the chaplains had passed a very strict resolution against sectarian preaching. At Dalton, Chaplain Stokes believed that "in the preaching you cannot tell to which denomination a man belongs."[17]

Although Protestants accounted for the overwhelming majority of clergy, there were a few Catholic priests. Chaplain James M'Neilly of the Forty-ninth Tennessee remembered that a priest had explained to him that his main function was to administer the sacrament of extreme unction. On the battlefield, he distinguished Catholics by the crucifixes around their necks or in their hands, and he frequently found more of them among the Yankee dead than his own. Father

Emmeran Blemiel, a young Irishman who served as the chaplain of
the Tenth and Fifteenth Tennessee, was killed at the Battle of Jonesboro while administering the last rites to a dying artilleryman. Services of worship were also held. "The Catholic Priest this morning
had mass, the service being held under the flies," wrote Captain Key
at Dalton. "It was indeed novel to see candles burning in daylight in
the wild forrest, while the worshippers bowed before God and
reverently crossed themselves."[18]

The presence of civilian ministers unquestionably aided the revival cause. "There is a meating to be in the regiment this evening
and it is nearly time for it, I think," jotted W. A. Stephens of the
Forty-sixth Alabama. "I must hasten so as to get to go for we have
some veary interesting Prechers hear to preach to us and I dont know
how long tha will stay with us, as tha dont belong to our Brigaid."[19]

The religious spirit transcended rank. Lieutenant General Polk, an
Episcopalian bishop in civil life, baptized Generals Johnston, Hardee, and Hood while at Dalton. Particularly touching was the baptism of Hood, who, unable to kneel because of his amputated leg,
supported himself on a crutch and bowed his head. Several generals
openly participated in the religious activity. A. P. Stewart, an elder in
the Presbyterian church, assisted in serving the sacrament of the
Lord's Supper in his division. Brigadier General M. P. Lowrey, a
former Baptist preacher, often closed his brigade's worship services
by giving the benediction. Pat Cleburne attended preaching with
most of his staff. What, if anything, this did to bond the soldiers to
these generals is undeterminable, but undoubtedly it served to im-
press, if not influence, many of the men. Commented a Mississippian: "Nearly all of our first generals have joined the church."[20]

Without question, it was the fear of death that drove many to the
altar. A Tennessean remembered that at Dalton the preachers ham-
mered away on the subject of death and the fact that many would
never see their loved ones again. Wrote an Alabamian, "every body
seams to be getting religion but I cannot [understand] why it is I do
no all aught to have religion for we do not no when we will be
killed."[21]

An incident at Dalton got the attention of the entire army. While
the men were clearing for camp sites, an old tree had been set on fire
and left smoldering for several days. During a prayer meeting on the

night of April 29, the pine suddenly burst into flames and came
crashing down on ten worshipers of the Fourth Tennessee, killing all instantly. The next day they were buried as a group in a most solemn ceremony. Three wagons carried their bodies, preceded by the division band playing the "Dead March." After a brief service, volleys were fired and a hymn sung. The entire army was deeply moved by the seemingly fateful event, and much theological debate ensued.[22]

What conclusions can be drawn from the revival phenomenon as it related to the Army of Tennessee? One writer has determined that the clergy served as the impetus for revival. This conclusion is true as far as it goes, but it fails to take into account that revivalism occurred in several units, such as Liddell's brigade, under near exclusive lay leadership. Additionally, this rationale fails to recognize the dual nature of the revivals—outreach and nurture. The chaplains were largely responsible for the former, but the lay-dominated soldier associations that were formed supported and cultivated the new converts. In April 1863, for example, a Young Men's Christian Association was formed in the Army of Tennessee with fifty men from all denominations, and efforts were made to start one in every brigade. Such support measurably assisted the revivals.[23]

Many thought that the revivals made a telling difference on the army. "I do not think there is so much wickedness in our regiment as there used to be," suggested one of Bragg's soldiers in July 1863. Captain Key came to the same conclusion: "There appears to be a wonderful reform among the soldiery, for they are leaving off card playing, profanity, and other vices, and are humbling themselves before God." A Mississippian was "greatly pleased since I have come to the Army of Tennessee. There is a better moral tone exhibited here than I have ever seen among the soldiers."[24]

Perhaps the most important aspect of the Dalton revival was its timing on the heels of the Missionary Ridge disaster and just before the expiration of the three-year enlistments. At this crucial moment, when the very life of the army was at stake, the revival extolled the virtues of sacrifice, commitment, obedience, discipline, and bearing hardships with patience. Thus the paradox—thousands proclaimed Christ as the Prince of Peace, yet this commitment ultimately improved morale and was in part responsible for lengthening the war.

On a deeper level, the revivals, according to one historian, "helped ready the Southern troops to look for an otherworldly triumph in the midst of more immediate defeats."[25] The failing of the revivals was their single dimension. They were personal and pastoral in nature, rather than social and prophetic. They extolled the virtues of individual piety but did not address the larger moral issues of war and slavery.

It would, of course, be a mistake to assume that all the men in the Army of Tennessee were deeply religious. Many ignored the call of the revivals, and it was not uncommon to see a blanket spread out on the ground and a game of dice or cards being played within hearing distance of a worship service. T. M. Webb of the Twenty-fourth Tennessee Battalion was convinced that "there is plenty of preaching here [Shelbyville] but it does no good, as I can see here a man preaching and there is one swearing, and over there is one singing a song to suit himself and right out there is a gang of them playing cards, and in fact every thing here at the same time."[26]

Comments from the soldiers also make it clear that the Christian pilgrimage in the Army of Tennessee was often a lonely one. "I would enjoy religion more if I had some companions who had respect for Christianity, but there is not one in our battalion," lamented a Reb at Tullahoma. Writing from the Chattahoochee River in 1864, a Georgian admitted: "I am lonesome for want of company (my kind of company) not so much as the greater portion of this Co. is they enjoy themselves mostly playing cards, and this enjoyment is not joy to me but sorrow they play cards every day for Money & Sunday (the 'Sabbath day') not excepted I enjoy myself reading religious Books that I borry from Citizens."[27]

Organized religious activity, of necessity, declined during active operations. General Hardee discouraged the congregating of soldiers during the Atlanta Campaign, fearing that it would draw the fire of the enemy. Yet there is ample evidence that both preaching and study persisted, albeit on a reduced scale. "Chaplain Stone preached to the 43d [Mississippi] under the shade of a tree without being disturbed, as only one minie-ball intruded itself in the congregation, which came while the preacher was at prayer and darted into the ground in the midst of the crowd," observed William Berryhill. Another Mississippian informed his wife: "We have prayer meeting occasionally on our lines when Mr. Sherman will allow it."

On July 17, 1864, a Southerner attended a Bible class in the morning, prayer meeting in the afternoon with the Thirty-fifth Alabama, and preaching that evening with the Forty-ninth Alabama. In Gist's brigade brush arbors were set up in rear positions during July and services were continued. Yet one Georgian complained on August 5 that he had not heard one sermon since leaving Dalton.[28]

Even during Hood's Tennessee Campaign there were many applications for church membership. One chaplain reported that the religious activity in the army continued in North Carolina in 1865. The evidence seems to indicate, however, that by then the revivals were few and small in scope.[29]

It would be unfair to treat the religious outpouring of the soldiers of the Army of Tennessee only as a sociological phenomenon. For most soldiers the transformation was genuine and deeply personal. For many it was the only thing that made life bearable and death hopeful in the midst of the horror of war. And for the army, religion proved to be one of the dominant factors in maintaining unity from 1863 to the end of the war.

9

We Are Dissatisfied and
We Don't Care Who Knows It

It was in the area of morale that the soldiers of the Army of Tennessee differed most from their comrades in Virginia. Though Lee's army had its defeats, they were interspersed with victories. In the West, there was a depressing accumulation of reverses. The problem ran deeper than simply the lack of success on the battlefield. One historian argues that low morale in the West was inevitable because of the homogeneity of the army. Not that there was "a pool of militarily deficient genes in the western states of the Confederacy," but "the all but total absence of Virginians from the Army of Tennessee deprived the western Confederates of a great deal of the mythical aura that surrounded the Rebels' eastern army." Richard McMurry concludes that this factor "inevitably affected" the morale of the western army.[1]

The deteriorating military situation in the West during the winter and spring months of 1862 led to the army's first crisis of morale. On March 7, 1862, Albert Sidney Johnston informed the president: "The fall of [Fort] Donelson disheartened some of the Tennessee troops and caused many desertions from some of the new regiments. I now consider morale restored." The letters and diaries suggest that this assessment may have been overly optimistic. A Mississippian at Corinth informed his wife before Shiloh, "I do not think a single man of this Regt. will reenlist unless things greatly change." A. H. Tarlske was convinced that "Tennessee is gone, unless things change very shortly. This war was premature. We were not ready." James Hall of the Ninth Tennessee informed his parents: "A great many men say they will go home when their time is out. I hope they think better of it." A disgruntled A. H. Mecklin believed that "a few leading characters have been the chief instigation of this war. The more I see of this war, the more fully satisfied am I that there is not religion about it." Concluded Josiah Knighton of the Fourth Louisiana on April 25: "I am afraid the Confederacy is gone forever."[2]

The Conscription Act was passed shortly thereafter, which not only drafted all men between the ages of eighteen and forty-four but also extended the service of the twelve-month volunteers to three years. It seems clear that had this not been done, a significant portion of the western army would have melted away. As it was, a majority of the troops accepted the law, though under protest, but some deserted and morale generally deteriorated. "We are doomed men for two years longer," thought Mecklin. Knighton was likewise appalled: "We received the mortifying intelligence a few days ago that the regiment was compelled to enlist for two years longer. We were never asked to reenlist again, but forced against our will," he informed his father. J. G. Law admitted that the "conscript act has caused some dissatisfaction among the troops, and a few have deserted." The most serious incident occurred when a Tennessee regiment demanded a furlough before the commencement of its next two years of service. Only after Bragg had a battery brought forward and the guns trained on the men did they relent. Diarist Rufus Daniel of the Sixth Arkansas wrote on June 16, 1862, "A heavy guard from our reg't to guard 7th Arks. reg't to keep the men from trying to go home."[3]

Both the desertion and absent without leave rates were affected.

On April 3, 1862, there were 46 officers and 1,334 men reported absent without leave in A. S. Johnston's army. After Shiloh the figures were 40 officers and 2,660 men, or 5 percent of the total. By the time the army reached Tupelo, desertions were commonplace. "I have said nothing about the desertions in our regiment, which of late has become quite popular among the cowardly devils that are in the Army," William Mott informed his wife on June 21, 1862. "I am sorry to say that Tennesseans are the only ones that are leaving in that disgraceful manner." Yet a staff officer observed that desertions were particularly high "from some of the Louisiana regiments composed of Irishmen. A whole company of them left their camp, none of them going over to the enemy, but merely attempting to make their way home under the plea that their time was out last April." Even Bragg was forced to concede "the shameful fact" that many officers and men were absent without sanction. A Texas Ranger was convinced that "some of them just enlisted to get the bounty and once they got it some morning finds them on their way back home. Such men are worthless."[4]

A study of A. P. Stewart's division reveals that desertions occurred in clusters rather than slow leaks. In the week ending June 2, 1862, for example, Preston Smith's First Brigade sustained a staggering 301 desertions, while the other two brigades of the division had a combined total of only 19. Leading the list was the Twenty-second Tennessee with 100 desertions, followed by the Thirteenth Tennessee with 81, Twelfth Tennessee with 77, Forty-seventh Tennessee with 6, and Bankhead's Tennessee Battery with 37. The week ending June 12, Smith's brigade reported only 9 deserters, 8 of whom were from the Twelfth Tennessee. For the week ending July 5, Stewart's Second Brigade counted 19 deserters, all but one from the Twenty-fourth Tennessee.[5]

The negative reaction to the Conscription Act was evidence of the growing lack of Southern nationalism. Loyalty to the Richmond government was at best dubious. That an additional two-year commitment was more than many had bargained for was an indication that a vacuum had been created when the original enthusiasm waned because of the hardships of soldier life and the reality of battle, and the void was not filled by an emerging nationalism.

Most of the men, of course, stayed at their posts. Joseph Lyman

did so because he was convinced that "this war is just and necessary." The motivation for Richard Pugh of the Washington Artillery
was more personal. After Shiloh he wrote to his wife that he "was
fighting for *you*, fighting to be able to sit down with [you] and look
out of 'that window,' fighting to get one more kiss from you." An
Alabama lieutenant wrote frankly that "the new conscription law is
much talked about of now: it don't worry me any, for I have always
considered myself 'in for the war.'" Rufus Catlin of the Nineteenth
Louisiana believed that "*for the cause* we must endure it. We must
fight the harder." Mecklin was equally candid in his reason for
staying: "I am desirous to escape, but do not know how."[6]

Following the Perryville and Murfreesboro setbacks, many became dissatisfied with Bragg's leadership. "Bragg is the laughing
stock of the whole army. Many of the Tennessee troops will desert,
and I can't say they are to blame," argued a cavalryman in January
1863. Frank Carter concurred: "There is no doubt but that Gen.
Bragg has in a great degree lost the confidence of the army and many
think that there was no reason for the [Murfreesboro] retreat."
Several months later an artilleryman wrote: "All confidence in Bragg
is lost, and I do not believe this army can win a victory under his
superintendence." Lieutenant William D. Cole of the Thirty-eighth
Alabama blamed Bragg for his failure to get a furlough and told his
wife: "I understand that Bragg says that he had rather see two men
die than to Furlough one. So you may imagine the chance at present.
I hope and I do believe that if there is any such place as Hell that he
will land safe to receive his reward." Writing still later, J. W. Harris
noted: "Everybody here curses Bragg," and if he were replaced "it
will put our troops in much better spirits." Van Buren Olden of the
Ninth Tennessee declared on October 31, 1863: "I am getting tired
of Bragg as a leader, he has conducted affairs so badly."[7]

Desertions remained high throughout the first quarter of 1863.
E. W. Treadwell of the Nineteenth Alabama expressed his concern:
"I am fearful that desertions will prove disastrous to our army. It is
now a common saying amon[g] the men that they will desert as soon
as the foliage are large enough to hide them good they speak of it as
though they are jesting but I fear many of them will carry it two far
for a joke." About three weeks later he wrote that "our army still to
desert as a rapid rate I learn to day that 2 left our Regt. last night

and 13 from the 25th [Alabama] most of whom carried their guns and 60 cartridges each."[8]

Much has been made of the duping of General William Rosecrans by phony Rebel deserters sent out by Bragg just before the Battle of Chickamauga. These decoys supposedly convinced the Federals of the demoralized state of the Confederate army. Yet Federal letters and diaries make it clear that there was a constant stream of legitimate deserters coming into Northern lines. For example, Alfred Hough informed his wife on August 20, 1863: "We have evidence every day that they are growing weaker out here, deserters are coming to us constantly, and they all tell the same tale—Bragg will make all the resistance in his power, but he is weak, his army is dissatisfied, badly fed, badly used and disheartened. We had yesterday 11 men from one Company of Louisians come to us, they all say thousands would come if they dared to make the attempt."[9]

The next day a Federal cavalry trooper told his mother that fifty Rebel deserters had come in. He continued: "One of them told me that most of his company would have deserted if possible, and that this is the case with the whole Rebel army." Federal General John Beatty noted on August 24, 1863: "Deserters are coming in almost every day. . . . Eleven from one company arrived yesterday." On September 7, 1863, an Indiana soldier informed his wife: "Deserters continue to come in to our lines. they give a sad statement of the condition of the rebel army. I heard a very intelligent one say that the rebellion must go down soon. . . . he says that they are sitting around in camp in little groups plotting how to desert."[10]

Major James Connolly, a Federal staff officer, revealed on September 16, 1863, that a Rebel mail had been captured at Tyner's Station, east of Chattanooga. He read two hundred letters and heard as many more read and was convinced that "such a gloomy, despondent bunch of manuscript, related to the Southern Confederacy, I never dreamed of. They all agreed that the Confederacy was ruined, that they were whipped, that it was no use fighting any longer, that they intended to desert etc. etc." Even an officer on General Simon Buckner's staff acknowledged to his sister that all was lost. Connolly wrote that two days earlier a Confederate captain and his entire company had marched into Federal lines. He concluded: "The newspapers don't tell one hundredth part of the facts in regard to deser-

*His name etched in his cartridge box, a youthful Private W. J. Cocker of
the Third Tennessee was photographed early in the war. His enthusiasm,
like so many others', waned, and during the spring of 1863 he deserted the
ranks. (Herb Peck)*

·tion from the rebel army; there is a perfect stampede . . . ; they are
swarming into our lines daily."[11]

It has traditionally been argued that desertions and low morale
during this time were the result of Bragg's inept leadership, harsh
discipline, and unpopularity with the troops. Yet scholars have too

long accepted at face value the idea that the soldiers mirrored the negative attitudes of most of the generals. Bragg's biographer, Grady McWhiney, has concluded that this interpretation is superficial and one-sided. There were men in the ranks, he claims, who supported Bragg. In addition to the sources that he quotes, others can be found to support this thesis. Following Murfreesboro, Frank Batchelor wrote "that he [Bragg] is a great general none can deny." In February 1863 Isaac Alexander explained: "I must say he [Bragg] has been a much abused man and I must further say he does not deserve it. The principal part of the abuse comes from editors and civilians and others who do not face the enemy." When it was rumored that Bragg would be replaced in the spring of 1863, an Alabama artillery captain noted: "I hope it is not so for no matter how much others may abuse him I like him as a General and I hope he will remain with the army."[12]

Some historians have failed to appreciate that there were contributing factors to low morale and desertions unrelated to Bragg's leadership. One of these was the consolidation of units. Following the Battle of Murfreesboro, some regiments had been reduced to approximately 100 men. It thus became necessary to combine outfits, a policy which, by the spring of 1864, resulted in the merger of forty-four regiments and two battalions into twenty-three consolidated regiments. Though entirely justified as an organizational necessity, this policy nevertheless resulted in discord among the troops. Unit pride and unfamiliarity with new officers were to blame. The Thirteenth Tennessee was merged with the 154th Tennessee in late 1862, which, according to a member of the former, caused "general dissatisfaction among all of the 13th Regiment." In January 1863 the Twenty-fourth Mississippi was consolidated with the Twenty-ninth Mississippi. "I don't like it much still I think we can get along," concluded Thomas Newberry, a member of the latter. In March one of Bragg's infantrymen noted: "The men and officers are now very much displeased with the field officers commanding them. Therefore the consolidating of Regts together causes confusion and dissatisfaction." Several weeks later the Thirty-seventh Tennessee, with 484 men, was merged with the Fifteenth Tennessee, 140 troops, and the colonel of the latter was placed in command. Thirteen officers of the Thirty-seventh immediately tendered their resignations, although they were not accepted.[13]

Unfortunately, Bragg sometimes exacerbated the situation by
shifting units among different brigades solely to disperse the anti-
Bragg element of generals. When his Florida battery was transferred
to another battalion in November 1863, Lieutenant A. J. Neal
expressed his opposition: "I do not care to leave this [Williams's]
battalion, as we have fought together and I know them to be good
and excellant troops." Likewise, W. S. Dillon balked when the
Fourth Tennessee was transferred from Cheatham's to Stewart's
division: "This creates a great deal of dissatisfaction amongst our
boys as they do not like Stewart as well as they do Cheatham." Van
Buren Olden of the Ninth Tennessee expressed displeasure at being
in Walker's division: "The boys all want to get back under Cheatham and Polk."[14]

Being far removed from their homes adversely affected the morale
of the trans-Mississippi troops. There were a number of desertions
in the Texas brigade when it was assigned to Bragg's army in 1863.
"We have sent up some 300d petitions to the War Department to
come west of the [Mississippi] river, both by our officers and privates, but we have never got a hearing from them yet," wrote a
Texan in January 1863. "Our boys has become dissatisfied they are
deserting evry day." There was anger when Bragg denied the Texans
furloughs on the grounds that their newly consolidated regiments
required drill and discipline, although one of their number admitted
with candor that "it is true for we near new what dissiplin was
before." In October 1863, one of Bragg's Texans noted that half of
his company had deserted to return to the trans-Mississippi. "We are
dissatisfied and we do not care who knows it," he concluded.[15]

Another factor was the presence in the Army of Tennessee of a far
greater proportion of mountaineer tories than were found in the
Army of Northern Virginia. In early 1863 General Gideon Pillow,
backed by companies of cavalry, conducted a stringent roundup of
conscripts in east Tennessee and north Alabama. He estimated that
there were eight to ten thousand absentees in the latter area alone,
some of whom had deserted two, three, and four times. By April 1,
his efforts had placed ten thousand conscripts into the ranks of the
Army of Tennessee, twelve hundred from the Chattanooga vicinity
alone. These men had avoided the war for two years and were
obviously being forced into the ranks. Quite apart from Bragg's
leadership, it should not be surprising that many of them subse-

quently deserted. Federal General John Beatty noticed this phenomenon. He remarked that hundreds of Tennesseans had deserted "and are now wondering about in the mountains, endeavoring to get to their homes. They are mostly conscripted men. My command has gathered up hundreds, and the mountains and caves in this vicinity are said to be full of them."[16]

Individual circumstances affected the morale of some units. In May 1863 Colonel Alfred Allen took advantage of a rumor he knew to be false. The report was circulating that his Fourth Alabama Cavalry had been requested for duty in Alabama by Nathan Bedford Forrest. Rather than correct the story, he instructed his troops to clean their clothes and wash their hair in preparation. It was also rumored that his outfit was about to be relieved from picket duty by another regiment, which also proved to be false. "Such things as these, cause desertion, by men that have no pride or self respect and there is a good many in the Regiment," thought William Fackler.[17]

Success and failure in other theaters likewise affected morale. Two deserters from Cleburne's division told their Federal captors in May 1863 that recent victories by Lee in Virginia had injected new life into Bragg's army. In February 1863 John Magee believed that "the star of the confederacy never shown brighter than it does now Everybody in good spirits." Subsequent news of the Vicksburg and Gettysburg losses changed his views. On July 9 he wrote in his diary: "This news [Vicksburg] causes a depression of spirits in the whole army. . . . From Virginia the news is less cheering than at first—we do not claim a victory at Gettysburg and our army is falling back rapidly."[18]

The talk of foreign intervention raised the hopes of many. "You may depend upon it that if this war is not over soon we will [have] England and France to put an end to it," attested Isaac Alexander. In January 1863 William Rogers penned: "Rumor says that France will recognize the Southern Confederacy this month." So certain were some of intervention that by mid-February, according to Hezekiah Rabb, many were "offering to bet that Peace will be made by the middle of March & some by the 4th of July & some are putting up the money." As late as August 1863 it was commonly believed that French activity in Mexico would ultimately aid the Southern cause.[19]

Even in the weeks following Chickamauga, the most smashing Confederate victory in the West, the rash of desertions continued. One of Bragg's infantrymen remarked on October 3, 1863, that "their has several diserted lately they was in a compiny going out last nite and their is servel thretning to leave but I am in hops that is more taulk than [action]." According to a Georgian, "Last week their was 5 of our brigade left the pieket line and went to the yankies."[20]

This phenomenon may sound strange to the modern observer, but there were extenuating circumstances. Lack of furloughs and homesickness resulted in despondency on the part of many. So deep were these feelings of melancholy that even a major victory failed to evaporate them. "I never did want to go home so bad in all my life as I do now," confessed a nineteen-year-old Georgian. "If I ever do go home and lives as happy as I did I can enjoy myself. I think while I was at home I thought that it was a bad place but I was a fool for thinking so. Home is the best place in the world that I hav ever seen." Shortly thereafter a sergeant in an Alabama regiment wrote to his wife: "My great desire is to see you and my people. Now, I never was so bad off to come home in my life before. The fact is if I did not so hate a deserter, I would soon come home."[21]

Pitiful stories of suffering at home plummeted the morale of others. When Isham Thomas left Grenada, Mississippi, his daughter Jenie was four months old. On October 8, 1863, while at Chickamauga Station, he received word from his wife that their daughter, now two, had died. "Oh! Angie how it pained my heart to hear it. I had entertained such high hopes of seeing my sweet little babe . . . well do I remember how she used to turn and look for me when ever she would hear my voice."[22]

Scanty rations also drove many away during the fall of 1863. Writing on November 13, 1863, Alexander Doss explained that "their is agate many men Disertin & going to the yankeys their was 32 men went out of one Brigaid yesterday. . . . the Reason they are Disertin so is for the want of Something to Eat." W. A. Stephens told a similar story: "I rote you last I rote that we was not getting a nuff to eat we get tolible plenty now. Think they found out that tha did not give more than tha was we would have no more men for the men was deserting to the Yankees every day."[23]

That men would desert for such seemingly insignificant reasons as poor rations is again indicative of the larger issue of a weak Southern nationalism. Clearly, loyalty to home was stronger for many men than loyalty to the Richmond government. The letters and diaries show no increase in references to the Confederacy, nation, or country. Issues of local concern were more likely to keep the men in the ranks, or, conversely, move them to desert. Whether the distance of the western army from Richmond affected the views of the troops cannot be precisely determined but would seem to be a contributing factor.

Continued desertions notwithstanding, morale appears to have remained high among the troops for some weeks following Chickamauga. Lieutenant Roderick Shaw wrote in amazement: "Having before been accustomed to defeat and retreat, no one can conceive what a change a victory so brilliant would make . . . unless he could see the joyous countenances of those veterans." Some weeks after the battle Washington Ives insisted, "Our Army never has been in better fighting trim and more anxious for a fight."[24]

The news of Bragg's removal following Missionary Ridge was received with mixed emotions by the men. "He has now left us and the confidence of the army has *wonderfully* revived," remarked an officer. Yet there were those who expressed remorse at his leaving. "A large portion of the army was very sorry to part with Gen. Bragg," wrote a cannoneer. James Hall explained to his father that though his company initially despised Bragg, he soon won them over, and "when he left us they considered it a dark hour. . . . They loved him and respected him while they feared him." A disgusted Lieutenant Neal felt that "Bragg has been hunted down by a discontented set of croakers who will in time be ready to cry down [his successor] Hardee." Contended a soldier of the Sixth Arkansas: "I believe this [Bragg's replacement] will have a bad effect upon our arm[y]. Though the citizens are down on him, yet the soldiers have the utmost confidence in him. Consequently, do not blame him."[25]

Thus, evaluating the effect of Bragg's leadership on morale is complex. Largely unaware of the bitter wranglings in high circles in the Army of Tennessee, many of the men in the ranks continued to offer their support to Bragg.[26] Even if these supporters represented a minority, they clearly were a significant minority. There is no overwhelming evidence in the letters and diaries one way or the other, for most do not mention him either way.[27] That may be significant, for it may mean that there was a certain lukewarmness on the part of the troops, that is, Bragg did not evoke strong positive or negative emotions. If so, the traditional assumption that Bragg was despised by his men is contradicted. The point is that the anti-Bragg/pro-Bragg feelings among the generals did not seem to filter down to the ranks to a similar degree, or at least there is no substantive evidence to support such a notion.

The winter of 1863–64 was bleak for the Army of Tennessee. W. A. Stephens was convinced that the war effort was all but finished. "The lives that is lost in this war now is for no good, I fear," he confided on December 24, 1863. There were others of like mind. Joel T. Haley of the Thirty-seventh Georgia was "hopeful that our cause will soon begin to brighten, it looks desperate enough now." B. L. Wyman noted that "a large number are for going back into the 'Union,'" and even Lieutenant W. A. Brown found himself admitting that he was "almost as much dispirited as the men." Wrote a frustrated John Barfield of the Forty-fifth Alabama: "I am tired of such a trifling life as this and it is a general thing with the soldiers. There is a good many that ses tha are going home."[28]

As morale plunged, desertions soared. The situation was particularly bad in the Thirty-sixth and Thirty-ninth Georgia, which were recruited from the counties in and around Dalton. Seemingly impotent in resolving the problem, the higher echelon punished those they could get their hands on—several captains in those regiments. Several men in the First Tennessee stole artillery horses and rode off to join Nathan Bedford Forrest in west Tennessee. This practice was common. It was estimated that two-thirds of Chalmer's and Roddey's cavalry brigades, operating in Mississippi and Alabama, were composed of infantry deserters from the Army of Tennessee. Hardee, temporarily commanding the army, attempted to restore order, but, according to one soldier, he was "not liked by all the men."[29]

Some men exhibited a certain understanding, if not sympathy, for deserters. One veteran told his wife that "the men are so badly disheartened that a good many are leaving here every night. Some call it deserting. Those that leave call it going to protect their families, which I think is a man's duty." A. J. Edge unashamedly confided plans for deserting to a female companion: "If I don't get a furlow to come home I will have to run away and then when I run away I am going to the north and I will stay thair tell the war ends and if it never ends I will all ways stay thair. I don't want you to read this letter to nobody that will tell anything."[30]

Yet most took a stern view toward deserters. Wrote L. W. Bigbe to his sister on December 3, 1863: "Well Sis I want to see you verry Bad But I dont no when I will get a chance to come hom I cant do like Wess and pervis did Desert I dont want to see you nor none of the rest of my People Bad a nuff for that." A Tennessee surgeon also informed his wife: "I hope you will know me too well to even mention that to me to desert my country at this time would be awful." He took some pleasure in informing his wife that her "old sweetheart deserted some time ago and is now driving a wagon in the Yankee army."[31]

Upon his arrival at Dalton in late December 1863, Johnston declared an amnesty for all absentees. Some 649 deserters ultimately returned to the ranks. Equally important, he established a system of furloughs. A leave of absence was not to extend over thirty days (based on how far away a person lived) and was to be granted at the ratio of one per twenty-five men, except in units that reenlisted for the war, in which case one furlough was granted per ten men. The prospect of going home, even for a brief time, lifted the spirits of the men. "The troops are better satisfied than I have seen them since the first of the war; the system of furloughs has rendered them so. They all say they are willing to reenlist but they want to go home first," attested J. W. Ward. Wrote Mississippian William Chambers on March 31, 1864: "I am compelled to say that it was the immediate prospect of obtaining furloughs that endured many of the men to reenlist." Unfortunately, the efforts of most to obtain a furlough were futile, and B. L. Wyman undoubtedly expressed the sentiments of many: "It seems as if every body can get a furlough but myself." Much to his dismay, Hezekiah Rabb discovered that furloughs came with strings attached: "I am provoked with the way I have been treated about a furlough to think that I have been in the service nearly two years & now they don't want to give me a furlough Except I reenlist." How many furloughs were ultimately given out is not known, but 3,399 men who did receive them returned in time for the spring campaign.[32]

Confidence in Johnston's leadership, furloughs, improved rations, and a well-timed religious revival all helped elevate the morale of the army at Dalton. The timing was particularly crucial, for the terms of many three-year men were about to expire. Specifically, however, it was the action of the 154th Tennessee that electrified the army when it unanimously reenlisted for the war. This lead was soon taken up by other regiments in Cheatham's division. One news correspondent reported that the "old army spirit" had been rekindled. This comment was echoed by a chaplain: "The enthusiastic spirit of 1861 is spreading abroad."[33]

A close examination reveals that the reenlisting fervor was not universally contagious. Lieutenant Shaw informed his sister on April 18, 1864, that though many had reenlisted, "none of the Florida troops have made a good start in that direction. They all want furloughs now and reorganization and no consolidation [of regiments]. Poor fools!" He dismissed the patriotism of the Tennesseans by noting that they "cannot return to their homes." One soldier also noticed that the Georgians and Alabamians were slow to respond. He thought this slowness was because "these states [civilians] are whipped and write discouraging letters to their friends in the army." Joel Haley believed that they were reluctant because volunteers were demanding to reorganize, "and unless it be granted, there will be a great deal of discontent." Lieutenant Smith also noted, "All the troops from across the Mississippi [River] are rather slow in reenlisting."[34]

The motives of some units for reenlisting for the duration of the war were highly dubious. It was widely rumored that the 154th Tennessee, the outfit that had initiated the enthusiasm, had been promised new uniforms from Charleston, Mobile, and Atlanta. All they got, however, were a few extra rations of flour. Just before the reenlisting call was made for the Eighteenth Alabama, whiskey was passed among the troops. Those who were known to want to reenlist were instructed to come running with a shout at the appropriate time. By the time the order was given, many in the regiment were drunk, and they blindly staggered up with the rest, shouting and yelling all the while.[35]

The majority of the men did reenlist simply because they knew that the war effort could not continue without them. J. W. Ward of the Twenty-fourth Mississippi remarked on February 4 that "the army is enlisting tolerable well for the war." Captain Blakemore noted in his diary: "The subject of reenlistments is making some stir in the army, but I believe our Division [Cleburne's] will all go in for the war cheerfully." By March 23, 1864, some 17,471 of 22,012 troops in Hardee's Corps had indicated that they were in for the war, a total of 70 percent.[36]

Morale continued to improve throughout the winter and spring months of 1864. Mississippian Sam Settles admitted that "they is some who are willing to give it up," but that "the majority are in favor of continuing the war for a while yet." Wrote Lieutenant Phillip Bond on February 6: "If some of our weak-kneed friends at home could have seen them [army] march past [on review], they would think there is some fight in us yet." Appraised another soldier on February 14: "The old [veteran] troops are not near as whipped as the citizens at home. Our regiment [Thirty-second Mississippi] has all re-enlisted with a few exceptions for the war." One veteran, who had served in the army for three years, remarked that he had never seen the troops in better spirits.[37]

As is true of Bragg, evaluating the influence of Johnston on morale is complex. One historian has done a study of Confederate morale in the Atlanta Campaign, being careful to distinguish postwar and contemporary accounts. Contrary to the traditional thesis, that is, that morale remained high under Johnston and subsequently plunged under Hood, Richard McMurry has discerned that the number of desertions under both commanders were about the same—approximately 142 a week. He concludes in a study of letters and diaries that though "many, perhaps most, Southerners, maintained their confidence in Johnston right up to the time he was relieved . . . feelings were nowhere near unanimous one way or the other." His contention is based on the letter and diary entries of eleven soldiers, most written in July and most anti-Johnston. I have expanded this base by including the entries from thirty additional soldiers and arranging the entire group according to month. A pattern then begins to emerge.[38]

In May there were eighteen comments made, twelve pro-Johnston

and the balance anti-Johnston. Examples of supporters include
Lieutenant John Davidson, who wrote on the twenty-first: "Our army is in fine spirits, no one but straglers think we are whiped." Captain Samuel Kelly thought that Johnston had the confidence of "nine-tenths of the army." On the other extreme was the letter of a Georgian written on the eighteenth: "I believe unless we get heavy reinforcements soon that the Yanks will take Atlanta easy. The truth is we have run until I am getting out of heart & we must make a stand soon or our army will be demoralized."[39]

In June there were eleven comments on morale, all but one of which were pro-Johnston. Examples include those of Hamilton Branch on the twenty-fifth: "Old Joe is all right and will give us the word in time." A Georgian wrote on the seventh: "Johnston is a great Gen. and our army has great confidence in him."[40]

During July there were twenty-six comments, twelve of which supported Johnston's leadership and fourteen that raised serious concerns or were outright opposed. The latter is represented by the perspective of Floridian Hugh Black: "I don't see the use in the Army trying to do anything more. I think that they have done their *best* and *lost*." On the ninth artillery Captain Dent expressed the fear that "Atlanta will be given up. If Johnston can be flanked out of every position from Dalton here I do not see why he cannot be flanked out of Atlanta." Calathiel Helms of the Sixty-third Georgia was blunt: "The men is all out of heart and say that Georgia will soon have to go under. . . . Johnston's army is very much demoralized as much as a army ever gets to be for all the news papers say that Johnston's army is in fine spirits but the papers has told nothing but lies."[41]

If these samplings are representative of the army at large, it would seem that when the campaign began in May the soldiers' feelings toward Johnston were mostly positive but that a significant minority questioned his strategy as the month wore on and he fell back from one position to another. By June he seems to have reached the peak of his popularity, with overwhelming support. By July the men not only had become more opinionated one way or the other (there were twice as many comments made that month as compared to May and over two and a half times as many as in June), but also there was a noticeable decline in confidence in Johnston's leadership. Clearly,

The face of a deserter. Private Jeremiah Jaco of the Thirty-fifth Tennessee deserted during the Atlanta Campaign. (Herb Peck)

those who claim that Johnston's retreats did not adversely affect morale do so in the face of significant evidence to the contrary.[42] His effect on morale cannot be properly evaluated unless it is seen in an evolutionary framework. Some men who had supported him in May had joined the "anti" column by July, as the army drew back to Atlanta. Judging from comments found in surviving letters and diaries from his troops, Johnston's confidence rating, which had risen from 70 percent in May to 90 percent in June, fell to only 50 percent in July.

An obvious question relates to why Johnston's confidence rating rose in June rather than continuing a slow decline. Some troops genuinely believed that his tactics of retreat were working. "We have got the best of every fight we have had with them," thought John Hill. "They report their loss since they commenced to advance to be 30,000, whilst ours is not over 10,000, if that many." There was also a widely held belief that trench warfare would not continue and that when Johnston gave the word a large Chickamauga-style battle would be fought and decide the campaign. In short, had the soldiers known in June what they found out in July, his confidence rating might have been significantly lower.[43]

That so many were questioning or opposing Johnston's leadership by July raises the issue of whether a pall was actually cast on the army when he was replaced, as traditional accounts claim. The truth can be found only by examining letters and dairies between July 18 and 20, for after that date Hood's sorties may have influenced opinion. Twelve accounts have been found for that period, all of which acknowledge that a crisis did exist. One of the more damaging comments came from a Texan: "For the first time, we hear men openly talk about going home by ten (10) and fifties (50). They refuse to stand guard, or do any other camp duty, and talk open rebellion against all Military authority—All over camp (not only among the Texas troops) can be seen this demoralization—and at all hours in the afternoon can be heard Hurrah Joe Johnston and god D——M Jeff Davis." A. J. Neal acknowledged the problem but was unyielding in his opinion: "I cannot regard it [the removal] as a calamity." In honor of their departing commanding general, the troops of Walker's division marched past Johnston's headquarters in complete silence "at the shoulder [arms], the officers saluting, and most of the latter and hundreds of men taking off their hats." At face value this would seem to support the traditional theme of Johnston's high popularity among the troops until it is remembered that there was a similar reaction, albeit to a lesser degree, when Bragg was replaced.[44]

Regret at Johnston's removal did not translate into disapproval of Hood. A Confederate wrote his father on July 25: "Army in good spirits—and confidence in General Hood unabated. The grief for the loss of General Johnston was painfully borne by the troops in silence. His removal fell upon them so unexpectedly that it made all feel sad—but we do not like confidence in our present commander." According to another, "All regret the removal of the former [Johnston] but are perfectly satisfied with the latter [Hood]." Captain Samuel Kelly was a solid Johnston supporter, but even he conceded that he did not "object to Hood and hope it is for the best." By August 1 D. G. Godwin was convinced that "Hood's popularity with the troops is growing daily."[45]

McMurry concludes that the reason for Hood's initial popularity was that the troops saw his sorties around Atlanta as victories—a point to be discussed in the next chapter. There was another unrelated factor that may have influenced the troops' feelings toward both Johnston and Hood. Polk's Army of Mississippi joined the Army of Tennessee early in the campaign. Throughout the summer of 1864, there were false but persistent rumors that additional reinforcements would be received. It was commonly said in the ranks that twenty-five thousand troops in the Army of Northern Virginia and all of Kirby Smith's trans-Mississippi army were on their way to Georgia. "We hear a great many things about reinforcements coming from the west side of the Miss. river, also about the movement of Lee's army in Va.," wrote a Southerner on July 12. Scribbled another the next day: "It is being rumored that Smith's troops from the Trans-Mississippi Department is on this side. We all believe it." On July 7 a Georgian recorded that "since we reached this place [Chattahoochee River] we have got the malistia of Ga. which is 10,000 [5,000] effective men & Ala. is ordered to send her malistia forward at once which will add to our strength 8 or 10 thousand more." W. J. Trask admitted on July 25, "Ten thousand rumors are current and many believe them all." One particular rumor then floating around was that fifteen thousand reinforcements had already arrived and "are now over the Chattahoochee River in Sherman's rear." Although the last sizable reinforcements (the Georgia militia) arrived about June 20, as late as August 2 a Rebel surgeon was writing: "We have got a reinforcement of twenty thousand in the last few days. They still keep coming in." On August 24 Raymond Harris entered in his diary: "I understand a

*This extremely rare photograph of a Confederate on horseback is that of
Lieutenant Nathan M. Robertson, who was later killed in action near
Atlanta. (Atlanta Historical Society)*

portion of the Alabama militia arrived last night and 6 or 8 thousand
more expected. This will be a considerable addition to our army in
numbers."[46]

Hood partially blamed the setbacks in the battles of Peachtree
Creek, Atlanta, and Ezra Church on the poor morale of the troops,
resulting from Johnston's continued retreats. "I cannot give a more
forcible, though homely, exemplification of the *morale* of the troops,
at that period, than by comparing the Army to a [mule] team which
has been allowed to balk at every hill: one portion will make strenuous efforts to advance, whilst the other will refuse to move and thus
paralyze the executions of the first. Moreover, it will work faultlessly
one day, and stall the next. No reliance can be placed upon it at any
stated time." According to Hood, his bloody sorties "greatly improved the *morale* of the Army, and arrested desertion."[47]

Surprisingly, Hood was partially correct concerning the effects of
his attacks on morale. Some did, indeed, view them as victories.

James Hall communicated on August 19: "I believe that fur the most part our troops are in good spirits." William M. Bowden of the Fifth Tennessee remarked on August 24: "The Boys are all well and in fine spirits what few of them is left. We are in full confidence of Driveing the Yankees out of Gorgia or at lest I dont think Sherman will go any furty in Gorgia." Yet the feelings concerning Hood's tactics were mixed. On July 21, Robert Patrick entered in his diary: "There seems to be a general dissatisfaction among the men on account of the headlong way in which they were out yesterday [Peachtree Creek], and they think that it costs more than it comes to." Cavalry trooper William Nugent evaluated on July 26: "He [Hood] gives us evidence of some ability—but at what fearful cost. We have lost *8,000* killed and wounded in the last two or three days. This sort of fighting, unless we meet with some more decided success, will dissipate our army very soon." By September 1 a Texan wrote bitterly: "He [Hood] has virtually murdered 10,000 men around Atlanta trying to do that which Joe Johnston said could not be done."[48]

Even after the fall of Atlanta, Hood was convinced that morale had not collapsed. He wrote Bragg in Richmond: "I think the officers and men of this army feel that every effort was made to hold Atlanta to the last. I do not think the army is discouraged." Again, the evidence is mixed. James Hall remained an optimist, claiming on September 4 that the army was "much less demoralized than you would suppose." Even Captain Dent, who was a pragmatist, concluded upon the fall of the city: "I do not think it renders our cause hopeless." On September 7, however, Lieutenant R. N. Colville wrote that "our troops are very much demoralized. They do not have the confidence in Hood that they had in Johnston." The important factor is that the men were not so dispirited as to leave en masse and the army was able to continue active campaigning.[49]

Morale seems to have been astonishingly good throughout the first half of the Tennessee Campaign during the fall of 1864. "The morale of the army is good all seem to want to go to Tenn.," said one. Captain Douglas thought that the men were "in fine spirits." Many believed the Battle of Franklin to be a great victory. Reflective of this amazing optimism was a story told by Hardin Fiquers. After that November battle, he found one poor Confederate sitting up, the bottom part of his jaw having been shot away and his lower lip and tongue hanging on his chest. When asked if anything could be done for him, the soldier scribbled on a piece of paper: "No; John B. Hood will be in New York in three weeks."[50]

Following the Nashville disaster, the men focused their despondency on Hood. Captain Samuel Foster angrily declared that the general had "butchered" ten thousand men around Atlanta and as many more around Franklin and Nashville. "He might command a Brigade—and even a division but to command the Army, he is not the man." G. W. Peddy was equally opinionated: "Our campaign has been the most disasterous of the war. Hood is a complete failure."[51]

By January 1865 the pitiful remnants of the Army of Tennessee had arrived at Tupelo. It was an unusually cold winter for that part of the country, and many were in want of winter clothing and blankets. Captain Robert M. Magill estimated that one-fourth of the men lacked shoes, and other estimates put the number higher. Some three thousand troops who lived in the vicinity were furloughed (many never to return to the ranks), leaving perhaps fifteen thousand. Morale, like the army, was totally shattered. Nightly desertions were commonplace. Concluded one soldier: "The regiment [Forty-third Mississippi] numbers one hundred and fifty men, about half of whom are barefoot. All are ragged, dirty, and covered with vermin. . . . The men are jovial enough in regard to their condition . . . but when it comes to discussing the prosecution of the war, they are entirely despondent, being fully convinced the Confederacy is gone."[52]

That morale was frequently low in the Army of Tennessee is not surprising when one considers the long string of defeats it endured. What is often underestimated was the army's indomitable spirit. Perhaps Federal General John M. Schofield best summarized the situation when he wrote: "I doubt if any soldiers in the world ever needed so much cumulative evidence to convince them that they were beaten."[53]

10

I Never Saw Braver Men

Battle was the ultimate experience for the soldier. It was the reason for the army's existence. Although combat occupied only a fraction of time, all else paled in significance to "seeing the elephant." It would be on the great battlefields of the West that the men of the Army of Tennessee would close in combat and meet the supreme test. On those fields they and their commanders would decide the fate of their nation.

What motivated the western soldiers to fight, despite frequent battlefield losses and lack of confidence in leadership? Punishments, a sense of commitment instilled through religious fervor, a bonding of the troops through shared suffering, and a certain perverse pride that arose from their common experiences of serving under losing gen-

erals explain the army's cohesiveness but not necessarily its fighting
motivation. Granted some soldiers fostered a passion for the Cause, but beyond that there were other compelling reasons.

One motivation was that the western troops often viewed the results of various battles from a perspective different from that of modern historians. For example, at Shiloh, Perryville, Murfreesboro, and Chickamauga, the Confederates achieved partial routs of the enemy in the first three and a near total rout in the last. Southern letters and diaries concentrate on this fact, detailing the large number of prisoners and cannon that were taken and the utter confusion that was inflicted upon the enemy. From their perspective, the Yanks had run on each of four consecutive battles. Wrote Tennessean Frank Carter after Murfreesboro: "There is no doubt but that the Yankees were *badly whipped,* having lost in killed and wounded at least five to our one, also about 5,000 prisoners, while our loss in prisoners was comparatively nothing." Yet modern historians see Shiloh and Murfreesboro as Confederate setbacks and Perryville as a strategic defeat.[1]

This concept is especially evident in the 1864 battles around Atlanta. Clearly Peachtree Creek (July 20), Atlanta (July 22), and Ezra Church (July 28) were Confederate defeats. Yet in examining the letters written between July 18 and August 30, one finds frequent references indicating that Southerners viewed these battles as victories. "On the 22nd [July] we charged the enemy's works and carried them capturing 8 14 [12-pounder] guns and several stacks of colors," wrote James Hall. An elated G. W. Athey told his sister: "We captured a good many prisoners in the first fight [July 22] and drove the yankes from thaire frunt lines of breast works." Hamilton Branch, likewise, informed his sister: "We have punished the enemy severely killing a great number and taking a quantity of prisoners and a number of guns."[2]

Even the Battle of Franklin was seen by some as a victory because the Confederates were left in possession of the field and many Federal prisoners were taken. "We captured a good many prisoners but I do not know the number. Some say a Brigade," Lieutenant Berryhill gleefully wrote. Historians, of course, consider Franklin a staggering defeat for the Rebels. The point is that many Southerners *believed* it to be otherwise.[3]

Thus the perception of battlefield victories motivated many men to fight on. If Shiloh, Perryville, and Murfreesboro resulted in strategic setbacks, they came on the heels of what were seen as tactical wins. Additionally, these perceived victories, it was commonly believed, were scored over numbers largely superior to their own, further validating their fighting prowess.

After the fall of Atlanta, another factor that motivated the troops to fight was the compelling desire to return to the army's birthplace and namesake—Tennessee. The army's morale was considerably elevated just by the knowledge that the men were returning "home." There was a uniqueness to that state, even for non-natives. Three cheers were given as the border was crossed. Captain Key, an Arkansan, wrote: "Last night we crossed the boundry between Ala. & Tenn., and this morning we are on the soil of the State that gave us birth." Under the circumstances, the desperate fighting at Franklin is understandable.[4]

Like other Civil War soldiers, western Confederates experienced a change of mind-set as the war progressed. Fear of combat lessened, an insensitivity to the grisly scenes of the battlefield developed, and a grudging respect for the enemy evolved.

Many westerners underwent their baptism of fire at Shiloh. The men watched aghast as their outfits began to sustain casualties. A. H. Mecklin saw "one of our Lieuts . . . shot through the hand accidentally by his own pistol and just as the same moment almost, our adjutant, the Lieut's brother, was stabbed in the thigh with a bayonet." A stunned member of the Crescent Regiment told his father that his outfit had no sooner gotten on the field then a "shell struck one of the drummers, carrying his head off his shoulders." After the battle, Richard Pugh vividly recalled "my feelings when I saw the first man killed. He was within thirty feet of me . . . and just as he was about to fire the gun [cannon], a ball [bullet] struck him in front of the ear, and he fell backwards expiring without a groan." On the first night of the battle, an orderly sergeant of the Washington Artillery proposed a prayer for all those killed in battle. "If daylight had suddenly broken upon us, it would have discovered tears stealing down the cheeks of nearly all present," wrote a member.[5]

Smartly outfitted Lieutenant Lawrence M. Anderson of the First Florida was mortally wounded at Shiloh. (Florida State Archives)

Even as late as Perryville, on October 8, 1862, the battlefield still offered some novelty for many. "The men stood right straight up on the open field, loaded and fired, charged and fell back as deliberately as if on drill," wrote an amazed E. J. Ellis. Sergeant Brown of Thomas J. Stanford's battery noted: "After the firing had entirely ceased, our lines began to cheer and it was taken up from one to the other. The line of battle could be marked out by the cheering of men. The Yankees replied with shots apparently of defiance. This roar of yells was kept up for sometime; then quiet settled on the two armies."[6]

In sharp contrast, the letters and diaries written during the Atlanta Campaign reveal how the soldiers had evolved into hardened veterans. "The minnie balls come over us fast sometimes. . . . They [troops] are so accustomed to them now they don't pay much attention to them," testified a Confederate. A Georgian matter-of-factly stated to his wife on June 20, 1864: "It is strange to me that I have no [more] fear than I have and it seems to me to be the case with most of us." About two weeks later he added, "We frequently get the dust sprinkled over us by the shells yet we don't feel much alarmed." Commented Captain Foster: "The Yankees commenced shelling us, as soon as we get into position, but it amounts to nothing. Shelling don't scare us as it used to and if they [shells] pass before they burst there is no danger in them."[7]

So, too, did the men change in the way they viewed the grisly sights of the battlefield. During the days following Shiloh, the men expressed a certain revulsion. "I have been through my first battle and I have had enough of war to last me a lifetime," stated a surgeon. Wrote Kentuckian J. H. Hines: "I was glad to hear the opening of the battle because I wished to satisfy my curiosity for seeing a battle and I thought it would do some good to see dead Federals. But I had not seen many before the sight became sickening." For a week or so after the battle, Richard Pugh observed that a certain quiet numbness had come over the army: "Everything was quiet as if the whole country was one church."[8]

Even in later battles, some expressed shock at the carnage of the battlefield. Thomas Warrick of the Thirty-fourth Alabama wrote his wife following Murfreesboro: "Martha . . . I can inform you that I have Seen the Monkey Show at last and I dont Waunt to see it no more[.] . . . Som [bodies] had there hedes [heads] shot of and som ther armes and leges Won was Shot in too in the midel I can tell you that I am tirde of Ware." Following Chickamauga a Texan wrote: "I went over a good deal of the battle ground and the dead were strewn for miles; such a sight I never saw before nor never want to see

again. . . . There was men shot all to pieces, some with their heads
busted open; some shot in two and arms and legs shot off, and every
where that they could be." Washington Ives saw men "swollen as
large as oxen and the stench is unbearable." During the Atlanta
Campaign, a Mississippi artilleryman witnessed "four men from the
36th Alabama buried in one grave stiff and rigid in death and their
bodies in the attitudes [positions] they were in when breath left
them."9

Yet it is clear that many men developed a certain insensitivity to
such scenes as the war progressed. One Confederate recalled that at
Murfreesboro his regiment was hotly engaged. A Federal in the
opposite line was suddenly hit, his death squeal sounding very much
like that of a hog when struck in the head with an ax. The entire
Tennessee regiment burst into laughter, even though there were men
in their own ranks being killed every few minutes. Stripping of
the dead also became commonplace. James Mitchell of the Thirty-
fourth Alabama told his wife following Murfreesboro: "There was a
great deal of pilferring performed on the dead bodies of the Yankees
by our men. Some of them left as naked as they were born, anything
in the world they had being taken from them." It was similar at
Chickamauga, where some Rebs robbed even their own dead without scruples. A popular souvenir was a laurel wood finger ring,
which the Federals had made in abundance while they were encamped around Lookout Mountain. In some instances the Confederates severed the fingers of the dead to obtain them.10

Even in an era of close combat, many of the men admitted that
they could not be certain if they actually killed anyone. "I have never
seen a single soldier who says that at any time he was closer than 150
yards to them," claimed James Searcy after Shiloh. John Johnson
told his family after Murfreesboro: "I will say nothing about what I
killed, for I can't swear I killed one." Alexander McGowin thought
he might have shot a Yank at Chickamauga but was uncertain. "It
was so smoky after the firing commenced that I could not see," he
admitted. During the Atlanta Campaign, John Hagan confessed: "I
do not know as I have killed a Yankee but I have been shooting
among them."11

At least one woman donned a Southern uniform and fought in the
ranks. Wrote Sergeant Hiram Holt: "There is a woman in the guard

house at Wartrace, who fought through the battles of Murfreesboro & Perryville. She was dressed like a man & is still. She and the other prisoners play cards together just as if she was another man. She will be sent home soon, what do you think of her."[12]

The troops often fought under less than ideal circumstances. At Chickamauga William Dillon of the Fourth Tennessee commented about the fighting on September 19, 1863: "Some old dry fences had taken fire and the wind blew the smoke in the faces of our men completely blinding them and giving [the] enemy a great advantage." During the early morning of September 20, a cannoneer in Swett's battery observed that the fog and smoke so obscured vision that "the colors of a regiment could not be distinguished half the length of a regiment." Major John Slaughter felt obliged to explain why his regiment, the Thirty-fourth Alabama, had to fall back during a charge on September 20. Half of his men had not had a drop of water in twenty-four hours. Additionally, in an earlier charge the men had to run one mile without time to rest and were then run back to the Lafayette Road. "This was done with their knapsacks and blankets on," he reported.[13]

The western army was engaged in three winter campaigns, and the weather was frequently a determining factor in combat performance. At Fort Donelson, on the night of February 13, 1862, the mercury plunged to ten degrees and the ground was blanketed with two inches of snow. There were numerous cases of frostbite, and it was believed that several men froze to death. At Murfreesboro the troops were in a cold, intermittent rain for a week before the battle, many with no camp fires. In the days preceding the Battle of Nashville there was a sleet storm that left an inch of ice on the ground. Related Captain Key: "The soldiers stand around their fires warming one side while the other side grows cold, and shed tears from the strong smoke that puffs in their eyes. . . . Our artillery carriages are frozen in the ground and half an inch of ice coats my brass guns." By the time of the battle the ground was thawing, resulting in thick mud, which greatly impeded the subsequent retreat.[14]

There were numerous examples of bravery on the battlefield. David Brand was proud of the performance of his regiment at Shiloh: "I never saw, nor do I think there was ever braver men than our 21st [Alabama]. I feel proud of the regiment." Similarly, Alex

Boyd of the Ninth Arkansas informed his sister: "Our regiment
suffered heavily [at Shiloh]. They made charges which other regiments would not." At Chickamauga, the colonel of the Tenth Mississippi singled out for valor in his report five captains, fifteen lieutenants, eight sergeants, six corporals, and twenty-eight privates. In
the Thirty-second Tennessee, a Private Mayfield was simultaneously
shocked by the explosion of a shell and struck in the thigh by a minié
ball. He was carried from the field on a litter but soon recovered.
Springing up, he shouted, "This will not do for me," and ran back
into the battle.[15]

The western army also had its share of cowards. At Shiloh, Lieutenant W. R. Morrow of the Fifth Tennessee left the field on the first
day's battle under the pretense of caring for a brother and was not
seen again until Corinth. The colonel of that regiment also noted the
character of a particular captain: "Several times I had to threaten to
shot him for hiding far back in the rear of his men." The entire Fifty-
fifth Tennessee broke and stampeded on its baptism of fire. The men
fled through the advancing Seventh Arkansas wildly shouting, "Retreat, retreat!" The Seventh's nearly eight hundred men virtually
melted away without having fired a shot, and order was restored
only by the determined efforts of many officers.[16]

Even in later battles there were numerous examples of individual
units breaking under fire and even greater numbers of shirkers. In
advancing at Murfreesboro, Washington Ives saw the Sixtieth North
Carolina "run like sheep." At Chickamauga Lieutenant Colonel
Watt Floyd of the Seventeenth Tennessee reported: "During this
awful struggle over the spur of Missionary Ridge hundreds [of
Southerners] were skulking behind the trees in our rear." During
an assault at Resaca on May 14, 1864, a Mississippian observed,
"Some of the men could not stand it, and remained behind [in the
breastworks], almost as pale as those who had already fallen."
At Spring Hill, during the Tennessee Campaign, Hamilton Branch
claimed that "Bate's men [division] seeing the [enemy] skirmish line
advancing ran like a scared dog."[17]

The rout at Missionary Ridge produced a panic of unprecedented
proportions. A disgusted Bragg condemned the conduct of the men,
and many in the ranks felt a similar embarrassment. "If we canot
hold as good a place as the Misherary ridge we had as well quit,"

concluded W. A. Stephens. A Louisiana soldier admitted that the men in his battalion acted disgracefully and "did not half fight." Joel Haley disassociated himself from those who fled: "Let it suffice that Bate's brigade, at least all of the Thirty-seventh [Georgia] regiment, was in no way responsible for the disorder that occurred." Yet William Chunn of the Fortieth Alabama thought that the troops were not to blame: "The firing was so terrible that the men could no longer stand it." James Hall attested that the Yankees flooded over the ridge by the thousands: "It required more courage to run than to stand still."[18]

The trench warfare of the Atlanta Campaign was a new combat experience for the men of the Army of Tennessee. The armies were rarely out of contact, skirmishing was incessant, and deadly snipers extracted a heavy toll. "To expose your head one second is to draw a dozen bullets," revealed Lieutenant Neal, who himself was struck down by a sniper's bullet only a few weeks later. At New Hope Church the Eleventh Tennessee lost six men to sharpshooters in an hour. Columbus Sykes estimated that sniper casualties in his brigade averaged six per day; Brigadier General Manigault claimed that his brigade lost ten or eleven per day. William Norrell expressed his revulsion: "This picket firing is beneath the dignity of civilized warfare, as it accomplishes nothing but murder and has nothing to recommend it. No Nation does it but ours and the Indian tribes we got it from that I know of. It is real 'bushwhacking' and nothing else."[19]

The picket line consisted of a regular line of breastworks about a quarter of a mile in front of the main line. About 150 yards in front of the picket line was a series of vidette posts. These consisted of pits, dug to accommodate four to six men and generally spaced about ten to fifteen yards apart. The enemy vidette posts were usually only 100 to 200 yards away. A sudden attack by the enemy could, and sometimes did, completely overrun these advanced positions. The entire Fortieth Alabama, 320 strong, was captured on June 15, 1864, while it was on the picket line. Several days later about 300 men of the Thirty-first Alabama were overrun in like fashion.[20]

Stray bullets posed a danger even to those in the rear. A private in the Nineteenth Alabama told of such to a lady friend: "We are not fighting at present, that is, our 'Co.' I hear a ball pass by me every syllable I take, and since I have been writing there has been two men shot through the body right here in camp. Poor fellows, I think they will die. I am sitting behind a tree to prevent being shot until I get this letter wrote, and the balls are constantly striking the tree that I am behind, but just so they don't strike me, I will not stop writing."[21]

A Mississippi cavalryman complained of the awful stench that came from the trenches. "There is a terrible exholation of odors from the ground near the trenches and in the vicinity of the camps; so much so as almost to sicken a hearty man." Several days later he wrote again: "I am extremely anxious, however, to get away from this big army and breath a little fresh air. The great number of dead horses, mules and human beings, make the air extremely offensive in the vicinity of the trenches."[22]

The veteran mind-set eventually developed a grudging respect for the enemy and even a surprising cordiality. Although there was some limited fraternization between the lines during the siege of Chattanooga, it was not until the Atlanta Campaign that this activity reached a peak. According to a Tennessean on June 30, 1864: "Some of our brigade met a squad of blue bellies on the half way ground and exchanged late papers, coffee, tobacco, etc. They have not weights and measures on the line: The Yanks give a shirt tail of coffee for a plug of tobacco." O. D. Chester told a similar story: "Pickets don't fire to each other now. We go down to the edge of the river on our side and the Yankees come down to their side and talk to each other." On one day an estimated two to three hundred Rebs and Yanks openly bathed together in the Chattahoochee River.[23]

There was still some danger, however, because there were some who did not participate in such open friendliness. Four soldiers of the Eighteenth Tennessee made a truce with a Michigan regiment on the Chattahoochee. When the Southerners showed themselves, the enemy opened fire, killing one. B. P. Weaver told his parents: "Our lines are some 600 yards apart. I can see some of the Blue Devils from where I sit—they got on their breastworks this morning and hollored to bring them some tobacco. They would give us a pound of coffee for a plug. We sent them an ounce of lead was our only reply."[24]

Another aspect of the changing character of the veterans was a reluctance to assault earthworks. Hood charged that the troops

Eighteen-year-old John M. W. Baird and Henry Clements were members
of the First Arkansas, a regiment that served in every major battle of the
Army of Tennessee from Shiloh to Nashville. Clements was captured at
Jonesboro, Georgia, on September 1, 1864, exchanged shortly thereafter,
and later wounded at Franklin. (Arkansas History Commission)

lacked spirit at Ezra Church on July 28 and Jonesboro on August 31,
1864. Some historians quickly dismiss the charge, yet several officers
made similar statements in their reports. At Ezra Church, Lieutenant
General S. D. Lee noted that the troops generally halted during the
charge; "the attack was a feeble one," he concluded. General John

Brown remarked that "the greater portion of Manigault's brigade
behaved badly." At Jonesboro a colonel noted that "the men seemed possessed of some great horror of charging breast-works, which no power, persuasion, or example could dispel." The color-bearer of the Thirteenth Louisiana attempted to lead his regiment forward, but the men cowered and refused to budge. The officers of the brigade were called upon but none responded. Major General Patton Anderson was livid in his censure: "I know that on other fields that regiment has acquitted itself with the highest honors, but I do say that if the men in question did belong to the Thirteenth Louisiana, as represented to me, they are unworthy comrades of a gallant color bearer."[25]

There were other officers who offered explanations—the intense heat, the lack of water, the exhausted condition of the men.[26] When all is said, however, did the troops lack their usual fighting intensity? The subject is not mentioned in the letters and diaries, but it is certainly possible. Four major assaults within six days may well have unnerved the men. The problem did not occur in the earlier battles of Peachtree Creek and Atlanta, thus pointing to the frequency of the attacks as a possible answer.

Whatever the cause, it was only temporary, for the Confederate assault against the Union works at Franklin on November 30, 1864, represented the model of a disciplined and courageous attack. Eighteen brigades, some eighteen thousand men, were involved, placing the attack on the scale of Pickett's Charge at Gettysburg. As the troops formed ranks, several brigade bands struck up "Dixie" and the "Bonnie Blue Flag," and scores of flags flapped in the autumn breeze. Realizing that a great slaughter was about to take place, men flocked around Chaplain James M'Neilly of Quarles's brigade, giving him watches, jewelry, letters, and photographs and asking that they be sent to their families in the event of death. These items had to be refused, however, for he was advancing with the troops. M'Neilly later recalled seeing several of these same men dead on the field.[27]

The bugler sounded forward and the order was shouted down the line: "Right shoulder shift arms. Forward. Quick time, march." The lines emerged from the woods in perfect order. One of Cleburne's soldiers recalled that he could see fixed bayonets the whole length of his division, so in step were the men. An advanced Federal battery tore large gaps into the advancing Rebel ranks—a single shell

*The dead were "lying heaped up all over the battleground," wrote a
Reb after the battle of Franklin. Private Thomas Murrell of the Sixth
Tennessee was counted among them. (Tennessee State Museum)*

dropped ten men in a heap. The line was cut to pieces as it ap-
proached the long ditch on the outside of the Federal breastworks at
the Carter house and nearby cotton gin. So filled was the ditch with
bodies that the wounded sometimes could not move because others
were atop them.[28]

Even to veterans accustomed to the slaughter of three years of
war, the carnage at Franklin caused a breathlessness. Granbury's
Texas brigade went into battle with 1,100 muskets and came out
with only 460. The Missouri brigade lost 447 of 687 men. Of the

120 troops of the Forty-ninth Tennessee, only 17 answered roll after
the battle. Thomas Taylor told his sister: "I have seen battlefields and have been in battles but I have never witnessed the amount of dead on as little ground as that where our division and Cleburne's fought." Testified Sam Vann of the Nineteenth Alabama: "Oh! you cannot have the slightest imagination of how many men were killed. They were lying heaped up all over the battleground. Such a slaughter of men never was seen on neither side. I counted 30 dead Yanks in a space of ground not larger than a common dwelling house." Related Texan William Stanton: "If you could only have seen that sight—our men laid like Railroad ties and puddles of blood." Alabamian Robert Bliss wrote shortly after the battle: "I have seen many battlefields, but none equal to this. The ground in front of the works . . . is covered with dead bodies and the ditch in front is filled with them." To Captain Douglas, the sight was "sickening, even to an old soldier."[29]

On December 16, 1864, the Confederate line at Nashville was broken. A rout resulted as the men ran to the rear in wild confusion. A cannoneer in Selden's Alabama Battery described the withdrawal as a "perfect stampede." His battalion lost eleven of twelve guns. Captain Thomas J. Key classified the panic as "one of the most disgraceful routs that it has been my misfortune to witness. All the batteries on the extreme left were captured . . . and hundreds if not thousands of the infantry fled in such shameful haste that they threw down their guns." Mississippi artilleryman E. T. Eggleston was bitter: "The infantry ran like cowards and the miserable wretches who were to have supported us refused to fight and ran like a herd of stampeded cattle. I blush for my countrymen and despair for the independence of the Confederacy if her reliance is placed in the army of Tennessee to accomplish it."[30]

The retreat was the most painfully miserable experience the army ever endured. M. Gillis of the Forty-sixth Georgia "thought of Bonepart's retreat from Moscow and Washington's going into winter quarters at Valley Forge. Two-thirds of the men were barefooted and their feet bleeding on the Pike which was covered with mud and ice. The suffering of the army was indiscribable." A civilian who witnessed Hood's retreating army described it as "the most broken down set I ever saw."[31]

*Lieutenant Robert B. Hurt, Jr., of the Fifty-fifth Tennessee was among the
1,750 Confederates slain at Franklin. (Library of Congress)*

Casualties in several western battles were nothing short of staggering, with some regiments being decimated within minutes. Accurate
casualty records were kept for the battles of Shiloh, Perryville, Murfreesboro, and Chickamauga. The Sixth Mississippi at Shiloh lost
300 of 425 men (70.5 percent) in the morning assault on the first
day. At Murfreesboro the Eighth Tennessee sustained losses of 68.2

percent and the Tenth Tennessee at Chickamauga 60 percent. Two

Southern regiments at Shiloh had casualties in excess of 45 percent,
one at Perryville, four at Murfreesboro, and eighteen at Chickamauga. Following the latter, a Confederate commented: "It makes
one sad to see an old warrior reg't pass on the march bearing a flag
with probably fifty holes through it and the names of from three to
twenty hard fought fields sometimes you will not see more than fifty
rank and file in a regiment. . . . Look at their flag and you generally
see (as in the case of the 20th Louisiana) the numbers of three or four
regiments consolidated. There are some regiments whose flags have
inscriptions of honor on them so numerous that it would be almost
impossible to crowd another name."[32]

Many men boasted of close calls on the battlefield. After Murfreesboro John Johnson informed his family: "I have been in places
that I can't see for my life how I came out safe. I am tempted to say
that a Yank can never kill me. I am Yankee-proof!" During the
fighting around Atlanta, a Tennessean claimed: "The boys regard a
severe wound now as equivalent to a furlough, and whenever one is
wounded they say he has got a furlough for thirty, sixty or ninety
days as the wound may be slight, severe, or serious."[33]

Thousands of others paid the ultimate sacrifice. Because the Army
of Tennessee retained possession of only two major battlefields
(Chickamauga and Franklin), Southern dead were frequently buried
by the Federals or local civilians in mass graves with no identifica-
tion. At Shiloh, for example, there were at least six burial pits, the
largest with 571 bodies, stacked in layers seven deep. Following the
Battle of Perryville, Henry P. Bottom, a local citizen, had 400 unidentified Rebs buried on the ground where Cheatham's division
made its assault. Some 2,000 Confederate dead were buried in a
mass pit at Murfreesboro and a like number in Jonesboro, Georgia.
After the Battle of Resaca, the women of the town gathered up 421
Southern dead and had them buried in a common grave.[34]

At Chickamauga individual graves were dug for the Southern
dead and wooden markers placed. Following the battle and continuing for some years after the war, efforts were made to remove
individual bodies to family and church cemeteries. About half of the
Confederate dead were thus removed. The other half, many of

whom were unidentified, were reburied in a mass grave of some 3,000 bodies at Marietta. Included also were Southern dead from Chattanooga and the Marietta vicinity. Fewer than 900 are identified. In the battles around Atlanta, many of the wounded were entered into city hospitals. Those who died of their wounds, along with some who died of disease, are buried in Oakland Cemetery in Atlanta. About 2,500 bodies were thus buried separately and most are identified. At Franklin burial parties dug long trenches and placed wooden markers for each of 1,750 Southern dead. Unfortunately, many of these markers were pulled out and used for firewood by civilians during the winter of 1864–65. In April 1866 Colonel John McGavock of Carton plantation hired men to locate these trenches and eventually 1,481 Confederates were reburied in a cemetery on his property.[35]

The government sent no formal notices to the relatives of the deceased. They were usually informed by the soldier's comrades, a company commander, chaplain, or relative in the army, or through casualty lists published in newspapers. Nothing so humanizes the war as these sad letters, the following of which serve as examples:[36]

> On the Line, New Hope Church
>   June 4, 1864
> Dear Sir:
> It becomes my painful duty to inform you of the death of your son, C. W. Lewis. He was killed by the enemy's sharpshooters on the 27 of May, having been pierced in the right side [by] 2 minnie balls at the same time, one entering the right side of his neck and ranging towards the left shoulder, the other penetrated his right side. He survived only about one hour, but was sensible to the last moment of his life, nor did he speak but a few words, said nothing about his wounds and pain nor about his friends or affairs. He died very easily without pain. I assisted to bury him that night. He is buried near New Hope Church in a grave with two others of the Battalion. Being a mess mate and a particular friend of mine I deeply deplore his loss and sympathize with you in your bereavement, but while we mourn his loss but trust in his eternal gain. He

was much respected by his brother soldiers as a good soldier
and a true patriot. He died like a hero at his post of duty falling for a holy cause. . . .
With much regret I am sir,

> Your Obit Serv't
> R. A. Allen
> Co. B, 4th La. Batt.
> Gibson's Brigade
> Army of Tenn.

Field Infirmary
D. H. Reynolds [Brigade]
Aug. 19, 1864
Dear Pa and Ma,
How shall I prepare you for the sad and heartrending tidings?
Our family, heretofore so fortunate during this struggle, must
now mourn the loss of a "loved one": Brother Jester is no more.
He now "sleeps the sleep that knows no waking," beneath
Georgia's blood-stained soil, a glorious martyr to the cause of
liberty. He was killed near Marietta, Georgia, June 22, while on
skirmish. Our skirmishers were ordered to attack the enemy's
line for the purpose of a demonstration and accordingly had
charged them three times, each time driving them from their en-
trenchments. At the beginning of the third charge he was
wounded slightly, but he would not retire from the field, and as
our skirmishers were falling back, the "Yanks" persuing them,
he stopped and turned to look back—just as he turned to look
back—just as he turned, the fatal ball popped him through the
chest, killing him almost instantly. . . .
I went to see him the morning of the 23rd but instead of meeting my Dear Brother, was told by his comrades that they had
just buried him—had given him a soldier's burial. His lieutenant
met me with tears streaming down his cheeks and told me that
his best friend and bravest soldier was gone. He was the beloved
of his company and the general favorite of his regiment. All
spoke of his piety—he died a Christian soldier. . . . We can meet
him again—it is a glorious thought—our only consolation. He

has only gone before, soon we shall follow. Our family circle
has been broken, may it be unbroken in heaven. . . .

> Your son, Affectionately,
> Milton [Walls]
> 25th Regt. Ark. Vols.
> D. H. Reynolds Brig.
> Walthal Division
> Stewart Corps
> Army of Tenn.

Hd. Qrs. Austin's Ba. SS
Florence, Ala.
November 15, 1864
To Mrs. Mary E. Devilbliss
Dear Madam,
It becomes my sad and painful duty to inform you of the death
of your beloved consort, Andrew Devilbliss, who was killed in
the attack on this place October 30, 1864. He was wounded
mortally by one of our own shells and expired almost immediately. His last words were "Lieutenant, write to my wife." In
fulfilling this his last request, I cannot but testify to his many
virtues as a soldier and a Christian. His greatest hope was that
he might live to see his children once more, as he talked constantly of you and them. He had a strong presentiment of his
approaching death, as he often (lately) told his comrades that in
the next engagement, he would fall; his words have been truly
verified. I have known Andrew since the commencement of the
war, and his only wish seems to have been to see the boys and
have them with him once more. . . . His body is interred in the
cemetery at this place and marked. . . . Sympathizing with you
in your affliction and knowing a just God will console you in
distress, I am very resp'y

> Lt. A. T. Martin

It is easy to envision the soldiers of the Army of Tennessee only in
the context of massed formations, yet each was unique. No fewer
than twelve thousand were killed and sixty-five thousand wounded
on its battlefields. They were the forgotten heroes of the Lost Cause.

By April 1865 the remnants of the Army of Tennessee, perhaps five thousand men, were in North Carolina, part of a hodgepodge army of twenty-one thousand, commanded by Joseph E. Johnston. On the fourteenth the general established communication with William T. Sherman concerning a meeting to discuss surrender terms. Such a meeting was arranged between the lines at the farmhouse of John Bennett at Durham on the seventeenth. Nine days later, on April 26, 1865, the terms were formalized.[37]

During the intervening period, Johnston's army, camped at Goldsboro, remained inactive. Numerous rumors concerning the surrender floated throughout the ranks, although no particulars were made available to the men. Discipline was lax to nonexistent. On April 18 Captain Foster entered in his diary: "Had battalion drill today to see if the men would drill." Many of the troops did not wait for the formal surrender and mass desertions were commonplace. Revealed a Mississippian on April 18: "A whole brigade and a reg't left yesterday. There was an appeal to souldiers today by General Loring to not take any ill advised measures, but to stand by the colors and that their officers would see that they have their rights. He begged them not to desert."[38]

Finally, the surrender terms did become known. The men were to retain their personal property and be allowed the use of army wagons and mules for the journey home. Each column was to have a number of guns that was equal to one-seventh of its strength. Recorded Foster on April 29: "Men [Granbury's brigade] are beginning to realize the situation; and are talking about going home to Texas. Our guns have all been turned in, to our Ordnance officers. And we suppose to save us from further humiliation there has not been a Yank in sight of us yet."[39]

The regiments that surrendered at Goldsboro were but a shell of their former strength. The Nineteenth Tennessee, which originally mustered 1,297, was down to 64. The First and Twenty-seventh Tennessee had 3,200 men in their combined ranks but surrendered only 65. The Thirteenth Tennessee, with a total of 1,200, counted 50. Indeed, the entire Tennessee contingent in the army consisted of only 1,312 men.[40]

It is perhaps ironic that in later years the Sons of Confederate Veterans would establish their national headquarters in Franklin, Tennessee, site of the bloodiest defeat of the Army of Tennessee. If courage is honored, however, there is no more fitting place. If the soldiers of the West were lacking in the refinement and esprit that characterized the army in Virginia, they never lacked in courage. As Captain Foster wrote in his diary on May 3, 1865: "After turning in our guns, and getting our paroles, we feel relieved. No more picket duty, no more guard duty, no more fighting, no more war. It is all over, and we are going home."

Notes

ABBREVIATIONS

ADAH	Alabama Department of Archives and History
AHS	Atlanta Historical Society
ATOR	Army of Tennessee Ordnance Records
CCNMP	Chickamauga-Chattanooga National Military Park
DU	Duke University
EU	Emory University
FC	Filson Club
FSU	Florida State University
GDAH	Georgia Department of Archives and History
GHS	Georgia Historical Society
GPL	Greenwood, Mississippi Public Library
GRPL	Grenada, Mississippi Public Library
KMNBP	Kennesaw Mountain National Battlefield Park
LC	Library of Congress

LHA	Louisiana Historical Association
LSU	Louisiana State University
MC	Museum of the Confederacy
MDAH	Mississippi Department of Archives and History
MVC	Mississippi Valley Collection
NA	National Archives
OR	*The War of the Rebellion: A Compilation of the Official Records of the Union and Confederate Armies*
PC	Private Collections
RG	Record Group
SHC	Southern Historical Collection
SNMP	Shiloh National Military Park
SRNBP	Stones River National Battlefield Park
TSLA	Tennessee State Library and Archives
TU	Tulane University
UA	University of Alabama
UG	University of Georgia
UM	University of Mississippi
USL	University of Southwestern Louisiana
USMHI	United States Military History Institute
UT	University of Texas
VNMP	Vicksburg National Military Park
WGC	West Georgia College
WKU	Western Kentucky University
WRHS	Western Reserve Historical Society
WTHS	West Tennessee Historical Society
YU	Yale University

INTRODUCTION

1. Roberts, "Review of the Army of Tennessee at Dalton, Ga.," 150; Tower, ed., *A Carolinian Goes to War*, 163.

2. "Reminiscences," 57; Connelly, *Autumn of Glory*, 251; McMurray, *History of the Twentieth Tennessee Regiment*, 188; Horn, ed., *Campaigns and Battles of the Sixteenth Regiment*, 320–21.

3. "Boy Company of the 45th Alabama," *Confederate Veteran* 10 (August 1902): 353; Collins, *Chapters from the Unwritten History*, 131; Brown, ed., *One of Cleburne's Command*, 43; Connelly, *Autumn of Glory*, 276; Madaus and Needham, *Battle Flags*, 91, 102.

4. Johnston, "Jefferson Davis and the Mississippi Campaign," 478–79; Dawes, "Confederate Strength in the Atlanta Campaign," 281; Clark, *Under the Stars and Bars*, 106–7; Garrett, ed., *Confederate Diary of Robert D. Smith*, 62; Hamilton Branch to mother, May 18, 1864, Branch Letters, UG.

5. Davis, *Orphan Brigade*, 8–9; Wiley, *Life of Johnny Reb*, 339; Samuel C. Kelly to wife, January 16, 1865, Kelly Letters and Diary, ADAH.

6. McMurry, *Hood*, 98; Rowland, *Official and Statistical Register of Mississippi*, 593, 695; Brewer, *Alabama*, 627, 632, 634, 448; Isaac Alexander to sister, April 18, 1863, Alexander Letters, SHC; Tower, ed., *A Carolinian Goes to War*, 21; Hoffman, *Confederate Collapse*, 23–24.

7. Hoole and Hoole, eds., *Historical Sketches*, 4; William Drennan to wife, May 30, 1863, Drennan Papers, MDAH; *Atlanta Intelligencer*, December 2, 1863; Hoffman, *Confederate Collapse*, 23; Robert Magill Diary, April 4, 1864, Wiley Collection, EU.

8. Brewer, *Alabama*, 640, 644, 647, 669.

9. Daniel, *Cannoneers in Gray*, 127–28; Tower, ed., *A Carolinian Goes to War*, 129–30; John (?) to cousin, March 9, 1864, Army of Tennessee Papers, LHA.

10. Morgan, "In the Army of Tennessee," 302; Rugeley, ed., *Batchelor-Turner Letters*, 44; Watson Diary, February 24, 1864, CCNMP. See also criticism of cavalry in Tower, ed., *A Carolinian Goes to War*, 129–30; Sykes, "Walthall's Brigade," 569.

11. *OR*, Ser. I, vol. 6, p. 808 (unless otherwise indicated, all citations are from Series I); Rowland, *Official and Statistical Register of Mississippi*, 527, 536, 608, 617–18, 624, 630, 559, 674, 726, 738; Brewer, *Alabama*, 633, 643, 662, 667–68; Walter R. Roher to cousin, March 31, 1864, Roher Letters, DU.

12. Roher to cousin, March 31, 1864, Roher Letters, DU; Clark, ed., *Histories of the Several Regiments and Battalions from North Carolina*, 2:728; Anderson, *Memoirs*, 80, 135–37.

13. Jones and Martin, eds., *Gentle Rebel*, 65.

14. James Hall to father, February 15, 1864, James Hall Letters, ADAH.

CHAPTER 1

1. W. A. Brown Diary, September 19, 1863, GPL. See also Wiley, ed., *Four Years on the Firing Line*, 141. Some Federals at Chickamauga noticed that Longstreet's troops wore mostly gray uniforms, while Bragg's soldiers were "go-as-you-please . . . with every imaginable variety of garments and head covering" (Hinman, *Story of Sherman's Brigade*, 422).

2. Connelly, *Army of the Heartland*, x.

3. Stanley, ed., *Autobiography of Sir Henry Morton Stanley*, 169; Haratio (?) to wife, April 11, 1862, Haratio (?) Letters, ADAH; Civil War Veterans' Questionnaires, TSLA.

4. McMurry, *Two Great Rebel Armies*, 105; Tower, ed., *A Carolinian Goes to War*, 15; Gill letter as quoted in McDonough and Jones, *War So Terrible*, 276. I have been unable to locate the original Gill letters and the microfilm copy at Emory University is, unfortunately, missing.

5. *Richmond Dispatch,* April 29, 1862.

6. Bailey, *Class and Tennessee's Confederate Generation,* 63–64.

7. Joseph T. Glatthaar, *The March to the Sea and Beyond: Sherman's Troops in the Savannah and Carolinas Campaigns* (New York, 1985), 52–65; Simpson Diary, June 17, 1864, TSLA; Rugeley, ed., *Batchelor-Turner Letters,* 38.

8. Cate, ed., *Two Soldiers,* 19.

9. Neil Gillis to Mary, October 22, 1864, Neil Gillis Letters, EU; Mitchell, *Civil War Soldiers,* 174.

10. *Atlanta Intelligencer,* July 7, 1864.

11. McDonough, *Shiloh,* 11–12; Tower, ed., *A Carolinian Goes to War,* 15; *New Orleans Picayune,* March 7, 1862.

12. Joseph Lyman to wife, April 19, 1862, Lyman Letters, YU; P. W. Watson to wife, July 11, 1862, Watson Letters, SRNBP; Robert Kennedy to mother, November 7, 1862, Kennedy Letters, USL; J. Morgan Smith to Miss Kittie, January 17, 1863, Smith Letters, SRNBP.

13. Lonn, *Foreigners in the Confederacy,* 203.

14. Civil War Centennial Commission, ed., *Tennesseans in the Civil War,* 1:174; "Famous Tenth Tennessee," 553; Stevenson, *Thirteen Months in the Rebel Army,* 36–37; McGrath, "In a Louisiana Regiment," 103–4. There was a scattering of about seven other foreign companies in the army, mostly Irish and Germans (Lonn, *Foreigners in the Confederacy,* 496–502).

15. Robert Patrick to sister, April 1, 1862, Patrick Letters, LSU; Thomas Butler to aunt, May 15, 1862, Butler Letters, LSU; Folmar, ed., *From That Terrible Field,* 88.

16. Thomas Warrick to wife, December 15, 1862, Warrick Letters, ADAH; Reuben Searcy to father, December 12, 1862, Reuben Searcy Letters, ADAH; Hall to sister, December 14, 1862, James Hall Letters, ADAH; Anderson, ed., *Campaigning with Parson's Texas Cavalry Brigade,* 123. See also Wommack, *Diary,* 75.

17. Williams Memoirs, EU; Douglas, ed., *Douglas' Texas Battery,* 132–33; Brown Diary, September 26, 1864, GPL; Watkins, "Co. Aytch," 214–15; Magill Diary, September 26, 1864, Wiley Collection, EU.

18. Fremantle, *Three Months in the Southern States,* 167; W. R. Montgomery to aunt, October 16, 1863, Montgomery Letters, CCNMP; Blackford, ed., *Letters from Lee's Army,* 224. See also comments by Lee's soldiers in Wiley, *Life of Johnny Reb,* 340.

19. Connelly, *Army of the Heartland,* xiii, 37–38.

20. Ibid., xiii.

CHAPTER 2

1. Connelly asserts that "the Army of Tennessee never attained a real *esprit* at a corps level" (*Army of the Heartland,* xiii). The idea that soldiers

imbued armies with a sense of family is presented in Mitchell, *Civil War Soldiers*, 17.

2. William D. Rogers to parents, April 17, 1863, Rogers Letters, SRNMP.

3. Lindsley, ed., *Military Annals of Tennessee*, 205, 223; *OR*, vol. 23, pt. 2, p. 757.

4. Thompson, *History of the Orphan Brigade*, 205, 223; Davis, *Orphan Brigade*, 170; Jackman Journal, May 19–23, 1863, LC.

5. Douglas, ed., *Douglas' Texas Battery*, 64–65; Brown Diary, May 12, 1863, GPL.

6. John M. Davidson to wife, February 8, 1863, Davidson Letters, AHS.

7. Fremantle, *Three Months in the Southern States*, 156–57.

8. Brown Diary, December 15, 1862, GPL.

9. Anderson, ed., *Campaigning with Parson's Texas Cavalry Brigade*, 108; Jones Diary, May 8, 1863, GRPL. See also Davidson to wife, March 31, 1863, Davidson Letters, AHS.

10. Black, ed., "William J. Rogers' Memorandum Book," 87.

11. *Columbus Enquirer*, January 15, 1864; *OR*, vol. 32, pt. 2, pp. 530–31, 751; *Atlanta Intelligencer*, April 1, 1864; W. H. Reynolds to wife, March 25, 1864, Reynolds Letters, GDAH; James Hall to father, February 15, 1864, James Hall Letters, ADAH; Y. H. Smith Diary, January 15, 1864, Wiley Collection, EU; Tower, ed., *A Carolinian Goes to War*, 168.

12. Grammer Diary, February 5, 1864, VNMP; Bond, "Alabama State Artillery," 331.

13. Dubose, *General Joseph Wheeler*, 274–75.

14. J. J. Davis to wife, February 6, 1864, Davis Letters, MVC; Moore, "Writing Home to Talladega," 76; Jackman Journal, February 5, 1864, LC.

15. Cate, ed., *Two Soldiers*, 66; *Memphis Appeal*, March 18, 1864; Andrew J. Neal to sister, March 8, 1864, Neal Letters, EU; Benedict Joseph Semmes to wife, March 16, 1864, Semmes Letters, SHC; Porter Diary, April 7, 1864, EU; Worsham, *Old Nineteenth Tennessee Regiment*, 108; Grammer Diary, April 7, 1864, VNMP; Mitchell, ed., "Letters of a Confederate Surgeon," 160; Garrett, ed., *Confederate Diary of Robert D. Smith*, 59; Jamison and McTigue, eds., *Letters and Recollections of a Confederate Soldier*, 91.

16. Cate, ed., *Two Soldiers*, 69; W. B. Shepard to wife, March 31, 1864, in Benjamin F. Cheatham Papers, TSLA; Neal to sister, March 23, 1864, EU.

17. *Memphis Appeal*, March 4, 1862; Lindsley, ed., *Military Annals of Tennessee*, 424, 215; Cabaniss, *Civil War Journal and Letters of Washington Ives*, 22; Davidson to wife, September 10, 1863, Davidson Letters, AHS. See also Warrick to wife, August 6, 1862, Warrick Letters, ADAH.

18. B. H. Green to parents, April 1, 1862, Green Letters, Wiley Collection, EU; Lyman to wife, April 13, 1862, Lyman Letters, YU; Folmar, ed., *From That Terrible Field*, 98; Biel, ed., "Evacuation of Corinth," 50–51.

19. James I. Hall, "Notes on the War," SHC; Simpson Diary, July 29, 1862, TSLA; Cabaniss, *Civil War Journal and Letters of Washington Ives*,

24; Warrick to wife, August 11, 1862, Warrick Letters, ADAH; Black, ed., "William J. Rogers' Memorandum Book," 64–65; *Memphis Appeal,* August 26, 1862; Robert L. Bliss to mother, August 25, 1862, Bliss Letters, ADAH.

20. Cabaniss, *Civil War Journal and Letters of Washington Ives,* 26; George Winchester Diary, July 27, 1862, TSLA; Simpson Diary, July 28, 1862, TSLA; Law, "Diary of J. G. Law," 218; Bliss to mother, September 6, 1862, Bliss Letters, ADAH.

21. J. W. Hill to sister, June 16, 1862, Hill Letters, UT; Magee Diary, August 9, 1862, DU; Jones Diary, August 4, 1862, GRPL.

22. Searcy to mother, August 31, 1862, James Searcy Letters, ADAH; Bolling Hall to father, August 11, 1862, Bolling Hall Letters, ADAH; Law, "Diary of J. G. Law," 392. See also Gammage, *The Camp, the Bivouac and the Battle Field,* 51.

23. Jackson, ed., *So Mourns the Dove,* 66.

24. Fremantle, *Three Months in the Southern States,* 155–56. In late September 1863, an Illinois infantryman talked to some pickets of a South Carolina regiment and described them as "a fine, handsome, stout lot of fellows, better dressed than we are, their uniforms being apparently new.... The Carolinians' uniform is a bluish gray . . . with sky blue pants" (Gates, ed., *Rough Side of War,* 94).

25. William M. Thompson to brother, June 21, 1864, Thompson Letters, PC; Jordon, ed., "Mathew A. Dunn Letters," 122; Haynes and Wilkins, eds., "Stanley Letters," 40; Steryx, ed., "Autobiography and Letters of Joel Murphree," 191; R. N. Colville to father, June 26, 1864, Colville Letters, KMNBP; Cash and Howorth, eds., *My Dear Nellie,* 185; Roundtree, ed., "Letters of a Confederate Soldier," 287. See also Wiley, ed., "Confederate Letters of John W. Hagan," 287; John McCorkle to wife, July 2, 1864, McCorkle Letters, GHS; J. N. Davis to wife, May 29, 1864, Davis Letters, UG.

26. *OR,* vol. 23, pt. 1, pp. 587, 591, and vol. 31, pt. 2, pp. 600, 645, 697; Martin, *Desertion of Alabama Troops,* 81; Robbins, "Desertion," 33; Bolling Hall to sister, January 12, 1864, Bolling Hall Letters, ADAH; "Monthly Inspection of Hood's Corps, March 7, 1864," Yerger Papers, MDAH. For other reports of sufficient shoes at Dalton see *Augusta Constitutionalist,* January 19, February 5, 1864; *Memphis Appeal,* March 27, 1864; *Montgomery Daily Mail,* April 14, 1864.

27. Davidson to wife, June 4, 1864, Davidson Letters, AHS; James Searcy to sister, May 23, 1864, James Searcy Letters, ADAH; Haynes and Wilkins, eds., "Stanley Letters," 40; Cash and Howorth, eds., *My Dear Nellie,* 182.

28. Wiley, ed., "Confederate Letters of John W. Hagan," 227; Davidson to wife, June 6, 1864, Davidson Letters, AHS; Jones and Martin, eds., *Gentle Rebel,* 32–33; Noyes, "Excerpts from the Civil War Diary of E. T. Eggleston," 345. See also Porter Diary, June 10, 1864, MDAH; Clark, *Under the Stars and Bars,* 100, 117.

29. Betts, ed., "Civil War Letters of Elbridge Littlejohn," 33; J. W. Ward to grandmother, October 18, 1864, Wiley Collection, EU; Jones and Martin, eds., *Gentle Rebel*, 107; Cate, ed., *Two Soldiers*, 146; Brown, ed., *One of Cleburne's Command*, 146; Cabaniss, *Civil War Journal and Letters of Washington Ives*, 15; E. M. Graham Diary, November 23, 1864, UT.

30. Thomas Roane to sister, October 21, 1864, Roane Letter, MVC.

31. Jones and Martin, eds., *Gentle Rebel*, 101; Brown, ed., *One of Cleburne's Command*, 138.

32. Cash and Howorth, eds., *My Dear Nellie*, 215.

33. James Lanning Diary, October 31, 1864, Wiley Collection, EU; M. A. Traynham to wife, November 13, 1864, Traynham Letters, EU; Brown, ed., *One of Cleburne's Command*, 144; Jones and Martin, eds., *Gentle Rebel*, 111; Cate, ed., *Two Soldiers*, 149.

34. Jones and Martin, eds., *Gentle Rebel*, 109; Jordon, ed., "Mathew A. Dunn Letters," 126; Betts, ed., "Civil War Letters of Elbridge Littlejohn," 33; Brown Diary, November 30, 1864, GPL; G. W. Athey to sister (undated), Athey Letters, ADAH; B. P. Weaver to wife, November 3, 1864, Weaver Letters, EU; Roundtree, ed., "Letters of a Confederate Soldier," 296; Mitchell, ed., "Letters of a Confederate Surgeon," 174; Lanning Diary, October 29, December 9, 1864, Wiley Collection, EU. See also Vann, "*Most Lovely Lizzie*," 18. During the third and fourth quarters of 1864 the Army of Tennessee was issued 45,412 jackets, 102,864 pairs of pants, 102,558 pairs of shoes, 108,937 pairs of drawers, 27,000 blankets, 45,853 hats, 61,860 cotton shirts, and 55,560 pairs of socks ("Resources of the Confederacy," 120).

35. OR, vol. 45, pt. 1, pp. 735–36.

36. Ibid., 747.

37. William E. Stanton to wife, March 30, 1865, Stanton Letters, UT; Andrews, *The South Reports the Civil War*, 490.

CHAPTER 3

1. Connelly, *Army of the Heartland*, 28; OR, 7:765. See also Jones, "Outfitting the Provisional Army of Tennessee," 258.

2. Enoch Hancock to daughter, June 16, 1861, Hancock Letters, TSLA; Mackey Diary, January 2, 1862, MC.

3. Johnston, *Johnston*, 323, 333; Davis, *Orphan Brigade*, 48; OR, 6:832.

4. Johnston, *Johnston*, 333; OR, 4:525.

5. Horn, *Army of Tennessee*, 82; OR, 7:910, 751; Worsham, *Old Nineteenth Tennessee Regiment*, 22; Lindsley, ed., *Military Annals of Tennessee*, 349–50.

6. OR, vol. 10, pt. 1, p. 575; Roman, *Military Operations of General Beauregard*, 1:260; Lindsley, ed., *Military Annals of Tennessee*, 499; "Ordnance Returns of the 1st Brigade, 1st Division, May 12, 1862," and "Ord-

nance Returns of the 2d Brigade, 1st Division, June 21, 1862," Yerger Papers, MDAH.

7. *OR*, 4:417, 430, 52:190; Atkinson, ed., *Civil War Letters of Fletcher*, 27.

8. Sword, *Firepower from Abroad*, 19, 21; *OR*, 4:828, 7:863, 872, 53:228; Lindsley, ed., *Military Annals of Tennessee*, 390; Thompson, *History of the First Kentucky Brigade*, 58, 87; McMurray, *History of the Twentieth Tennessee Regiment*, 124–26, 204, 212–13, 390; Mecklin Diary, March 13, 1862, MDAH; R. P. Boswell to E. Lee, March 29, 1862, Boswell Letters, TSLA.

9. *OR*, vol. 10, pt. 1, p. 379; Jarman, "History of Co. K, 27th Mississippi Infantry," MDAH; Chisolm, "Gen. B. J. Hill's Old Regiment at Shiloh," 211.

10. "Ordnance Returns of the 1st Brigade, 1st Division, May 12, 1862," Yerger Papers, MDAH.

11. *OR*, vol. 16, pt. 1, pp. 1094, 1097; Garrett, ed., *Confederate Diary of Robert D. Smith*, 29; Lindsley, ed., *Military Annals of Tennessee*, 187; Rugeley, ed., *Batchelor-Turner Letters*, 32.

12. McWhiney and Jamieson, *Attack and Die*, 49; Hezekiah Rabb to wife, May 23, 1863, Rabb Letters, EU.

13. "Report of Arms in Bragg's Army, April 30, 1863," Bragg Papers, WRHS.

14. *OR*, vol. 23, pt. 2, p. 763; Oladowski to Gorgas, July 25, 1863, Letters Sent, Ordnance Officer, Army of Tennessee (ATOR), Chap. IV, vol. 141, RG 109, NA.

15. Sword, *Firepower from Abroad*, 118–19; *OR*, vol. 30, pt. 1, pp. 822–26, pt. 2, pp. 43, 386, vol. 31, pt. 2, p. 100; Rennolds, *History of Henry County Commands*, 62–63; Oladowski to Wright, October 17, 1863, ATOR. Confederate records reveal that 23,281 arms were picked up on the Chickamauga battlefield. Since thousands of these were dropped by wounded Southerners, the Federal figure probably more closely represents the net gain.

16. Garrett, ed., *Confederate Diary of Robert D. Smith*, 51; Walker, *Rolls and Historical Sketch of the Tenth Regiment, South Carolina Volunteers*, 74.

17. Oladowski to Wright, December 20, 1863, to Gorgas, December 28, 1863, to Humphries, January 9, 1864, to Wright, January 25, 1864, ATOR; Wright to Gorgas, March 18, 1864, Letters and Telegrams Sent, Atlanta Arsenal, 1862–64, Chap. IV, vol. 16, RG 109, NA.

18. *OR*, vol. 38, pt. 4, p. 782; "Monthly Inspection of Hood's Corps, March 7, 1864," Yerger Papers, MDAH.

19. "Report of Equipage of the 5th Tennessee Volunteers, March 28, 1862," and "Weekly Return of 2d Brigade, 1st Division, 1st Corps, Army of the Mississippi, June 21, 1862," Yerger Papers, MDAH.

20. Fremantle, *Three Months in the Southern States,* 156; *OR,* vol. 23, pt. 2, p. 758; Oladowski to Mackall, July 14, 19, 1863, ATOR.

21. *OR,* vol. 23, pt. 2, p. 758; Oladowski to Gorgas, July 23, 1863, and "Ammunition Expended in Polk's Corps at Chickamauga," October 29, 1863, ATOR.

22. Wright to Gorgas, February 12, 1864, Letters and Telegrams Sent, Atlanta Arsenal, 1862–64, Chap. IV, vol. 16, RG 109, NA; *OR,* vol. 32, pt. 2, pp. 768–69; "Monthly Inspection of Hood's Corps, March 7, 1864," Yerger Papers, MDAH.

23. Daniel and Gunter, *Confederate Cannon Foundries,* 104–8.

24. *OR,* vol. 16, pt. 1, p. 1097, pt. 2, p. 1157, vol. 23, pt. 2, p. 762; Civil War Centennial Commission, ed., *Tennesseans in the Civil War,* 1:138; Oladowski to Wright, January 17, May 22, September 25, 1863, and to Gorgas, September 25, 1863, ATOR; William Harris Bragg, *Joe Brown's Army,* 72.

25. *OR,* vol. 30, pt. 1, pp. 238–39, pt. 2, pp. 41–42, vol. 31, pt. 1, pp. 99–100.

26. Daniel, *Cannoneers in Gray,* 128–29, 180.

27. McDonough, "Battle of Stones River," 29.

CHAPTER 4

1. James I. Hall to parents, June 9, 1861, and to children, June 11, 1861, Hall Letters, SHC; Theodore Mandeville to wife, December 29, 1862, Mandeville Letters, LSU; Musick, ed., " 'This Is War—Glorious War,' " 37; *New Orleans Crescent,* September 14, 1861. See also Fall, "Civil War Letters of Albert Boult Fall," 159, 162.

2. Green to father, March 12, 1862, Green Letters, Wiley Collection, EU; Samuel R. Shelton Diary, April 12, May 24, 1862, in *Memphis Commercial Appeal,* April 29, 1962; Williams and Wooster, eds., "With Terry's Texas Rangers," 305.

3. Roman, *Military Operations of General Beauregard,* 1:383.

4. *OR,* vol. 10, pt. 1, p. 776, and pt. 2, p. 572; Searcy to mother, June 17, 1862, James Searcy Letters, ADAH; Warrick to mother, July 22, 1862, Warrick Letters, ADAH. On April 30, 1862, the government ration was one pound of beef or ten ounces of pork or bacon, one and one-quarter pounds of flour or meal, and to each one hundred rations eight quarts of beans or fifteen pounds of rice, four quarts of vinegar, four pounds of soap, and one pound of candles (*OR,* vol. 10, pt. 2, pp. 478, 530–31).

5. *New Orleans Crescent,* January 23, 1862; *OR,* vol. 10, pt. 2, p. 572.

6. Eqlantine Aquors to cousin, February 20, 1862, Aquors Letters, DU; Martin Busk to brother, February 2, 1862, Busk Letters, TSLA; *OR,* vol. 10, pt. 1, p. 782, pt. 2, p. 572; Jackson, ed., *So Mourns the Dove,* 25.

7. *OR*, 7:334, 876; Worsham, *Old Nineteenth Tennessee Regiment*, 30; Law, "Diary of J. G. Law," 25; Harrison, "Confederate View of Southern Kentucky," 170.

8. Little and Maxwell, *History of Lumsden's Battery*, 29; Lindsley, ed., *Military Annals of Tennessee*, 207; Crow and Teague, eds., *Diary of a Confederate Soldier*, 27; *OR*, vol. 10, pt. 1, p. 783; Blakemore Diary, June 10, 1862, TSLA; James Searcy to father, June 20, 1862, James Searcy Letters, ADAH.

9. *Mobile Advertiser and Register*, November 9, 11, 1862; Shingleton, "With Loyalty and Honor as a Patriot," 247; Bailey, ed., "Reminiscences of the Civil War by T. J. Walker," 51.

10. Garrett, ed., *Confederate Diary of Robert D. Smith*, 36; James Hays to wife, August 30, 1862, Hays Letters, GDAH; Doss to wife, October 29, 1862, Doss Letters, KMNBP; Jones Diary, October 19, 24, 1862, GRPL; Brown Diary, October 20, 1862, GPL.

11. Dennis, ed., *Kemper County Rebel*, 18, 30, 40; James Searcy to sister, November 15, 1862, James Searcy Letters, ADAH; Hill to sister, December 8, 1862, Hill Letters, UT.

12. *OR*, vol. 23, pt. 2, p. 647.

13. Ibid., 769–70; Connelly, *Autumn of Glory*, 114.

14. *OR*, vol. 25, pt. 2, pp. 687, 730, and vol. 51, pt. 2, p. 738. Richard D. Goff concludes that during this time shortages were limited mostly to the Army of Northern Virginia, and the "incomplete evidence suggests that the field armies in the Southwest . . . ate their fill" (*Confederate Supply*, 87). He also states that Bragg drew heavily from the reserve meat supply in Atlanta, although he "had his own meat packing plant at Fayetteville, Tennessee" (p. 82).

15. *OR*, vol. 23, pt. 2, p. 759; Isham W. Thomas to wife, March 11, 1863, Thomas Letters and Diaries, GPL; Doss to mother, April 4, 1863, Doss Letters, KMNBP; Mathis, ed., *In the Land of the Living*, 68. See also Dennis, ed., *Kemper County Rebel*, 70. For the daily ration of the Army of Tennessee on March 31, 1863, see *OR*, vol. 23, pt. 2, p. 770.

16. McDonald quoted in Wommack, *Call Forth the Mighty Men*, 248; Garrett, ed., *Confederate Diary of Robert D. Smith*, 50; Jackson, ed., *So Mourns the Dove*, 53; Mathis, ed., *In the Land of the Living*, 62.

17. Rogers to parents, April 26, 1863, Rogers Letters, SRNBP; Joel H. Puckett to wife, February 10, 1863, Puckett Letters, UT; Hay, ed., *Cleburne and His Command*, 126; Emmanuel, "Historical Sketch of the Georgetown Rifle Guards" (pages unnumbered). See also James Searcy to brother, May 9, 1863, James Searcy Letters, ADAH.

18. *OR*, vol. 23, pt. 2, pp. 647, 680, 688, 695, 700; William J. Hardee to B. R. Johnson, January 21, 1863, Hardee Papers, ADAH.

19. *OR*, vol. 30, pt. 4, p. 550.

20. Ibid., 547–48, 550–52; Taylor, "Rebel Beef," 19.

21. Warrick to wife, August 2, 1863, Warrick Letters, ADAH; Partin, "A Confederate Sergeant's Report to His Wife," 306; Anderson, ed., *Campaigning with Parson's Texas Cavalry Brigade*, 120. See also Ward to father, August 26, 1863, Ward Letters, Wiley Collection, EU.

22. Watson Diary, October 19, 28, 29, 30, 1863, CCNMP; Doss to wife, October 25, 1863, Doss Letters, KMNBP. See also Alex McGowin to family, September 27, 1863, McGowin Letters, SRNBP.

23. Charles Weaver to father, November 18, 1863, Charles Weaver Letters, ADAH; W. C. Athey to mother, November 12, 1863, Athey Letters, ADAH; *Atlanta Intelligencer*, December 18, 1863. See also Watson Diary, November 2, 1863, CCNMP; E. K. Flournoy to wife, November 2, 1863, Flournoy Letters, ADAH; Watkins, "*Co. Aytch*," 121–22; J. W. Harris to mother, November 19, 1863, Harris Letters, TSLA. Between November 8 and 13, 1863, Hardee's and Breckinridge's corps received 561 head of cattle, but they averaged only 154 pounds each (various vouchers, November 8–18, 1863, Bragg Papers, WRHS).

24. *OR*, vol. 32, pt. 3, p. 860; Andrew Edge to wife, December 8, 1863, Edge Letters, EU; Brown Diary, December 8, 1863, GPL; Anderson, ed., *Campaigning with Parson's Texas Cavalry Brigade*, 127–28; Kirwan, ed., *Johnny Green of the Orphan Brigade*, 119; Jackman Journal, December 15, 1863, LC. See also W. R. Hurst to wife, December 3, 1863, Hurst Letters, KMNBP; Cabaniss, *Civil War Journal and Letters of Washington Ives*, 54.

25. *OR*, vol. 32, pt. 2, pp. 510, 557, 603, 608, 612; Jackson, ed., *So Mourns the Dove*, 77; Mitchell, ed., "Letters of a Confederate Surgeon," 164; John A. Harris to wife, April 25, 1864, Harris Letters, LSU. For complaints about food shortages see A. J. Martin to parents, April 30, 1864, A. J. Martin Letters, KMNBP; James Hall to father, February 15, 1864, James Hall Letters, ADAH. The opposite view can be found in Doss to wife, January 27, 1864, Doss Letters, KMNBP; Jamison and McTigue, eds., *Letters and Recollections of a Confederate Soldier*, 88.

26. Lewis, "A Confederate Officer's Letters," 492.

27. *OR*, vol. 32, pt. 3, pp. 574–75; Watkins, "*Co. Aytch*," 126.

28. Wiley, "Billy Yank and Johnny Reb in the Campaign for Atlanta," 18; Unidentified Diary, Sixty-fifth Georgia, various entries between January 14 and March 8, 1864, KMNBP; Unidentified Diary, March 4, 1864, quoted in Wiley, *Life of Johnny Reb*, 95; *Memphis Appeal*, January 21, 1864.

29. Jones and Martin, eds., *Gentle Rebel*, 40; Garrett, ed., *Confederate Diary of Robert D. Smith*, 70; Collins, *Chapters from the Unwritten History*, 223; Jordon, ed., "Mathew A. Dunn Letters," 121; Brown, ed., *One of Cleburne's Command*, 103; Simpson Diary, June 25, 1864, TSLA; Edwin Davis to editor, July 26, 1864, Davis Letters, GDAH.

30. Wiley, ed., "Confederate Letters of John W. Hagan," 283; O. D. Chester to sister, July 14, 1864, Chester Letters, KMNBP; *OR*, vol. 32, pt. 2, p. 608; Crittenden to wife, June 28, 1864, Crittenden Letters, UT; Trask

Journal, June 21, 1864, EU; Steryx, ed., "Autobiography and Letters of Joel Murphree," 183; Jones and Martin, eds., *Gentle Rebel*, 40; Neal to parents, July 13, 1864, Neal Letters, EU; Mitchell, ed., "Letters of a Confederate Surgeon," 165; Wiley, "Billy Yank and Johnny Reb in the Campaign for Atlanta," 18.

31. Puckett to wife, May 21, 1863, Puckett Letters, UT; Hall to children, July 8, 1864, Hall Letters, SHC; Columbus Sykes to wife, June 29, 1864, Sykes Letters, KMNBP; Charles H. Thiot to wife, June 26, 1864, Thiot Letters, EU; Betts, ed., "Civil War Letters of Elbridge Littlejohn," 26; Z. T. Armistead to brother, May 31, 1864, Armistead Letters, GDAH; Helms to wife, May 26, 1864, Helms Letters, GDAH; Aiken, ed., "Letters of the Offield Brothers," 124; Douglas, ed., *Douglas' Texas Battery*, 108. For the opposite view see a Reb's comments in Wiley, "Life of Billy Yank and Johnny Reb in the Campaign for Atlanta," 18; Trask Journal, May 16, 1864, EU.

32. Tower, ed., *A Carolinian Goes to War*, 167–68; Steryx, ed., "Autobiography and Letters of Joel Murphree," 179; Mathis, ed., *In the Land of the Living*, 103; Smith, *Company K*, 115.

33. Mathis, ed., *In the Land of the Living*, 100. See also Hall to father, February 15, 1864, Hall Letters, SHC.

34. Goodners Diary, September 11, 1864, AHS; Brown, ed., *One of Cleburne's Command*, 137; Diary, October 28, 1864, TSLA; Warrick to wife, November 13, 1864, Warrick Letters, ADAH; B. P. Weaver to wife, November 13, 1864, Weaver Letters, EU; Anderson, ed., *Campaigning with Parson's Texas Cavalry Brigade*, 153. See also Lanning Diary, September 26, 1864, Wiley Collection, EU.

35. Cabaniss, *Civil War Journal and Letters of Washington Ives*, 15–19.

36. Cate, ed., *Two Soldiers*, 177; Cavanaugh, *Confederate Record*, 16. See also Vann, "Most Lovely Lizzie," 20.

27. McMurry, *Two Great Rebel Armies*, 72.

CHAPTER 5

1. McGrath, "In a Louisiana Regiment," 112; Clark and Riley, eds., "Medical Department," 59. See also *New Orleans Crescent*, September 28, 1861; J. R. Pope to mother, January 26, 1862, Pope Letters, DU.

2. Johnston, *Johnston*, 337, 443; L. P. Yandell to father, October 9, 1861, Yandell Letters, FC; *OR*, 4:524–25, and 7:746; Magee Diary, December 1, 1861, DU; Connelly, *Army of the Heartland*, 70; Boswell to E. Lee, December 1, 1861, Boswell Letters, TSLA; W. E. Coleman to parents, January 19, 1862, Coleman Letters, TSLA; Hancock to brother, November 22, 1861, Hancock Letters, TSLA; Carter, *Cavalryman's Reminiscences*, 19; Silver, ed., *Confederate Soldier*, 37.

3. Bailey, *Class and Tennessee's Confederate Generation*, 81.

4. Baird, *David Wendell Yandell*, 38–40; LaPointe, "Hospitals in Memphis," 327.

5. Clark and Riley, eds., "Medical Department," 59; Johnston, *Johnston*, 493, 519.

6. Anderson, "After the Fall of Fort Donelson," 289–90.

7. J. W. Collom to wife, April 10, 1862, Collom Letter and Memoirs, PC.

8. Lindsley, ed., *Military Annals of Tennessee*, 531–32; H. O. Beasley to wife, April 8, 1862, Beasley Letters, SNMP.

9. *Charleston Courier*, April 22, 1862; Charles J. Johnson to wife, April 11, 1862, Johnson Letters, LSU; "Miss Ella Palmer," 72; Stevenson, *Thirteen Months in the Rebel Army*, 124; Cunningham, *Doctors in Gray*, 49; Garrett, ed., *Confederate Diary of Robert D. Smith*, 6.

10. "Report of Killed, Wounded and Missing of 2d Corps, Army of the Mississippi, at the Battle of Shiloh, 1862," Chap. II, vol. 220½, RG 109, NA (hereafter cited as "Casualty Report"); *Memphis Appeal*, April 12, 16, 23, 1862.

11. Stevenson, *Thirteen Months in the Rebel Army*, 124–25; Lyman to wife, April 19, 1862, Lyman Letters, YU; Harwell, ed., *Kate*, 25; "Casualty Report."

12. *Memphis Appeal*, April 12, 15, 17, 1862; *Natchez Weekly Courier*, April 23, 1862; Bessham, " 'Through a Mist of Powder and Excitement,' " 132–33.

13. "Casualty Report."

14. *OR*, vol. 10, pt. 1, p. 784; Wiley, *Life of Johnny Reb*, 247–48; Worsham, *Old Nineteenth Tennessee Regiment*, 48–49.

15. Folmar, ed., *From That Terrible Field*, 57; Lindsley, ed., *Military Annals of Tennessee*, 810; *OR*, vol. 10, pt. 1, pp. 776, 784; Bliss to mother, April 21, 1862, Bliss Letters, ADAH; James Searcy to mother, May 18, 1862, James Searcy Letters, ADAH; Mecklin Diary, May 27, 1862, MDAH; Cox, ed., "R. L. Davis Letters," 41; Andrew Devilbliss to wife, April 19, 1862, Devilbliss Letters, TU; Bergeron, ed., *Reminiscences of Uncle Silas*, 61.

16. Butler to wife, May 15, 1862, Butler Letters, LSU; "Report of Sick and Wounded in Western Department Commanded by Generals Beauregard and Bragg, May and June 1862," Jones Collection, TU.

17. Tower, ed., *A Carolinian Goes to War*, 20; Hughes, ed., *Liddell's Record*, 72; Polignac, "Polignac's Diary," 17; "Miss Ella Palmer," 73; *OR*, vol. 10, pt. 1, p. 177.

18. *Medical and Surgical History*, 1:252, 255; Beers, *Memoirs*, 80–82.

19. "Battle of Perryville as Told in a Letter by J. A. Bruce," 117.

20. Clark and Riley, eds., "Medical Department," 67; "Reminiscences of Murfreesboro," 255.

21. Hardee to Breckinridge, February 18, 1863, Hardee Papers, ADAH.

22. "Medical Director's Consolidated Report of Sick and Wounded, January 1–May 31, 1863," Jones Collection, TU; Lindsley, ed., *Military Annals of Tennessee,* 215; William D. Cole to wife, June 24, 1863, Cole Letters, USMHI.

23. "Medical Director's Consolidated Report of Sick and Wounded, January 1–May 31, 1863," Jones Collection, TU; Lindsley, ed., *Military Annals of Tennessee,* 215.

24. "Medical Director's Consolidated Report of Sick and Wounded, January 1–May 31, 1863," Jones Collection, TU; Black, ed., "William J. Rogers' Memorandum Book," 76–77.

25. "Consolidated Weekly Report of Bragg's Hospitals, September 30, 1863," Stout Papers, UT.

26. *OR,* vol. 20, pt. 1, pp. 228–29; Roberts, "Field and Temporary Hospitals," 258, 260; McMicken to Flewellyn, April 23, 1863, Stout Papers, UT; *Medical and Surgical History,* 1:274, 276–77.

27. Duncan, *Medical Department of the United States Army,* 302–3; Howell Memoirs, ADAH.

28. Tower, ed., *A Carolinian Goes to War,* 102; Harwell, ed., *Kate,* 152–54.

29. Noll, ed., *Doctor Quintard,* 90; Clark and Riley, eds., "Medical Department," 71–73; Stout to Moore, October 10, 1863, Stout Papers, UT.

30. Ambulance Train Reports of Wiley M. Baird, October 22, November 30, C. Miller, September 26, G. W. Garmoney, November 25, W. J. Sneed, November 29, J. E. Nagle, November 30, Frank M. Dennis, October 22, 1863, Stout Papers, UT.

31. Stout to Moore, October 10, 1863, Stout Papers, UT; Duncan, *Medical Department of the United States Army,* 303, 305.

32. *OR,* vol. 31, pt. 2, p. 684; "Service with the Twentieth Tennessee Regiment," 139.

33. Wyman to mother, December 11, 1863, Wyman Letters, ADAH; Hurst to wife and family, December 23, 1863, Hurst Letters, KMNBP; "Tabular Statement of Medical Officers on Duty and the Number of Beds Occupied and Unoccupied, March 31, 1864," Stout Papers, UT.

34. Breeden, "Medical History," 41, 54, 56.

35. Ibid., 43–44; Steryx, ed., "Autobiography and Letters of Joel Murphree," 179; Porter Diary, June 13, 1864, MDAH; Garrett, ed., *Confederate Diary of Robert D. Smith,* 71.

36. Breeden, "Medical History," 46, 48–49; Mitchell, ed., "Letters of a Confederate Surgeon," 171.

37. Breeden, "Medical History," 53–56.

38. John Davis to wife, August 1, 1864, John Davis Letters, GDAH.

39. Dyer, *Reminiscences,* 235–37.

40. Chaplain W. T. Bennett to Sister Davis, August 18, 1864, and Dr. Will Somers to Miss John J. Davis, August 23, 1866, Davis Letters, MVC.

41. Collins, *Chapters from the Unwritten History*, 232; Norrell Diary, June 6, 1864, KMNBP.

42. "Report of Stewart's Corps, September 20, 1864," Jones Collection, TU.

43. Smith Diary, October 20, 1864, TSLA; Warrick to wife, November 10, 1864, Warrick Letters, ADAH; J. K. P. Martin to parents, October 12, 1864, J. K. P. Martin Letters, KMNBP.

44. Roberts, "Field and Temporary Hospitals," 256, 258; Holmes, *Diary*, 23.

45. Brown, ed., *One of Cleburne's Command*, 154.

46. Ibid., 157–58; Holmes, *Diary*, Smith, *Company K*, 129; Crumpton, "Closing Scenes with Johnston's Army," 5–6.

CHAPTER 6

1. Boswell to aunt and uncle, August 3, 1861, Boswell Letters, TSLA; Hall to wife, June 9, 1861, Hall Letters, SHC; Mitchell, ed., "Letters of a Confederate Surgeon," 342.

2. Hall to wife, June 9, 1861, and to children, June 11, 1861, Hall Letters, SHC; Mitchell, ed., "Letters of a Confederate Surgeon," 342; *Memphis Appeal*, October 25, 1861; Green to father, March 19, 1862, Green Letters, Wiley Collection, EU.

3. Folmar, ed., *From That Terrible Field*, 52; Robert T. Moore to Thomas Alderson, April 21, 1862, Moore Letters, ADAH; Cox, ed., "R. L. Davis Letters," 40. See also James Searcy to father, April 19, 1862, James Searcy Letters, ADAH.

4. Jackson, ed., *So Mourns the Dove*, 25; Folmar, ed., *From That Terrible Field*, 51.

5. Warrick to wife, March 22, 1863, Warrick Letters, ADAH; Sam Settles to wife, September 29, 1863, Settles Letters, PC; Cate, ed., *Two Soldiers*, 31. See also Law, "Diary of J. G. Law," 27; Wiley, ed., *Fourteen Hundred and 91 Days in the Confederate Army*, 278; Puckett to wife, July [?], 1862, Puckett Letters, UT; Taylor, ed., *Reluctant Rebel*, 172; Brown, ed., *One of Cleburne's Command*, 80; Thiot to wife, June 22, 1864, Thiot Letters, EU; Watson Diary, September 15, 1863, CCNMP; Collins, *Chapters from the Unwritten History*, 223.

6. Hubbard, *Notes of a Private*, 6; Little and Maxwell, *History of Lumsden's Battery*, 39; Kirwan, ed., *Johnny Green of the Orphan Brigade*, 41; Hay, ed., *Cleburne and His Command*, 136. See also Garrett, ed., *Confederate Diary of Robert D. Smith*, 67–68.

7. Boswell to E. Lee, December 28, 1861, Boswell Letters, TSLA; Mecklin Diary, June 2, 1862, MDAH; Nixon, ed., "An Alabamian at Shiloh," 149; Grammer Diary, January 27, 1864, VNMP; Watkins, "Co. Aytch," 83–84.

8. Folmar, ed., *From That Terrible Field,* 58; *New Orleans Crescent,* February 19, 1862; Hay, ed., *Cleburne and His Command,* 132; *Macon Telegraph,* January 18, 1864.

9. Coleman Diary, February 15, 16, 17, 18, 20, 21, 1863, SHC.

10. Johnson to wife, September 8, 1861, Johnson Letters, LSU; *New Orleans Crescent,* September 14, 28, December 11, 1861, January 14, 1862; Alderson, ed., "Civil War Diary of Captain James Litton Cooper," 158; M. H. Parsons to sister, December 22, 1861, Parsons Letters, SNMP.

11. Brown Diary, 9, GPL; S. R. Latta to wife, December 31, 1861, Latta Letters, LSU; Jones Diary, December 1, 1861, GRPL; Mott, "War Journal," 237–38; Parsons to sister, December 22, 1861, Parsons Letters, SNMP; *Memphis Appeal,* December 27, 1861.

12. Wommack, *Diary,* 76; Black, ed., "William J. Rogers' Memorandum Book," 80; Mathis, ed., *In the Land of the Living,* 41, 61; Dennis, ed., *Kemper County Rebel,* 53; *OR,* vol. 23, pt. 2, p. 758; Warrick to wife, April 8, 1863, Warrick Letters, ADAH; Campbell, "From Hoover's Gap to Chattanooga," 44; Moorman, "Moorman Memorandum," 76.

13. Roberts, "In Winter Quarters at Dalton, Ga.," 274; *Memphis Appeal,* January 21, 1864; J. K. Weaver to mother, January 8, 1864, J. K. Weaver Letters, ADAH; Curry, "History of Company B," 191; Cater, *As It Was,* 180–81; Kirwan, ed., *Johnny Green of the Orphan Brigade,* 118; Jackman Journal, December 22, 1863, LC; Cate, ed., *Two Soldiers,* 12; Jones Diary, January 25, 1864, GRPL; Mathis, ed., *In the Land of the Living,* 92; Davis to wife, January 2, 1864, Davis Letters, UG; Reisnor Etter Diary, December 11, 1863, SRNBP.

14. John ? to cousin, March 9, 1864, John ? Letters, Army of Tennessee Papers, LHA; Belser L. Wyman to mother, March 29, 1863, Wyman Letters, ADAH; *Memphis Appeal,* March 15, 1864. See also Mecklin Diary, May 7, 1862, MDAH; James Searcy to wife, June 10, 1862, James Searcy Letters, ADAH; Curry, "History of Company B," 191; Ward to grandmother, February 4, 1864, Ward Letters, Wiley Collection, EU; Dillon Diary, January 7, 1862, UM.

15. Davis to wife, May 29, 1864, Davis Letters, UG; Jones and Martin, eds., *Gentle Rebel,* 52, 65, 67; Jordon, ed., "Mathew A. Dunn Letters," 118; Chattahoochee Valley Historical Society, ed., *War Was the Place,* 100; Mathis, ed., *In the Land of the Living,* 103.

16. Brown, ed., *One of Cleburne's Command,* 104–5; Norrell Diary, June 24, 1864, KMNBP.

17. Kennedy to sister, June 20, 1863, Kennedy Letters, USL. See also Davis, *Orphan Brigade,* 168–69.

18. *New Orleans Crescent,* October 29, 1861; *Memphis Appeal,* March 9, 24, 1864; James Hall to father, December 25, 1862, Hall Letters, TSLA; James Hall to brother, April 18, 1864, James Hall Letters, ADAH; Cabaniss, *Civil War Journal and Letters of Washington Ives,* 65–66.

19. James Searcy to wife, May 25, 1862, James Searcy Letters, ADAH; Cabaniss, *Civil War Journal and Letters of Washington Ives,* 55; "Return of A. P. Stewart's Division, May 5, 1862," Yerger Papers, MDAH; Cate, ed., *Two Soldiers,* 30. See also Daniel Weaver to sister, January 22, 1864, Daniel Weaver Letters, ADAH; Atkinson, ed., *Civil War Letters of Captain Elliot H. Fletcher,* 31.

20. Worsham, *Old Nineteenth Tennessee Regiment,* 96; Wiley, ed., *Four Years on the Firing Line,* 204. See also Wiley, "Billy Yank and Johnny Reb in the Campaign for Atlanta," 22; Kerr, ed., *Fighting with Ross' Texas Cavalry Brigade,* 152.

21. Smith, "Sketch of the 24th Tennessee," 85; Magee Diary, August 9, 1862, DU.

22. Davis, *Orphan Brigade,* 168–69; Jones Diary, March 21, November 17, 1864, GRPL; *Mobile Advertiser and Register,* March 30, 1864; *Atlanta Intelligencer,* April 1, 1864.

23. Fall, "Civil War Letters of Albert Boult Fall," 162; Magill Diary, February 15, 1864, Wiley Collection, EU; *New Orleans Crescent,* October 29, 1861. See also Folmar, ed., *From That Terrible Field,* 52; S. R. Latta to wife, February 14, 1862, Latta Letters, LSU.

24. Nye, "Jake Donelson"; Thompson, *History of the Orphan Brigade,* 252, 253.

25. "Daily Rebel Banner," 344; *Daily Rebel Banner,* April 4, 1863, TSLA.

26. Roberts, "In Winter Quarters at Dalton, Ga.," 274; Joyce, "Orphan Brigade Glee Club," 413–15; Collins, *Chapters from the Unwritten History,* 240; Little and Maxwell, *History of Lumsden's Battery,* 36; Duke, *Reminiscences,* 164–65; Ridley, *Battles and Sketches of the Army of Tennessee,* 283.

27. Jarman, "History of Co. K," MDAH; Wiley, ed., *Four Years on the Firing Line,* 175–76; Brown Diary, March 27, 1864, GPL; *Memphis Appeal,* March 27, 1864; *Atlanta Intelligencer,* April 1, 1864; Baker Diary, March 22, 1864, MDAH; Wiley, *Life of Johnny Reb,* 64.

28. Bentley, "Great Snowball Fight," 22–23; Vaughn, *Personal Record,* 89–95; Worsham, *Old Nineteenth Tennessee Regiment,* 107–8; Rennolds, *History of Henry County Commands,* 71; Unidentified Diary, Sixty-fifth Georgia, March 22, 1864, KMNBP; Bailey, ed., "Reminiscences," 58; Magill Diary, March 22, 1864, Wiley Collection, EU; Watkins, "*Co. Aytch,*" 130; Jackman Journal, March 22, 1864, LC.

29. Neal to sister, March 25, 1864, Neal Letters, EU; Wiley, *Life of Johnny Reb,* 65.

30. Faust, "Christian Soldiers," 79; Lyman to wife, March 15, 16, 1862, Lyman Letters, YU; Watson Diary, October 29, 1863, CCNMP. See also Partin, "Confederate Sergeant's Report," 295; Wiley, *Life of Johnny Reb,* 357, n. 46.

31. Wommack, *Diary,* 9; Unidentified Diary, March 24, 1862, Fourth

Tennessee File, SNMP; Dillon Diary, March 24, 1862, UM; McMurray, *History of the Twentieth Tennessee Regiment,* 189; Mecklin Diary, March 6, 1862, MDAH; Mathis, ed., *In the Land of the Living,* 73; "Famous Tenth Tennessee," 553.

32. Brown, "Reminiscences of a Private Soldier," 449; Magee Diary, August 14, 1862, DU.

33. Boswell to E. Lee, December 28, 1861, Boswell Letters, TSLA; Black, ed., "William J. Rogers' Memorandum Book," 77; McMurray, *History of the Twentieth Tennessee Regiment,* 224; Brown Diary, December 24, 1863, GPL.

34. Brown, ed., *One of Cleburne's Command,* 73; Jackman Journal, May 14, 1864, LC; Clark, *Histories of the Several Regiments and Battalions from North Carolina,* 2:743.

35. Kirwan, ed., *Johnny Green of the Orphan Brigade,* 119–20; Stevenson, *Thirteen Months in the Rebel Army,* 46; *Mobile Advertiser and Register,* February 5, 1864; *Memphis Appeal,* January 21, 1864.

36. Mecklin Diary, April 25, 1862, MDAH; James T. Talbert to wife, May 15, 1862, Talbert Letters, GPL; Warrick to wife, December 24, 1862, Warrick Letters, ADAH.

37. Collins, *Chapters from the Unwritten History,* 170.

38. Dennis, ed., *Kemper County Rebel,* 74; Hall, "Notes on the War," SHC; Dillon Diary, April 16, 1863, UM; Joyce, "Dalton during the Winter of 1863–64," 464–65.

39. *New Orleans Crescent,* January 8, 1862.

40. Harris to wife, May 16, 1863, Harris Letters, LSU.

41. Wiley, *Life of Johnny Reb,* 55–56.

42. "Consolidated Report of Sick and Wounded in Western Department Commanded by Generals Beauregard and Bragg, June–November 1862," and "Medical Director's Consolidated Report of Sick and Wounded, Army of Tennessee, January–May 1863," Jones Collection, TU.

43. Cate, ed., *Two Soldiers,* 20–21; Wiley, *Life of Johnny Reb,* 53.

44. Breeden, "Medical History," 39, 47. Breeden concludes that the number of reported cases was small "for the attitude of society toward such maladies led to their concealment except for cases of an advanced or painful nature."

45. Anderson, ed., *Campaigning with Parson's Texas Cavalry Brigade,* 128.

CHAPTER 7

1. Watkins, "*Co. Aytch,*" 56.

2. *New Orleans Crescent,* September 14, 1861.

3. Davis, *Orphan Brigade,* 53; Bock, ed., "One Year at War," 176; Trask Journal, 82–83 (undated entry), EU; Wiley, *Life of Johnny Reb,* 223.

4. *New Orleans Crescent,* September 25, December 21, 1861; Johnson to wife, December 9, 1861, Johnson Letters, LSU.

5. Harrison, ed., "Confederate View of Southern Kentucky," 172; *New Orleans Crescent,* December 21, 1861; Magee Diary, August 14, 1862, DU.

6. John Farris to wife, December 26, 1863, Farris Letters, EU.

7. *New Orleans Crescent,* October 29, 1861; Little and Maxwell, *History of Lumsden's Battery,* 32–33.

8. Special Orders No. 42, June 21, 1862, Yerger Papers, MDAH.

9. Mecklin Diary, March 18, 1862, MDAH; Dickey to wife, July 13, 1864, GDAH; Doss to wife, January 27, 1864, Doss Letters, KMNBP; Treadwell to wife, April 27, 1863, Treadwell Letters, ADAH.

10. McMurray, *History of the Twentieth Tennessee Regiment,* 223–24.

11. Johnson to wife, September 8, 1861, Johnson Letters, LSU; Oliver Strickland to mother, January 27, 1864, Strickland Letters, EU.

12. Wiley, *Life of Johnny Reb,* 225; Dennis, ed., *Kemper County Rebel,* 88.

13. Special Order No. 41, June 20, 1862, Yerger Papers, MDAH; *Montgomery Daily Mail,* March 21, 1863; Kelly Diary, March 2, 1864, ADAH.

14. General Order No. 4, February 1863, and General Order No. 66, March 29, 1863, Orders and Circulars, Army of Tennessee, Chap. II, vol. 53, RG 109, NA; Black, ed., "William J. Rogers' Memorandum Book," 82; *Montgomery Daily Mail,* March 12, 1863.

15. Hay, ed., *Cleburne and His Command,* 128–29; *OR,* vol. 23, pt. 2, p. 654; James Hall to father, January 17, 1862, James Hall Letters, ADAH.

16. Harris to wife, June 13, 1863, Harris Letters, LSU; Wyman to mother, April 3, 1863, Wyman Letters, ADAH; James Searcy to mother, June 20, 1863, James Searcy Letters, ADAH; Talley, "History of Havis Georgia Battery," KMNBP; Little and Maxwell, *History of Lumsden's Battery,* 33.

17. Davis, *Orphan Brigade,* 54–55.

18. "Severe Discipline," 374.

19. General Order No. ?, April 26, 1862, Army of the Mississippi, in Army of Tennessee Papers, LHA; *Augusta Constitutionalist,* July 19, 1863. In June 1862 Private I. T. Taylor of the Fifth Tennessee Cavalry was sentenced to be hanged for the murder of a lieutenant at Cumberland Gap in December 1861 (General Order 71, June 14, 1862, Beauregard-Bragg Correspondence, LHA).

20. *New Orleans Crescent,* January 11, 1862; Tower, ed., *A Carolinian Goes to War,* 166; *OR,* vol. 30, pt. 2, pp. 234, 386, and vol. 38, pt. 5, p. 909.

21. Tower, ed., *A Carolinian Goes to War,* 166.

22. Special Orders No. 42, June 21, 1862, and Special Orders No. 18, May 25, 1862, Yerger Papers, MDAH; *OR,* vol. 23, pt. 2, pp. 954–55; Black, ed., "William J. Rogers' Memorandum Book," 85; Martin, *Desertion of Alabama Troops,* 227–28.

23. *Memphis Appeal,* December 28, 1861.

24. Watkins, "Co. Aytch," 55–57; Dillon Diary, May 27, 1862, UM;

Daniel Diary, June 28, 1862, USMHI. In June 1862 three members of Company G, Tennessee Artillery, were lashed and branded at Tupelo for desertion (General Order No. 70, June 12, 1862, Beauregard-Bragg Correspondence, LHA).

25. Jackson, ed., *So Mourns the Dove*, 29; Watson Diary, December 7, 1863, CCNMP; Owens, "Penalties for Desertion," 235; Martin, *Desertion of Alabama Troops*, 227; Roundtree, ed., "Letters of a Confederate Soldier," 283; Cabaniss, *Civil War Journal and Letters of Washington Ives*, 56; Curry, "History of Company B," 192.

26. Garrett, ed., *Confederate Diary of Robert D. Smith*, 6; Fremantle, *Three Months in the Southern States*, 157. A deserter at Corinth attempted to reach the federal lines at night to take the oath of allegiance, got lost in the darkness and ended back in the Rebel lines. He openly admitted his desire to take the oath and was shot without benefit of trial (*Memphis Avalanche*, May 24, 1862).

27. Watkins, "Co. Aytch," 72.

28. Ridley, "Camp Scenes around Dalton," 66–67; Watson Diary, September 28, 1863, CCNMP; Wiley, ed., *Fourteen Hundred and 91 Days in the Confederate Army*, 163; Roundtree, ed., "Letters of a Confederate Soldier," 280; Gallagher, ed., *Fighting for the Confederacy*, 307; General Order No. 225, December 5, 1863, Orders and Circulars, Army of Tennessee, Chap. II, vol. 53, RG 109, NA.

29. Blakemore Diary, June 26, 30, 1862, TSLA; Magee Diary, June 10, 1862, DU; Jackson, ed., *So Mourns the Dove*, 32; Aughey, *Tupelo*, 175–77; Daniel Diary, June 30, 1862, USMHI; Watkins, "Co. Aytch," 56.

30. Urquhart, "Bragg's Advance and Retreat," 609; *OR*, vol. 23, pt. 2, pp. 954–55; Cabaniss, *Civil War Journal and Letters of Washington Ives*, 26; Hall to sister, July 12, 1862, Tom Hall Letters, ADAH.

31. Watkins, "Co. Aytch," 84–85. See also James Parrott to wife, June 15, 1863, quoted in Wommack, *Call Forth the Mighty Men*, 262.

32. Crittenden to wife, December 20, 1862, Crittenden Letters, UT; James Hall to father, December 22, 1862, Hall Letters, TSLA.

33. Worsham, *Old Nineteenth Tennessee Regiment*, 77; Noll, ed., *Doctor Quintard*, 83–86; Jones Diary, June 12, 1863, GRPL.

34. Smith, "Sketch of the 24th Tennessee," 86–87.

35. Dennis, ed., *Kemper County Rebel*, 36; Cabaniss, *Civil War Journal and Letters of Washington Ives*, 32; *Chattanooga Daily Rebel*, February 6, 1863; Fremantle, *Three Months in the Southern States*, 157; Alderson, ed., "Civil War Diary of Captain James Cooper," 151; *Southern Confederacy*, January 3, 1863; "Three Deserters Shot at Shelbyville," 128.

36. Davis, *Orphan Brigade*, 147–48; Kirwan, ed., *Johnny Green of the Orphan Brigade*, 59–61. This was Lewis's second desertion.

37. Only sixteen executions for desertion can be documented as having occurred under Bragg during his year-and-a-half tenure. By contrast, at least thirty-one executions for desertion occurred at Dalton under Johnston.

38. Davis to wife, January 2, 1864, Davis Letters, UG; Cabaniss, *Civil War Journal and Letters of Washington Ives,* 60, 62, 65; Watson Diary, February 21, 1864, CCNMP; Garrett, ed., *Confederate Diary of Robert D. Smith,* 57; Collins, *Chapters from the Unwritten History,* 201; Jackman Journal, March 25, 1864, LC; Warrick to wife, April 13, 1864, Warrick Letters, ADAH; *Atlanta Intelligencer,* April 16, 1864; McKee, "Events of Camp Life," 113.

39. Owens, "Penalties for Desertion," 235.

40. Brown Diary, May 4, 1864, GPL; Kelly to wife, May 6, 1864, Kelly Letters and Diary, ADAH; Magill Diary, May 4, 1864, Wiley Collection, EU; Davenport Diary, May 4, 1864, TSLA; Hampton, *Eyewitness,* 41–42; Mitchell, ed., "Letters of a Confederate Surgeon," 167; Stephens to wife, May 7, 1864, Stephens Letters, EU; Lindsley, ed., *Military Annals of Tennessee,* 478.

CHAPTER 8

1. Law, "Diary of J. G. Law," 507; Harrison, ed., "Confederate View of Southern Kentucky," 175; James Searcy to brother, April 20, 1862, James Searcy Letters, ADAH; Lyman to wife, March 23, 1862, Lyman Letters, YU. The notable exception was a Dr. Palmer, a renowned New Orleans clergyman, who preached to large crowds at Corinth. See *Memphis Avalanche,* May 22, 23, 1862; *Memphis Appeal,* May 13, 1862.

2. Johnson to wife, October 12, 1861, Johnson Letters, LSU; Prim, "Born Again in the Trenches," 251.

3. "Incidents in Army Life," 520.

4. Wiley, *Life of Johnny Reb,* 183–84; Norton, "Revivalism in the Confederate Army," 411; Faust, "Christian Soldiers," 68, 72–73.

5. *Southern Presbyterian,* April 12, 1863; Jones, *Christ in Camp,* 489; Bennett, *Narrative of the Great Revival,* 265–66, 280–81; DeWitt Diary, March 9, 1863, TSLA; Fitzgerald, *John B. McFerrin,* 273.

6. Estes Diary, May 19, 1863, MC; Davidson to wife, May 10, 1863, Davidson Letters, AHS; Black, ed., "William J. Rogers' Memorandum Book," 87.

7. Dennis, ed., *Kemper County Rebel,* 80; Coleman Diary, March 8, 1863, SHC; Prim, "Born Again in the Trenches," 252–53.

8. *Southern Presbyterian,* August 27, 1863.

9. Noll, ed., *Doctor Quintard,* 78–79.

10. Jones, *Christ in Camp,* 594; M'Neilly, "A Day in the Life of a Confederate Chaplain," 397–98, 471–72; DeWitt Diary, March 9, 1863, TSLA; Fitzgerald, *John B. McFerrin,* 275; Hall, "Religion in the Army of Tennessee," 129–31; Norton, *Rebel Religion,* 81–83; Romero, *Religion in the Rebel Ranks,* 41.

11. Black, ed., "William J. Rogers' Memorandum Book," 87; Partin,

"Confederate Sergeant's Report to His Wife," 295; Reuben Searcy to mother, July 6, 1862, Reuben Searcy Letters, ADAH; Thiot to wife, June 23, 1864, Thiot Letters, EU; Crittenden to wife, July 15, 1864, Crittenden Letters, UT.

12. Jones, *Christ in Camp*, 577; D. L. Kelly to Miss Hinnell, September 12, 1863, Kelly Letters, EU.

13. Lewis, ed., "Confederate Officer's Letters on Sherman's March to Atlanta," 492; Warrick to wife, April 8, 1864, Warrick Letters, ADAH; Elkins, ed., *Letters from a Civil War Soldier*. See also Porter Diary, April 25, 1864, MDAH; Jamison and McTigue, eds., *Letters and Recollections of a Confederate Soldier*, 91; Godwin to wife, May 8, 1864, Godwin Letters, AHS; Thomas Taylor to sister, May 7, 1864, Taylor Letters, Wiley Collection, EU.

14. McFerrin, "Religion in the Army of Tennessee," 281–82; Davenport Diary, March 31, 1864, TSLA.

15. Gay, *Life in Dixie*, 67–74.

16. Prim, "Born Again in the Trenches," 262–64; Jones, *Christ in Camp*, 583; Davenport Diary, May 4, 1864, TSLA; Fitzgerald, *John B. McFerrin*, 276.

17. McDonald, *History of the Cumberland Presbyterian Church*, 421, 430; Fitzgerald, *John B. McFerrin*, 277; *Southern Presbyterian*, June 25, 1863; Gay, *Life in Dixie*, 71.

18. Norton, *Rebel Religion*, 58–59; Meany, "Valiant Chaplain of the Bloody Tenth," 46; Cate, ed., *Two Soldiers*, 12.

19. Stephens to wife, April 17, 1864, Stephens Letters, EU.

20. Shattuck, *A Shield and Hiding Place*, 103; Lacy, *Revivalism in the Midst of Years*, 128; Cash and Howorth, eds., *My Dear Nellie*, 180.

21. Clark Memoirs, CCNMP; Jacob Weaver to sister, May 3, 1864, Jacob Weaver Letters, ADAH.

22. Worsham, *Old Nineteenth Tennessee Regiment*, 108–9; Roberts, "In Winter Quarters at Dalton, Ga.," 275; Lindsley, ed., *Military Annals of Tennessee*, 278; Rennolds, *History of Henry County Commands*, 71–72; Godwin to unknown, May 8, 1864, Godwin Letters, AHS; Ridley, *Battles and Sketches*, 283; Taylor to sister, May 7, 1864, Taylor Letters, Wiley Collection, EU.

23. Shattuck, *A Shield and Hiding Place*, 101; Jones, *Christ in Camp*, 582; Norton, *Rebel Religion*, 57. See also Larkin Weaver to mother, July 16, 1863, Larkin Weaver Letters, ADAH.

24. Robert E. Hill to sister, June 21, 1863, quoted in Prim, "Born Again in the Trenches," 255; Cate, ed., *Two Soldiers*, 77; Cash and Howorth, eds., *My Dear Nellie*, 180.

25. Shattuck, *A Shield and Hiding Place*, 102.

26. Quoted in Wommack, *Call Forth the Mighty Men*, 266. See also Law, "Diary of J. G. Law," 298; Collins, *Chapters from the Unwritten History*, 226; Clark Memoirs, CCNMP.

27. Coleman Diary, February 8, 1863, SHC; Muir, "Battle of Atlanta," 111.

28. Prim, "Born Again in the Trenches," 266; Jones and Martin, eds., *Gentle Rebel*, 37; Jordon, ed., "Mathew A. Dunn Letters," 120, 125; Goodloe, *Confederate Echoes*, 430–31; McFerrin, "Religion in the Army of Tennessee," 281.

29. Prim, "Born Again in the Trenches," 267–68.

CHAPTER 9

1. McMurry, *Two Great Rebel Armies*, 90–91. McMurry's contention is based on Michael Adams's (*Our Masters the Rebels*) thesis that a series of nineteenth-century myths influenced the way the Civil War was conducted.

2. Johnston to Davis, March 7, 1862, Letter Book of the Headquarters of the Western Department, Kuntz Collection, TU; John Cato to wife, March 27, 1862, Cato Letters, MDAH; A. T. Tarlske to wife, March 23, 1862, Tarlske Letters, MDAH; Hall to parents, April 22, 1862, Hall Letters, SHC; Mecklin Diary, May 27, 1862, MDAH; Knighton to sister, April 25, 1862, Knighton Letters, LSU.

3. Mecklin Diary, April 19, 1862, MDAH; Knighton to father, April 20, 1862, Knighton Letters, LSU; Law, "Diary of J. G. Law," 465; Watson, *Life in the Confederate Army*, 368; Daniel Diary, June 16, 1862, USMHI. See also Wall and McBride, eds., "Extraordinary Perseverance," 331.

4. *OR*, vol. 10, pt. 1, pp. 398–99, and vol. 20, pt. 2, p. 407; Mott, "War Journal," 448; Polignac, "Polignac's Diary," 17; Hill to sister, June 16, 1862, Hill Letters, UT.

5. Weekly Return of 1st Brigade, 1st Division, 1st Corps, Army of the Mississippi, June 2, 12, 1862, and Weekly Return of 2d Brigade, 1st Division, 1st Corps, Army of the Mississippi, July 5, 1862, Yerger Papers, MDAH.

6. Lyman to wife, March 12, 1862, Lyman Letters, YU; Richard Pugh to wife, April 13, 1862, Pugh Letters, LSU; Folmar, ed., *From That Terrible Field*, 58; Rufus Catlin to sister, May 24, 1862, Catlin Letters, LC; Mecklin Diary, April 22, 1862, MDAH.

7. J. L. Hammer to mother, January 5, 1863, Hammer Letters, WTHS; Carter to wife, January 6, 1863, Carter Letters, DU; Cole to wife, June 12, 1863, Cole Letters, USMHI; J. W. Harris to George, October 31, 1863, Harris Letters, TSLA; Olden Diary, October 31, 1863, TSLA. McWhiney also quotes from the anti-Bragg letters of John Buie and John Ellis ("Braxton Bragg," 44).

8. Treadwell to wife, April 5, 9, 1863, Treadwell Letters, ADAH.

9. Athearn, ed., *Soldier in the West*, 129–30.

10. Colton, ed., *Column South*, 84; Ford, ed., *Memoirs of a Volunteer*, 238; Carmony, ed., "Jacob W. Bartmess Civil War Letters," 69.

11. Angle, ed., *Three Years in the Army of the Cumberland,* 121–22.

12. In support of his thesis, McWhiney quotes from the pro-Bragg letters of soldiers J. H. Frayser and John Ellis. See McWhiney, "Braxton Bragg," 44; Rugeley, *Batchelor-Turner Letters,* 42; Alexander to brother, February 26, 1863, Alexander Letters, SHC; Mathis, ed., *In the Land of the Living,* 64.

13. Black, ed., "William J. Rogers' Memorandum Book," 77; Mitchell, ed., "Civil War Letters of Thomas Jefferson Newberry," 55; Dennis, ed., *Kemper County Rebel,* 69; Lindsley, ed., *Military Annals of Tennessee,* 503.

14. Connelly, *Autumn of Glory,* 251–52; Neal to father, November 20, 1863, Neal Letters, EU; Dillon Diary, November 9, 1863, UM; Olden Diary, December 7, 1863, TSLA.

15. Anderson, ed., *Campaigning with Parson's Texas Cavalry Brigade,* 127; Marsh, "Confederate Letters," 24; Wiley, ed., *Fourteen Hundred and 91 Days,* 166. On December 13, 1863, Marsh wrote: "I maid an application for a leeve of absence for 60 days to come home but like all applications sent in by Tex and Ark [troops] it came back not approved."

16. Connelly, *Autumn of Glory,* 109; *OR,* vol. 23, pt. 2, p. 758; Beatty, *Memoirs,* 218.

17. William Fackler to wife, May 5, 1863, Fackler Letters, DU.

18. Beatty, *Memoirs,* 218; Magee Diary, February 24, July 9, 1863, DU. See also Fielder Diary, July 9, 15, 1863, TSLA.

19. Alexander to sister, July 16, 1862, Alexander Letters, SHC; Black, ed., "William J. Rogers' Memorandum Book," 79; Rabb to wife, February 13, 1863, Rabb Letters, EU; Simpson, ed., *The Bugle Softly Blows,* 37. See also Hill to sister, December 8, 1862, Hill Letters, UT; Fackler to sister, March 26, 1863, Fackler Letters, DU.

20. Mathis, ed., *In the Land of the Living,* 77; Roundtree, ed., "Letters of a Confederate Soldier," 280.

21. Roundtree, ed., "Letters of a Confederate Soldier," 278; Partin, ed., "Confederate Sergeant's Report to His Wife," 303.

22. Thomas to wife, October 8, 1863, Thomas Letters and Diary, GPL. See also Warrick to wife, October 26, 1863, Warrick Letters, ADAH.

23. Doss to wife, November 13, 1863, Doss Letters, KMNBP; W. A. Stephens to wife, November 24, 1863, Stephens Letters, EU.

24. Roderick Shaw to sister, October 8, 1863, Shaw Letters, FSU; Cabaniss, *Civil War Journal and Letters of Washington Ives,* 41. See also Marsh, "Confederate Letters," 29.

25. Frank Carter to wife, December 3, 1863, Carter Letters, DU; Wyman to mother, December 11, 1863, Wyman Letters, ADAH; James Hall to father, January 31, 1863, James Hall Letters, ADAH; Neal to sister, December 6, 1863, Neal Letters, EU; Daniel Diary, December 2, 1863, USMHI.

26. There were some men who did know about the feuding between Bragg and his generals. See *OR,* vol. 31, pt. 3, p. 209.

27. A good example would be the Holmes diary, which, although quite complete, fails to mention any specific feelings about Bragg. He does mention a rumor that Johnston would replace Bragg but does not comment on it (Dennis, ed., *Kemper County Rebel*, 29).

28. Stephens to wife, December 24, 1863, Stephens Letters, EU; Haley to E. Faw, January 30, 1864, Haley Letters, TSLA; Wyman to mother, December 11, 1863, Wyman Letters, ADAH; Brown Diary, January 14, 1863, GPL. See also Anderson, ed., *Campaigning with Parson's Texas Cavalry Brigade*, 126; C. O. Bailey to mother, February 16, 1864, Bailey Letters, FSU.

29. Magill Diary, December 25, 1863, Wiley Collection, EU; Cannon, *Reminiscences*, 45; *OR*, Ser. IV, vol. 2, p. 775; Wyman to mother, December 11, 1863, Wyman Letters, ADAH.

30. Jackson, ed., *So Mourns the Dove*, 80; Edge to companion, March 26, 1864, Edge Letters, EU.

31. Mathis, ed., *In the Land of the Living*, 81; Mitchell, ed., "Letters of a Confederate Surgeon," 155.

32. Smith Diary, January 3, 1864, Wiley Collection, EU; *OR*, vol. 32, pt. 2, pp. 558, 582; Chambers, "My Journal," 311–12; Thomas to wife, March 5, 1864, Thomas Letters and Diary, GPL; Wyman to wife, January 5, 1864, Wyman Letters, ADAH; Rabb to wife, February 18, 1864, Rabb Letters, EU; Dawes, "Confederate Strength in the Atlanta Campaign," 281. See also Mathis, ed., *In the Land of the Living*, 92; Stephens to wife, April 17, 1864, Stephens Letters, EU.

33. Pickett, "Re-Enlistments by the Confederates," 171; Porter, "Re-Enlistments in the Army of Tenn.," 351–52; "More about Re-Enlistments at Dalton," 399; Bryson, "Bate's Second Tennessee Regiment," 19; "Camp of the 154th Tennessee, January 14, 1864," WTHS; *Memphis Appeal*, January 18, 20, 21, 26, 27, 1864; *Macon Telegraph*, February 1, 11, 1864.

34. Shaw to sister, April 16, 1864, Shaw Letters, FSU; Jamison and McTigue, eds., *Letters and Recollections of a Confederate Soldier*, 89; Haley to E. Faw, January 30, 1864, Haley Letters, TSLA; Smith Diary, January 3, 1864, Wiley Collection, EU.

35. Lynn, "Re-Enlistments in the Western Army," 259; Jones, "History of the 18th Alabama Regiment," ADAH; M. A. Cameron to brother, January 24, 1864, Cameron Letters, UA.

36. Ward to grandmother, February 4, 1864, Ward Letters, Wiley Collection, EU; Blakemore Diary, January 23, 1864, TSLA; *OR*, vol. 32, pt. 3, p. 670.

37. Settles to wife, January 24, 1864, Settles Letters, PC; Bond, "Alabama State Artillery," 331; Neal F. Hensely to brother, February 14, 1864, DU; *Memphis Appeal*, March 27, 1864. See also Mitchell, ed., "Letters of a Confederate Surgeon," 159; Colville to father, April 29, 1864, Colville Letters, KMNBP; James Hall to father, April 5, 1864, James Hall Letters, ADAH.

38. McMurry, "Confederate Morale in the Atlanta Campaign," 229, 238. McMurry also uses the correspondence of two soldiers of the Georgia militia, but for the purposes of this study only the letters and diaries of "regulars" will be considered.

39. Davidson to wife, May 21, 1864, Davidson Letters, AHS; Kelly to wife, May 29, 1864, Kelly Letters and Diary, ADAH; Wiley, ed., "Confederate Letters of John W. Hagan," 272. McMurry quotes three soldiers—two pro-Johnston and one anti-Johnston. In addition to the above see also the "pro" entries of Thompson to brother, May 20, 1864, Thompson Letters, PC; Puckett to wife, May 21, 1864, Puckett Letters, UT; Noyes, ed., "Excerpts from the Civil War Diary of E. T. Eggleston," 342; Osborn, ed., "Civil War Letters of Robert W. Banks," 211; Branch to mother, May 4, 1864, Branch Letters, UG; Ward to cousin, May 25, 1864, Ward Letters, USMHI; Wright, ed., "Some Letters to His Parents," 369. Other anti-Johnston letters include Warrick to sister, May 21, 1864, Warrick Letters, ADAH; Thurmond to Miss Porterfield, May 21, 1864, Thurmond Letters, GDAH; Cole to wife, May 21, 1864, Cole Letters, USMHI.

40. Branch to mother, June 5, 1864, Branch Letters, UG; Roundtree, ed., "Letters of a Confederate Soldier," 288. McMurry quotes one pro- and one anti-Johnston letter. Other "pro" letters include Wiley, ed., "Confederate Letters of John W. Hagan," 273; Bond, "Alabama State Artillery," 337; Cash and Howorth, eds., *My Dear Nellie*, 184; Thiot to wife, June 14, 1864, Thiot Letters, EU; Aiken, ed., "Letters of the Offield Brothers," 123; J. T. Terrell to parents, June 6, 1864, quoted in Wiley, *Life of Johnny Reb*, 149.

41. Black to wife, July 20, 1864, Black Letters, FSU; Mathis, ed., *In the Land of the Living*, 103; Haynes and Wilkins, eds., "Stanley Letters," 43; Helms to wife, July 6, 1864, Helms Letters, GDAH.

McMurry quotes five anti-Johnston letters. See also Jones and Martin, eds., *Gentle Rebel*, 52; Branch to mother, July 7, 1864, Branch Letters, UG; Stephens to wife, July 9, 1864, Stephens Letters, EU; Davis to wife, July 6, 1864, Davis Letters, UG; Wiley, ed., "Confederate Letters of John W. Hagan," 282.

Other pro-Johnston entries during July include Dixon Diary, July 3, 1864, KMNBP; C. H. Eastman to mother, July 10, 1864, Eastman Letters, TSLA; Haynes and Wilkins, eds., "Stanley Letters," 43; Jones and Martin, eds., *Gentle Rebel*, 46; Puckett to wife, July 13, 1864, Puckett Letters, UT; Cash and Howorth, eds., *My Dear Nellie*, 188; Jones Diary, July 10, 1864, GRPL; Jordon, ed., "Mathew A. Dunn Letters," 119; Anderson, ed., *Campaigning with Parson's Texas Cavalry Brigade*, 143; W. H. Staggers to Miss Jessie, July 14, 1864, Staggers Letters, WTHS; Hammond to sister, July 7, 1864, Hammond Letters, Wiley Collection, EU; Betts, ed., "Civil War Letters of Elbridge Littlejohn," 26.

42. See, for example, McNeil, "Survey of Confederate Soldier Morale,"

13. McNeil claims that there was only a small degree of dissatisfaction with Johnston's leadership. Surprisingly, even Bell Wiley writes: "The writer has yet to find an unfavorable remark from a man in the ranks about this officer's [Johnston] Fabian generalship, while compliments are frequently found" (*Life of Johnny Reb*, 240).

43. Hill to sister, June 11, 1864, Hill Letters, UT; Ward to cousin, May 25, 1864, Ward Letters, USMHI; Porter Diary, June 9, 1864, MDAH; Leonidas Mackey to family, July 5, 1864, Mackey Letters, AHS; Cash and Howorth, eds., *My Dear Nellie*, 20; Jordon, ed., "Mathew A. Dunn Letters," 119.

44. Brown, ed., *One of Cleburne's Command*, 106–7; Neal to father, July 20, 1864, Neal Letters, EU; *OR*, vol. 38, pt. 3, p. 717. See also Douglas, ed., *Douglas' Texas Battery*, 114; Jones and Martin, eds., *Gentle Rebel*, 57–58; Steryx, ed., "Autobiography and Letters of Joel Murphree," 184; Branch to mother, July 18, 1864, Branch Letters, UG; Black to wife, July 20, 1864, Black Letters, FSU; Cate, ed., *Two Soldiers*, 89–90; Wiley, ed., "Confederate Letters of John W. Hagan," 286; Gill to wife, July 18, 1864, quoted in McMurry, "Confederate Morale in the Atlanta Campaign," 235; Fielder Diary, July 18, 1864, TSLA; Olden Diary, July 18, 1864, TSLA.

45. Osborn, ed., "Civil War Letters of Robert W. Banks," 215; George W. Peddy to wife, July 21, 1864, Peddy Letters, EU; Kelly Diary, July 27, 1864, ADAH; Godwin to Miss Bettie, August 1, 1864, Godwin Letters, AHS.

46. Brown, ed., *One of Cleburne's Command*, 104; Puckett to wife, July 13, 1864, Puckett Letters, UT; Wiley, ed., "Confederate Letters of John W. Hagan," 284; Trask Journal, July 25, 1864, EU; Peddy to wife, August 2, 1864, Peddy Letters, EU; Harris Diary, August 24, 1864, UT. See also Richard F. Eddons to sister, August 24, 1864, Eddons Letters, USMHI.

47. Hood, *Advance and Retreat*, 183, 191.

48. James Hall to brother, August 19, 1864, James Hall Letters, ADAH; Taylor, ed., *Reluctant Rebel*, 199; Cash and Howorth, eds., *My Dear Nellie*, 190; William Bowden to sister, August 24, 1864, Bowden Letters, UM; Brown, ed., *One of Cleburne's Command*, 129.

49. James Hall to father, September 4, 1864, James Hall Letters, ADAH; Mathis, ed., *In the Land of the Living*, 111; Colville to father, September 7, 1864, Colville Letters, KMNBP. For other indications of poor morale see Jones and Martin, eds., *Gentle Rebel*, 91; Neil Gillis to wife, September 8, 1864, Neil Gillis Letters, EU.

50. Ward to father, October 18, 1864, Ward Letters, Wiley Collection, EU; Douglas, ed., *Douglas' Texas Battery*, 143. For other examples of high morale see McMurry, *Hood*, 178.

51. Brown, ed., *One of Cleburne's Command*, 158; Peddy to wife, December 27, 1864, Peddy Letters, EU.

52. Magill Diary, January 1, 1865, Wiley Collection, EU; Dan Gillis to father, January 1, 1865, Dan Gillis Letters, EU; *OR*, vol. 45, pt. 2, p. 788;

Anderson, ed., *Campaigning with Parson's Texas Cavalry Brigade,* 155–56; Chambers, "My Journal," 356.

53. Schofield, *Forty-Six Years in the Army,* 248.

CHAPTER 10

1. Carter to wife, January 4, 15, 1863, Carter Letters, DU. For other examples of this view see John H. Maury to father, July 29, 1862, Maury Letters, DU; Blakemore Diary, April 9, 1862, TSLA; Foxworth Diary, May 8, 1862, p. 143, MDAH; Johnston S. Vandiver to wife, April 15, 1862; John Johnson to family, January 10, 1863, Johnson Letters, GDAH.

2. James Hall to father, July 31, 1864, James Hall Letters, ADAH; Athey to sister, August 2, 1864, Athey Letters, ADAH; Branch to sister, July 23, 1864, Branch Letters, UG. For other quotes proving the same conclusion see McMurry, "Confederate Morale in the Atlanta Campaign," 235–37, and McDonough and Jones, *War So Terrible,* 239.

3. Jones and Martin, eds., *Gentle Rebel,* 124. See also McMurry, *Hood,* 178. Some soldiers clearly understood the truth of Franklin, however. See Brown, ed., *One of Cleburne's Command,* 150–51.

4. Cate, ed., *Two Soldiers,* 158. See also Cabaniss, *Civil War Journal and Letters of Washington Ives,* 15.

5. Mecklin Diary, April 6, 1862, MDAH; "H.R." to father, April 11, 1862, USMHI; Pugh to wife, April 10, 11, 1862, Pugh Letters, LSU.

6. Ellis to mother, October 21, 1862, Ellis Letters, LSU; Brown Diary, October 8, 1862, GPL.

7. Dixon Diary, June 24, 1864, KMNBP; Hurst to wife, June 20, 1864, Hurst Letters, KMNBP; Brown, ed., *One of Cleburne's Command,* 116.

8. Alison Diary, April 9, 1862, SHC; J. H. Hines to sister, April 22, 1862, Hines Letters, WKU; Pugh to wife, April 21, 1862, Pugh Letters, LSU.

9. Warrick to wife, January 11, 1863, Warrick Letters, ADAH; Anderson, ed., *Campaigning with Parson's Texas Cavalry Brigade,* 122; Cabaniss, *Civil War Journal and Letters of Washington Ives,* 44; Noyes, "Excerpts from the Civil War Diary of E. T. Eggleston," 343.

10. Bailey, "Reminiscences," 52; James B. Mitchell to wife, January 13, 1863, Mitchell Letters, LC; "Second Tennessee at Chickamauga," 54.

11. James Searcy to brother, April 20, 1862, James Searcy Letters, ADAH; Johnson to family, January 10, 1863, Johnson Letters, GDAH; McGowin to sister, October 3, 1863, McGowin Letters, SRNBP; Wiley, ed., "Confederate Letters of John W. Hagan," 227.

12. Partin, ed., "Confederate Sergeant's Report to His Wife," 301.

13. Dillon Diary, September 19, 1863, UM; Brown Diary, September 20, 1863, GPL; *OR,* vol. 30, pt. 2, p. 354.

14. *OR,* 7:295–96, 318, 327, 334, 381; Dennis, ed., *Kemper County*

Rebel, 35–36; Cate, ed., *Two Soldiers,* 165–66. See also Goodners Diary, December 10, 1864, UT; Brown, ed., *One of Cleburne's Command,* 153.

15. David Brand to brother, April 9, 1862, Brand Letters, ADAH; Alex Boyd to sister, April 25, 1862, Boyd Letters, USMHI; *OR,* vol. 30, pt. 2, p. 325.

16. *OR,* vol. 10, pt. 1, pp. 582–83, 589, 403, 577, 591.

17. Cabaniss, *Civil War Journal and Letters of Washington Ives,* 35; *OR,* vol. 30, pt. 2, pp. 380, 328; Brown Diary, May 15, 1864, GPL.

18. Chattahoochee Valley Historical Society, ed., *War Was the Place,* 101; Haley to E. Faw, January 30, 1864, Haley Letters, TSLA; William A. Chunn to wife, December 1, 1863, DU; Hall to father, December 2, 1863, James Hall Letters, ADAH.

19. Neal to father, May 15, 1864, Neal Letters, EU; Lindsley, ed., *Military Annals of Tennessee,* 298; Columbus Sykes to wife, August 14, 1864, Sykes Letters, KMNBP; Tower, ed., *A Carolinian Goes to War,* 239; Norrell Diary, May 30, 1864, KMNBP. See also W. H. Tucker to wife, August 18, 1864, Tucker Letters, DU; H. T. Howard to wife, August 22, 1864, Howard Letters, GDAH.

20. Anderson, *Memoirs,* 388–89; Garrett, ed., *Confederate Diary of Robert D. Smith,* 69; Rennolds, *History of Henry County Commands,* 79; Chambers, "My Journal," 331; Cox, *Atlanta,* 100; Kelly Diary, June 19, 1864, ADAH; *OR,* vol. 38, pt. 3, p. 770.

21. Vann, *"Most Lovely Lizzie,"* [not numbered].

22. Cash and Howorth, eds., *My Dear Nellie,* 185.

23. Garrett, ed., *Confederate Diary of Robert D. Smith,* 72; Chester to wife, July 15, 1864, Chester Letters, KMNBP; Noyes, ed., "Excerpts from the Civil War Diary of E. T. Eggleston," 347. See also Kerr, ed., *Fighting with Ross' Texas Cavalry Brigade,* 148–49; Jones Diary, July 9, 1864, GRPL; Norrell Diary, June 14, 1864, KMNBP.

24. Hampton, *Eyewitness,* 57; Daniel Weaver to parents, August 18, 1864, Daniel Weaver Letters, ADAH.

25. *OR,* vol. 38, pt. 3, pp. 764, 768, 835, 774.

26. Ibid., 768, 800.

27. Boyce, "Missourians in the Battle of Franklin," 101–3; Rea, "A Mississippian in the Confederacy," 287–89; Rennolds, *History of Henry County Commands,* 104; Bailey, "Reminiscences," 69; Bevier, *History of the First and Second Missouri Confederate Brigades,* 251.

28. Shapard, "At Spring Hill and Franklin Again," 138–39; Boyce, "Missourians in the Battle of Franklin," 101–3, 138; Rea, "A Mississippian in the Confederacy," 287–89; Jones and Martin, eds., *Gentle Rebel,* 122–23.

29. Bevier, *First and Second Missouri Confederate Brigades,* 254; M'Neilly, "49th Tennessee in Battle of Franklin," 172–73; Thomas Taylor to sister, December 15, 1864, Taylor Letters, Wiley Collection, EU; Stanton to Mary Moody, March 30, 1865, Stanton Letters, UT; Bliss to mother,

December 1, 1864, Bliss Letters, ADAH; Douglas, ed., *Douglas' Texas
Battery*, 212.

30. Harwell, ed., *Kate*, 253; Cate, ed., *Two Soldiers*, 163; Noyes, ed.,
"Excerpts from the Civil War Diary of E. T. Eggleston," 357.

31. Gillis to father, January 2, 1865, M. Gillis Letters, EU; McMurry,
Hood, 180.

32. Cabaniss, *Civil War Journal and Letters of Washington Ives*, 49.

33. Johnson to family, January 10, 1863, Johnson Letters, GDAH; Jamison and McTigue, eds., *Letters and Recollections of a Confederate Soldier*,
93.

34. One of six Shiloh burial pits is located just outside the park on private
property.

35. The National Park Service estimates that about one-half of the Confederate dead at Chickamauga were reburied in private and church cemeteries (James Ogden to Daniel, October 15, 1989). There are two Confederate cemeteries in Chattanooga. One, known as the Confederate Cemetery,
has 749 known and 156 unknown dead, and the Silverdale Cemetery has
approximately 155 unknown dead. These were all deaths that occurred in
Rebel hospitals in that city and are not battlefield-related (Ned Irwin to
Daniel, August 9, 1989). For information on the Franklin burials see McDonough and Connelly, *Five Tragic Hours*, 157–58.

36. R. A. Allen to Dear Sir, June 4, 1864, Allen Letters, KMNBP; Milton
Walls to parents, August 19, 1864, USMHI; A. T. Martin to Dear Madam,
November 15, 1864, Devilbliss Letters, TU.

37. Horn, *Army of Tennessee*, 425–27.

38. Brown, ed., *One of Cleburne's Command*, 164–65; Porter Diary,
April 18, 1865, MDAH.

39. Pollard Memoirs, TSLA; Lindsley, ed., *Military Annals of Tennessee*,
368; Brown, ed., *One of Cleburne's Command*, 171.

40. Horn, *Army of Tennessee*, 427; Watkins, "*Co. Aytch*," 243; Vaughn,
Personal Record, 35.

Bibliography

MANUSCRIPTS

Alabama Department of Archives and History, Montgomery
    William Wirt Adams Papers
    G. W. Athey Letters (W. C. Athey Papers)
    Robert Lewis Bliss Letters
    David Brand Letters (Twenty-first Alabama File)
    E. K. Flournoy Letters
    Bolling Hall Letters (Bolling Hall Papers)
    James Hall Letters (Bolling Hall Papers)
    Tom Hall Letters (Bolling Hall Papers)
    Haratio ? Letters (Twenty-second Alabama File)
    William J. Hardee Papers
    William P. Howell Memoirs (Twenty-fifth Alabama File)
    Edgar D. Jones, "History of the 18th Alabama Regiment" (Eighteenth
        Alabama File)
    Samuel C. Kelly Letters and Diary (Thirtieth Alabama File)

L. D. G. Letter (Gage's Alabama File)
Robert T. Moore Letters (Nineteenth Alabama File)
James T. Searcy Letters
Reuben Searcy Letters (James Searcy Letters)
Henry C. Semple Letters
E. W. Treadwell Letters (Nineteenth Alabama File)
Thomas Warrick Letters
Charles Weaver Letters (Charles M. Gary Papers)
Daniel Weaver Letters (Charles M. Gary Papers)
J. K. Weaver Letters (Charles M. Gary Papers)
Larkin Weaver Letters (Charles M. Gary Papers)
Belser L. Wyman Letters
Arkansas Department of Archives and History, Little Rock
Peter Hotze Letters
Atlanta Historical Society, Atlanta
John Davidson Letters
Hosea Garrett Letters
D. G. Godwin Letters
B. C. Goodners Diary
William O. Howell Diary
Leonidas W. Mackey Letters
J. S. Speir Letters
Chickamauga-Chattanooga National Military Park
Carroll H. Clark Memoirs
G. E. Goudelock Letters
W. R. Montgomery Letters
Robert Watson Diary
Duke University, Perkins Library, Durham, North Carolina
Eqlantine Aquors Letters
John Buie Letters
Frank Carter Letters (Pope-Carter Collection)
William A. Chunn Letter
William Fackler Letters
Neal F. Hensley Letter (Bryant Wright Letters)
John E. Magee Diary
John H. Maury Letters (Richard L. Maury Papers)
John S. Palmer Letters
J. R. Pope Letters (Pope-Carter Collection)
A. Purviance, Jr., Diary
Walter R. Roher Letters (James Willcox Papers)
W. H. Tucker Letters
Emory University, Woodruff Library, Atlanta
John Barfield Letters
James Brother Letters

H. Davis Letters
Andrew Edge Letters
John Farris Letters
Dan Gillis Letters (Gillis Family Papers)
M. Gillis Letters (Gillis Family Papers)
Neil Gillis Letters (Gillis Family Papers)
William Jewell Letters
Andrew J. Neal Letters
W. P. Porter Diary
Hezekiah Rabb Letters
William A. Stephens Letters
Oliver Strickland Letters
Charles H. Thiot Letters
W. J. Trask Journal
M. A. Traynham Letters
James W. Watkins Letters
B. P. Weaver Letters
Bell I. Wiley Collection
    Adrian B. Carruth Diary
    J. M. Emmerson Letters
    B. H. Green, Jr., Letters
    J. L. Hammond Letters
    James Lanning Diary
    N. W. E. Long Letters
    Chris C. McKinney Letters
    Robert M. Magill Diary
    Frank Richardson Letters
    Y. H. Smith Diary
    Thomas Taylor Letters
    J. W. Ward Letters
Benjamin S. Williams Memoirs
Evans Memorial Library, Aberdeen, Mississippi
    A. J. Brown Diary
Filson Club Historical Society, Louisville, Kentucky
    Jim A. Cochran Letters
    Jim Crozier Letters
    D. W. Yandell Letters
Florida State University, Tallahassee
    C. O. Bailey Letters
    Hugh Black Letters
    Roderick Shaw Letters
Georgia Department of Archives and History, Atlanta
    Z. T. Armistead Letters
    W. E. Canning Letters

J. C. Carthright Letters
A. B. Clonts Letters
Albert M. Colton Letters
Edwin T. Davis Letters
John Davis Letters
William J. Dickey Letters (Dickey Family Papers)
Blaton Fortson Letters
E. T. Hawkins Letters
James Hays Letters
Calathiel Helms Letters
H. T. Howard Letters
John E. Jeffares Letters
John Johnson Letters
Jack King Letters
W. B. McDowell Letters
Lavandor R. Ray Letters
William Reed Letters
W. H. Reynolds Letters (Dickey Family Papers)
W. K. Thompson Letters
Bolton Thurmond Letters
Georgia Historical Society, Savannah
John McCorkle Letters
Greenwood Public Library, Greenwood, Mississippi
W. A. Brown Diary
James B. Talbert Letters (Thomas-Gattas Papers)
Isham W. Thomas Letters and Diary (Thomas-Gattas Papers)
Grenada Public Library, Grenada, Mississippi
George W. Jones Diary
Hardin County Historical Society, Elizabethtown, Kentucky
Squire Helm Bush Diary
Historic New Orleans Collection, New Orleans
Unknown Diarist—Orleans Guard Regiment (Walton-Ghenny Papers)
Kennesaw Mountain National Battlefield Park, Marietta, Georgia
R. A. Allen Letters
O. Davant Chester Letters
R. N. Colville Letters
M. H. Dixon Diary
Alexander Doss Letters
W. R. Hurst Letters
R. B. Ledbetter Letters
A. J. Martin Letters
J. K. P. Martin Letters
William O. Norrell Diary
Columbus Sykes Letters
William R. Talley, "A History of Havis Georgia Battery"

Unidentified Diary, Twenty-eighth Alabama
Unidentified Diary, Sixty-fifth Georgia
"Wallace" Letter
Kentucky Historical Society, Frankfort
  George W. Johnson Letters
Library of Congress, Washington, D.C.
  Rufus Catlin Letters
  John S. Jackman Journal
  James B. Mitchell Letters
Louisiana Historical Association, New Orleans
  Army of Tennessee Papers
  Beauregard-Bragg Correspondence
Louisiana State University, Department of Archives and History,
    Baton Rouge
  John Bryan Letters (Morris-Sibley Papers)
  Thomas Butler Letters
  John Ellis Letters
  John A. Harris Letters
  Charles J. Johnson Letters
  Josiah Knighton Letters
  S. R. Latta Letters
  Theadore Mandeville Letters
  Robert Patrick Letters
  Richard Pugh Letters
Memphis State University, Mississippi Valley Collection, Memphis
  J. J. Davis Letters
  Thomas Roane Letter
Mississippi Department of Archives and History, Jackson
  Otis T. Baker Diary
  J. A. Bigger Diary
  John H. Cato Letters
  William Drennan Papers
  Jobe M. Foxworth Letters and Diary
  George S. Galloway Letters
  Robert A. Jarman, "The History of Co. K, 27th Mississippi Infantry"
  A. H. Mecklin Diary
  Augustus Q. Porter Diary
  A. T. Tarlske Letter (George S. Galloway Letters)
  William Yerger Papers
Museum of the Confederacy, Eleanor S. Brockenbrough Library, Richmond
  William Estes Diary
  James T. Mackey Diary
National Archives, Washington, D.C.
  Letters and Telegrams Sent, Atlanta Arsenal, 1862–64, Chap. IV, Vol.
    16, RG 109

Letters, Orders, Circulars Sent and Received, Medical Director, Army of Tennessee, 1863–65, Chap. IV, Vol. 748, RG 109

Letters Sent, Ordnance Officer, Army of Tennessee, Chap. IV, Vol. 141, RG 109

Letters, Telegrams and Orders Issued and Received, Medical Purveyor, Army of Tennessee, 1863, Chap. IV, Vol. 750, RG 109

Orders and Circulars, Army of Tennessee, Chap. II, Vol. 53, RG 109

Record Book of Major A. L. Landis, Quartermaster in the Army of Tennessee, 1863–64, Chap. IV, Vol. 226, RG 109

"Report of Killed, Wounded and Missing of 2d Corps, Army of the Mississippi, at the Battle of Shiloh, 1862." Chap. II, Vol. 220½, RG 109

Private Collections

Jeremiah Collom Letter and Memoirs

Sam Settles Letters

William N. Thompson Letters

Shiloh National Military Park, Shiloh, Tennessee

H. O. Beasley Letters (Lindsay's Mississippi Cavalry File)

M. H. Parsons Letters (154th Tennessee File)

D. S. Purvine Letters (First Mississippi Cavalry File)

D. Ridley Letter (Ninth Texas File)

Lemuel A. Scarbrough Letters (Thirtieth Tennessee File)

Ben A. Shepard Letters (154th Tennessee File)

Unidentified Diary (Fourth Tennessee File)

Unidentified Diary (154th Tennessee File)

J. H. Wiley Letters (Twenty-second Alabama File)

Stones River National Battlefield Park, Murfreesboro, Tennessee

Reisnor Etter Diary (Sixteenth Tennessee File)

Alexander L. McGowin Letters (Sixteenth Alabama File)

Hezekiah F. Nuckols Letters (Fourth Kentucky File)

William D. Rogers Letters (First Florida File)

L. Jackson Sanders Diary (Thirtieth Tennessee File)

G. E. Sealy Letters (Forty-first Alabama File)

J. Morgan Smith Letters (Thirty-second Alabama File)

P. W. Watson Letters (Forty-fifth Alabama File)

Tennessee State Library and Archives, Nashville

George T. Blakemore Diary

R. P. Boswell Letters

O. D. Brown Diary

Robert Franklin Bunting Papers

Martin Busk Letters

Civil War Veterans' Questionnaires

David Clark Letters

W. E. Coleman Letters

Thomas H. Davenport Diary

Marcus B. DeWitt Diary
W. F. Dillon Letters
Henry H. Doak Memoirs
C. H. Eastman Letters (Small Collection)
James Caswell Edenton Diary
Albert Fielder Diary
Perry Franklin Letters
John E. Gold Memoirs
Joel T. Haley Letters
James Hall Letters (Walter K. Hoover Collection)
Enoch Hancock Letters
John W. Harris Letters
Stephen A. Jordon Diary
William L. McKay Memoirs
Perry F. Morgan Letters
Van Buren Olden Diary
William M. Pollard Memoirs
Joseph A. Rogers Letters
W. B. Shepard Letter (Benjamin F. Cheatham Papers)
S. R. Simpson Diary
William Austin Smith Diary
W. H. Williams Letters
George Winchester Diary
Tulane University, Howard Tilton Memorial Library, New Orleans
Andrew Devilbliss Letters
Joseph Jones Collection
Kuntz Collection
Clement Stanford Watson Letters
United States Military History Institute, Carlisle Barracks, Pennsylvania
Quintan Adams Letter (Adams Family Collection)
George W. Bolton Letters (Early M. Hess Collection)
Alex Boyd Letters (Civil War Misc. Collection)
William D. Cole Letters (Civil War Misc. Collection)
Rufus W. Daniel Diary (Civil War Misc. Collection)
Richard F. Eddons Letters (Civil War Times Collection)
F. M. Goodman Letters (Lewis Leigh Collection)
"H.R." Letter (Civil War Times Collection)
Charles Stewart Letters (Civil War Times Collection)
John S. Vandiver Letter (Civil War Misc. Collection)
William S. Ward Letters (Lewis Leigh Collection)
Milton Walls Letter (Civil War Times Collection)
John Weston Letters (Lewis Leigh Collection)
University of Alabama, William Stanley Hoole Special Collections
    Library, Tuscaloosa
M. A. Cameron Letters

University of Georgia, Hargrett Rare Book and Manuscript Library,
Athens
  Hamilton Branch Letters
  J. N. Davis Letters
University of Mississippi, John Davis Williams Library, Oxford
  William A. Bowden Letters
  William S. Dillon Diary
University of North Carolina, Southern Historical Collection, Chapel Hill
  Isaac Alexander Letters
  Joseph Dill Alison Diary
  D. Coleman Diary
  James I. Hall Letters
  James I. Hall, "Notes on the War"
  Aristide Hopkins Diary
  Benedict J. Semmes Letters
  C. P. Simonton, "History of the 9th Tennessee" (James Hall Papers)
  I. B. Ulmer, Jr., Diary
University of Southwestern Louisiana, Southwestern Archives and
    Manuscripts Collection, Lafayette
  Robert C. Kennedy Letters (Givens-Hopkins Collection)
University of Texas, Barker Texas History Center, Austin
  John Crittenden Letters
  B. C. Goodners Diary
  E. M. Graham Diary (John Benjamin Long Papers)
  T. B. Hampton Letters
  Raymond B. Harris Diary
  John W. Hill Letters
  Joel H. Puckett Letters
  Sebron Sneed Letters
  William E. Stanton Letters
  Samuel H. Stout Papers
Vicksburg National Military Park, Vicksburg, Mississippi
  George A. Grammer Diary
Western Kentucky University, Kentucky Building, Manuscripts Section,
    Bowling Green
  John H. Hines Letters
Western Reserve Historical Society, Cleveland
  Braxton Bragg Papers (William P. Palmer Collection)
West Georgia College Library, Carrolton
  Joseph Hutcheson Letters
West Tennessee Historical Society Collection, Memphis State Univer-
    sity
  "Camp of the 154th Tennessee, January 14, 1864"
  J. H. Hammer Letters

W. H. Staggers Letters
Daniel Stout Letters
Yale University Library, New Haven, Connecticut
Joseph Lyman Letters

NEWSPAPERS

Atlanta Intelligencer
Augusta Constitutionalist
Charleston Courier
Chattanooga Daily Rebel
Columbus Enquirer
Daily Rebel Banner
Kennesaw Gazette
Macon Telegraph
Memphis Appeal
Memphis Avalanche
Memphis Commercial Appeal
Mobile Advertiser and Register
Montgomery Daily Mail
Natchez Weekly Courier
New Orleans Crescent
New Orleans Picayune
Richmond Dispatch
Southern Confederacy
Southern Presbyterian

GOVERNMENT PUBLICATIONS

*The Medical and Surgical History of the War of the Rebellion, 1861–
    1865.* 5 vols. Washington, D.C., 1870.
*The War of the Rebellion: A Compilation of the Official Records of the
    Union and Confederate Armies, 1861–1865.* 128 vols. Washington,
    D.C., 1880–1901.

PUBLISHED PRIMARY SOURCES

Confederate Letters and Diaries

Aiken, Leona T., ed. "Letters of the Offield Brothers, Confederate Soldiers
    from Upper East Tennessee." *East Tennessee Historical Society
    Publications* 46 (1974): 116–25.

Anderson, John Q., ed. *Campaigning with Parson's Texas Cavalry Brigade, CSA.* Hillsboro, Tex., 1967.

Atkinson, J. H., ed. *The Civil War Letters of Captain Elliot H. Fletcher.* Little Rock, 1963.

Bailey, Hugh C., ed. "An Alabamian at Shiloh: The Diary of Liberty Independence Nixon." *Alabama Review* 11 (April 1958): 144–55.

"Battle of Perryville as Told in a Letter by J. A. Bruce." *Confederate Veteran* 10 (April 1902): 117.

Betts, Vicki, ed. "The Civil War Letters of Elbridge Littlejohn." *Chronicles of Smith County, Texas* 18 (Summer 1979): 11–50.

Biel, John Q., ed. "The Battle of Shiloh: From the Letters and Diary of Joseph Dimmit Thompson." *Tennessee Historical Quarterly* 17 (September 1958): 250–74.

————. "The Evacuation of Corinth: From the Diary and Letter of Joseph Dimmit Thompson." *Journal of Mississippi History* 24 (January 1962): 40–56.

Black, Roy W., Sr., ed. "William J. Rogers' Memorandum Book." *West Tennessee Historical Society Papers* 9 (1955): 59–92.

Blackford, Charles M., ed. *Letters from Lee's Army, or Memoirs of Life in and out of the Army in Virginia during the War between the States.* New York, 1947.

Bock, H. Riley, ed. "One Year at War: Letters of Capt. Geo. W. Dawson, C.S.A." *Missouri Historical Review* 73 (January 1979): 165–97.

Bond, Phillip. "The Alabama State Artillery." *Alabama Historical Quarterly* 20 (1958): 312–38.

Bowman, Larry G., and Jack B. Scroggs, eds. "Diary of a Confederate Soldier." *Military Review* 62 (February 1982): 20–33.

Brown, Norman D., ed. *One of Cleburne's Command: The Civil War Reminiscences and Diary of Captain Samuel T. Foster, Granbury's Texas Brigade, CSA.* Austin, 1980.

Cabaniss, Jim R. *Civil War Journal and Letters of Washington Ives, 4th Fla. C.S.A.* N.p., 1987.

Cash, William M., and Lucy W. Howorth, eds. *My Dear Nellie: The Civil War Letters of William L. Nugent to Eleanor Smith Nugent.* Jackson, Miss., 1977.

Cate, Wirt A., ed. *Two Soldiers: The Campaign Diaries of Thomas J. Key C.S.A. and Robert J. Campbell U.S.A.* Chapel Hill, 1938.

Chambers, William P. "My Journal." *Publication of the Mississippi Historical Society,* Century Series, 5 (1928): 221–386.

Chattahoochee Valley Historical Society, ed. *War Was the Place: A Centennial Collection of Confederate Soldiers' Letters.* Bulletin 5. Chambers County, Ala., 1961.

Cox, Brent A., ed. "R. L. Davis Letters." *Sons of the South* 3 (April 1986): 34–40.

Crenshaw, Edward. "Diary of Captain Edward Crenshaw." *Alabama Historical Quarterly* 1 (Fall 1930): 261–70; (Winter 1930): 438–52.

Crow, Mattie, and Lou Teague, eds. *The Diary of a Confederate Soldier: John Washington Inzer, 1834–1928.* Huntsville, 1977.

Dennis, Frank A., ed. *Kemper County Rebel: The Civil War Diary of Robert Masten Holmes C.S.A.* Jackson, Miss., 1973.

Dodd, Ephraim S. *Diary of Ephraim Shelby Dodd.* Austin, 1914.

Dougan, Michael B., ed. "An Ozark Boy in the Confederate Ranks: The Soldier Letters of W. V. Stark." *Mid-South Folklore* 6 (Summer 1978): 37–42.

Douglas, Lucia R., ed. *Douglas' Texas Battery, C.S.A.* Waco, Tex., 1966.

Elkins, Vera Dockery, ed. *Letters from a Civil War Soldier.* New York, 1969.

Fall, Albert B. "Civil War Letters of Albert Boult Fall, Gunner for the Confederacy." *Register of the Kentucky Historical Society* 49 (April 1961): 150–68.

Folmar, John F., ed. *From That Terrible Field: Civil War Letters of John M. Williams, Twenty-First Alabama Infantry.* University, Ala., 1981.

Fremantle, Arthur J. L. *Three Months in the Southern States, April–June 1863.* New York, 1864.

Garrett, Jill K., ed. *The Civil War Diary of Andrew Jackson Campbell, 1861–1863.* Columbia, Tenn., 1965.

———. *Confederate Diary of Robert D. Smith.* Columbia, Tenn., 1975.

Griffeth, Lucille, ed. *Yours Till Death: Civil War Letters of John W. Cotton.* University, Ala., 1951.

Harrison, Lowell H., ed. "A Confederate View of Southern Kentucky, 1861." *Register of the Kentucky Historical Society* 70 (July 1972): 163–78.

———. "The Diary of an 'Average' Confederate Soldier." *Tennessee Historical Quarterly* 29 (Fall 1970): 256–71.

Harwell, Richard B., ed. *Kate: The Journal of a Confederate Nurse.* Baton Rouge, 1959.

Haynes, Mary K., and James Wilkins, eds. "The Stanley Letters." *Pike County Historical Society Papers* 4 (April 1965): 1–50.

Holmes, Henry M. *Diary of Henry McCall Holmes, Army of Tennessee Assistant Surgeon Florida Troops with Related Letters, Documents, Etc.* State College, Miss., 1968.

Jackson, Alto L., ed. *So Mourns the Dove: Letters of a Confederate Infantryman and His Family.* New York, 1965.

Jamison, Henry D., and Marguerite J. McTigue, eds. *Letters and Recollections of a Confederate Soldier, 1860–1865.* Nashville, 1964.

Johnson, Kenneth R., ed. "The Early Civil War in Southern Kentucky as Experienced by Confederate Sympathizers." *Register of the Kentucky Historical Society* 68 (April 1970): 176–79.

Jones, Mary M., and Leslie J. Martin, eds. *The Gentle Rebel: The Civil War Letters of William Harvey Berryhill Co. D, 43d Regiment, Mississippi Volunteers.* Yazoo City, Miss., 1982.

Jordon, Weymouth T., ed. "Mathew Andrew Dunn Letters." *Journal of Mississippi History* 1 (April 1939): 110–27.

Kerr, Homer L., ed. *Fighting with Ross' Texas Cavalry Brigade, C.S.A.: Diary of Lieut. George L. Griscom, Adjutant, 9th Texas Cavalry Regiment.* Hillsboro, Tex., 1976.

Law, J. G. "Diary of J. G. Law." *Southern Historical Society Papers* 10 (July 1882): 378–81; 11 (January 1883): 175–81; (April–May 1883): 297–303; (October 1883): 460–65; 12 (January–February 1884): 22–28; (May 1884): 215–19; (July–September 1884): 390–95; (October–December 1884): 538–43.

Lewis, Davis W. "A Confederate Officer's Letters on Sherman's March to Atlanta." *Georgia Historical Quarterly* 51 (December 1967): 491–94.

Marsh, Bryan. "The Confederate Letters of Bryan Marsh." *Chronicles of Smith County, Texas* 14 (Winter 1975): 9–30, 43–55.

Marshall, Elizabeth H. "Watch on the Chattahoochee: A Civil War Letter." *Georgia Historical Quarterly* 43 (1959): 427–28.

Mathis, Ray, ed. *In the Land of the Living: Wartime Letters by Confederates from the Chattahoochee Valley of Alabama and Georgia.* Troy, Ala., 1981.

Mitchell, Enoch L., ed. "The Civil War Letters of Thomas Jefferson Newberry." *Journal of Mississippi History* 10 (January 1948): 44–80.

——. "Letters of a Confederate Surgeon in the Army of Tennessee to His Wife." *Tennessee Historical Quarterly* 4 (December 1945): 341–53; 5 (March 1946): 61–81; (June 1946): 142–81.

Moore, William H. "Writing Home to Talladega." *Civil War Times Illustrated* 29 (November–December 1990): 56, 71–78.

Moorman, Hiram C. "The Moorman Memorandum." *Confederate Chronicles of Tennessee* 3 (1989): 59–95.

Mott, Charles R., Jr. "War Journal of Confederate Staff Officer Charles R. Mott, Jr." *Tennessee Historical Quarterly* 5 (September 1946): 234–48.

Muir, Andrew F. "The Battle of Atlanta as Described by a Confederate Soldier." *Georgia Historical Quarterly* 42 (March 1958): 109–11.

Musick, Michael, ed. " 'This Is War—Glorious War': The Diary of Corporal Westwood James." *Civil War Times Illustrated* 17 (October 1978): 34–42.

Nixon, Hugh C., ed. "An Alabamian at Shiloh: The Diary of Liberty Independence Nixon." *Alabama Review* 12 (April 1958): 44–55.

Noyes, Edward. "Excerpts from the Civil War Diary of E. T. Eggleston." *Tennessee Historical Quarterly* 17 (December 1958): 336–58.

Osborn, George C., ed. "Civil War Letters of Robert W. Banks: Atlanta Campaign." *Georgia Historical Quarterly* 27 (June 1943): 208–16.

Partin, Robert. "An Alabama Confederate Soldier's Report to His Wife." *Alabama Review* 3 (January 1950): 22–35.

———. "A Confederate Sergeant's Report to His Wife during the Campaign from Tullahoma to Dalton." *Tennessee Historical Quarterly* 12 (December 1953): 291–308.

Polignac, Camille Armand Jules. "Polignac's Diary—Part I." *Civil War Times Illustrated* 19 (August 1980): 14–18.

Rietti, J. C. "Diary of J. C. Rietti." *Military Annals of Mississippi Confederate*, 97–103. Spartanburg, S.C., 1976.

Roundtree, Benjamin, ed. "Letters of a Confederate Soldier." *Georgia Review* 18 (Fall 1964): 267–97.

Rugeley, H. J. H., ed. *Batchelor-Turner Letters, 1861–1864, Written by Two of Terry's Texas Rangers*. Austin, 1961.

"Rutledge's Battery." *Confederate Veteran* 36 (June 1928): 260.

Shelton, Samuel R. "Diary." *Memphis Commercial Appeal*, April 9, 1961.

Simpson, Harold B., ed. *The Bugle Softly Blows: The Confederate Diary of Benjamin M. Seaton*. Waco, Tex., 1965.

Steely, Will F., and Arville W. Taylor, eds. "Bragg's Kentucky Campaign: A Confederate Soldier's Account." *Register of the Kentucky Historical Society* 57 (January 1959): 49–55.

Steryx, H. E. "Autobiography and Letters of Joel Murphree of Troy, Alabama, 1864–1865." *Alabama Historical Quarterly* 19 (1957): 170–208.

Taylor, F. Jay, ed. *Reluctant Rebel: The Secret Diary of Robert Patrick*. Baton Rouge, 1959.

Thompson, Joseph D. "The Battle of Shiloh: From the Letters and Diary of Joseph Dimmit Thompson." *Tennessee Historical Quarterly* 17 (Summer 1958): 250–74.

Vann, Samuel King. *"Most Lovely Lizzie": Love Letters of a Young Confederate*. Birmingham, 1958.

Wiley, Bell I., ed. "Confederate Letters of John W. Hagan." *Georgia Historical Quarterly* 38 (September 1954): 268–90.

———. *Fourteen Hundred and 91 Days in the Confederate Army* by W. W. Heartsill. Jackson, Tenn., 1954.

———. *This Infernal War: The Confederate Letters of Sgt. Edwin H. Fay*. Austin, 1958.

Williams, Robert W., and Ralph A. Wooster, eds. "With Terry's Texas Rangers: The Letters of Dunbar Affleck." *Civil War History* 9 (September 1963): 299–319.

Williamson, Edward C., ed. "Francis P. Fleming in the War for Southern Independence." *Florida Historical Quarterly* 28 (January 1981): 335–39.

Wommack, J. J. *The Civil War Diary of J. J. Wommack*. McMinnville, Tenn., 1961.

Wright, Gilbert, ed. "Some Letters to His Parents by a Floridian in the Confederate Army." *Florida Historical Quarterly* 36 (April 1958): 353–72.

Federal Letters and Diaries

Angle, Paul M., ed. *Three Years in the Army of the Cumberland: The Letters and Diary of James A. Connolly.* Bloomington, 1959.

Athearn, Robert G., ed. *Soldier in the West: The Civil War Letters of Alfred Lacy Hough.* Philadelphia, 1957.

Beatty, John. *Memoirs of a Volunteer, 1861–1863.* New York, 1946.

Campbell, Henry. "From Hoover's Gap to Chattanooga." *Civil War Times Illustrated* 2 (January 1964): 42–45.

Carmony, Donald W., ed. "Jacob W. Bartmess Civil War Letters." *Indiana Magazine of History* 52 (March 1956): 49–74.

Colton, J. Ferrell, ed. *Column South: With the Fifteenth Pennsylvania Cavalry.* Flagstaff, 1960.

Ford, Harvey S., ed. *Memoirs of a Volunteer, 1862–1863.* New York, 1946.

Gates, Arnold, ed. *The Rough Side of War.* Garden City, N.Y., 1987.

Postwar Accounts, Memoirs, and Histories

Alderson, William T., ed. "The Civil War Diary of Captain James Litton Cooper, September 30, 1861 to January 1865." *Tennessee Historical Quarterly* 15 (June 1956): 141–73.

———. "The Civil War Reminiscences of John Johnson, 1861–1865." *Tennessee Historical Quarterly* 13 (March 1954): 65–82; (June 1954): 156–78; (September 1954): 244–76; 14 (March 1955): 43–81; (June 1955): 142–75.

Anderson, Charles W. "After the Fall of Fort Donelson." *Confederate Veteran* 4 (September 1896): 289–90.

Anderson, Ephraim McD. *Memoirs: Historical and Personal; Including the Campaigns of the First Missouri Confederate Brigade.* St. Louis, 1868.

Aughey, John H. *Tupelo.* Lincoln, Neb., 1888.

Bailey, Russell B., ed. "Reminiscences of the Civil War by T. J. Walker." *Confederate Chronicles of Tennessee* 1 (1986): 37–74.

Banks, R. W. *The Battle of Franklin, November 30, 1864: The Bloodiest Engagement of the War between the States.* New York, 1908.

Barron, S. B. *The Lone Star Defenders: A Chronicle of the Third Texas Cavalry, Ross' Brigade.* New York, 1908.

Beers, Fannie A. *Memoirs.* Philadelphia, 1889.

Bennett, William W. *A Narrative of the Great Revival Which Prevailed in the Southern Armies.* Philadelphia, 1877.

Bergeron, Arthur W., ed. *Reminiscences of Uncle Silas: A History of the 18th Louisiana Infantry Regiment by Silas T. Grisamore*. Baton Rouge, 1981.

Bessham, Ben. " 'Through a Mist of Powder and Excitement': A Southern Artist at Shiloh." *Tennessee Historical Quarterly* 47 (Fall 1988): 131–41.

Bevier, R. S. *History of the First and Second Missouri Confederate Brigades, 1861–1865*. St. Louis, 1879.

Blackburn, J. K. P. *Reminiscences of the Terry Rangers*. Austin, 1919.

Bogle, Joseph. *Some Recollections of the Civil War*. Dalton, Ga., 1911.

"Boy Company of the 45th Alabama." *Confederate Veteran* 10 (August 1902): 353.

Boyce, Joseph. "Missourians in the Battle of Franklin." *Confederate Veteran* 24 (March 1916): 101–3, 138.

Brown, A. H. "Reminiscences of a Private Soldier." *Confederate Veteran* 17 (September 1909): 449.

Bryson, George C. "Bate's Second Tennessee Regiment." *Confederate Veteran* 11 (June 1903): 19.

Cannon, Newton. *Reminiscences of Sergeant Newton Cannon*. Franklin, Tenn., 1963.

Carter, Howell. *A Cavalryman's Reminiscences of the Civil War*. New Orleans, 1979.

Cater, D. J. *As It Was*. N.p., 1981.

Cavanaugh, John. *Confederate Record: Historical Sketch of Obion Avalanche, Company H, 9th Tennessee Infantry*. Union City, Tenn., 1922.

Chisolm, Alex R. "Gen. B. J. Hill's Old Regiment at Shiloh." *Confederate Veteran* 8 (May 1900): 211.

Clark, Sam L., and H. D. Riley, eds. "Outline of the Organization of the Medical Department of the Confederate Army and Department of Tennessee by Samuel H. Stout." *Tennessee Historical Quarterly* 16 (Spring 1957): 55–82.

Clark, Walter A. *Under the Stars and Bars: Or Memoirs of Four Years Service with the Oglethorpes, of Augusta, Georgia*. Augusta, 1900.

Clark, Walter A., ed. *Histories of the Several Regiments and Battalions from North Carolina in the Great War, 1861–1865*. Raleigh, 1901.

Collins, R. M. *Chapters from the Unwritten History of the War between the States*. St. Louis, 1893.

Cox, Jacob B. *Atlanta*. New York, 1882.

Crumpton, W. B. "Closing Scenes with Johnston's Army." *Confederate Veteran* 33 (January 1925): 5–6.

Curry, J. H. "A History of Company B, 40th Alabama Infantry, C.S.A." *Alabama Historical Quarterly* 17 (1955): 159–222.

Dacus, Robert H. *Reminiscences of Company "H," First Arkansas Mounted Rifles*. Dardanelle, Ark., 1897.

"The Daily Rebel Banner." *Confederate Veteran* 4 (October 1896): 344.

Dawes, E. C. "The Confederate Strength in the Atlanta Campaign." In Robert V. Johnson and Clarence C. Buel, eds., *Battles and Leaders of the Civil War.* 4 vols. 1887–88. Reprint. New York, 1956, 281–83.

"Dr. E. A. Flewellyn." *Confederate Veteran* 20 (January 1912): 33.

Duke, Basil W. *Reminiscences of General Basil W. Duke, C.S.A.* New York, 1911.

Duncan, Thomas D. *Recollections of Thomas D. Duncan: A Confederate Soldier.* Nashville, 1922.

Dupree, J. G. "Reminiscences of Service with the First Mississippi Cavalry." *Publications of the Mississippi Historical Society* 7 (1903): 88–99.

Dyer, John Will. *Reminiscences: Or Four Years in the Confederate Army, 1861 to 1865.* Evansville, Ind., 1898.

Emmanuel, S. *An Historical Sketch of the Georgetown Rifle Guards and as Co. A of the Tenth Regiment of South Carolina Volunteers, in the Army of the Confederate States.* N.p., 1909.

"The Famous Tenth Tennessee." *Confederate Veteran* 12 (December 1905): 553.

Fitzgerald, Oscar P. *John B. McFerrin: A Biography.* Nashville, 1888.

Fletcher, William A. *Rebel Private Front and Rear.* Austin, 1954.

Gallagher, Gary W., ed. *Fighting for the Confederacy: The Personal Recollections of General Edward Porter Alexander.* Chapel Hill, 1989.

Gammage, W. L. *The Camp, the Bivouac and the Battle Field: Being a History of the Fourth Arkansas Regiment, from Its Organization Down to the Present Date.* Jackson, Tenn., 1958.

Gay, Mary A. H. *Life in Dixie during the War.* Atlanta, 1894.

Goodloe, Albert T. *Confederate Echoes: A Voice from the South in the Days of Secession and the Southern Confederacy.* Nashville, 1907.

Gower, Herschel, and Jack Allen, eds. *Pen and Sword: The Life and Journals of Randal W. McGavock.* Nashville, 1959.

Graber, H. W. *A Terry Texas Ranger: The Life Record of H. W. Graber.* Austin, 1987.

Grainger, Gervis D. *Four Years with the Boys in Gray.* Franklin, Ky., 1902.

Guild, George B. *A Brief Narrative of the Fourth Tennessee Cavalry Regiment.* Nashville, 1913.

Hall, W. T. "Religion in the Army of Tennessee." *The Land We Love* 4 (December 1867): 129–31.

Hampton, N. J. *An Eyewitness to the Dark Days of 1861–65.* Nashville, 1898.

Harwell, Richard B., ed. *Cities and Camps of the Confederate States.* Urbana, 1958.

Hay, Thomas R., ed. *Cleburne and His Command by Irving A. Buck.* Jackson, Tenn., 1959.

Hill, Andrew M. "Personal Recollections of Andrew Malone Hill."
    Alabama Historical Quarterly 20 (1958): 85–91.

Hinman, Wilbur F. *The Story of Sherman's Brigade.* N.p., 1897.

Hood, John Bell. *Advance and Retreat: Personal Experiences in the
    United States and Confederate States Armies.* Bloomington, 1959.

Hoole, William S., and Martha D. Hoole, eds. *Historical Sketches of
    Barton's (Later Stovall's) Georgia Brigade, Army of Tennessee, C.S.A.
    by Joseph Bogle and William L. Calhoun.* University, Ala., 1984.

Horn, Stanley F., ed. *Campaigns and Battles of the Sixteenth Regiment,
    Tennessee Volunteers, in the War between the States, with Incidental
    Sketches of the Part Performed by Other Tennessee Troops in the Same
    War, 1861–1865 by Thomas A. Head.* McMinnville, Tenn., 1961.

Hubbard, John M. *Notes of a Private.* Memphis, 1909.

Hughes, Nathaniel C., ed. *Liddell's Record: St. John Richardson Liddell,
    Brigadier General, CSA.* Dayton, 1985.

"Incidents in Army Life." *Confederate Veteran* 23 (November 1915): 520.

Johnston, Joseph E. "Jefferson Davis and the Mississippi Campaign." In
    Robert C. Johnson and Clarence C. Buel, eds., *Battles and Leaders of
    the Civil War.* 4 vols. 1887–88. Reprint. New York, 1956, 3:472–82.

Johnston, William Preston. *The Life of Gen. Albert Sidney Johnston,
    Embracing His Service in the Armies of the United States, the Republic
    of Texas, and the Confederate States.* New York, 1879.

Jones, J. William. *Christ in Camp or Religion in Lee's Army.* Atlanta,
    1867.

Joyce, Fred. "Dalton during the Winter of 1863–64." *Southern Bivouac* 2
    (June 1884): 464–65.

———. "Orphan Brigade Glee Club." *Southern Bivouac* 2 (May 1884):
    413–15.

Kirwan, Albert D., ed. *Johnny Green of the Orphan Brigade.* Lexington,
    Ky., 1956.

Lindsley, John B., ed. *Military Annals of Tennessee.* Nashville, 1886.

Little, George, and James R. Maxwell. *A History of Lumsden's Battery.*
    Tuscaloosa, Ala., 1905.

Long, J. M. "A Seventeen Year Old Boy at Shiloh." *Blue and Gray* 3
    (1894): 8–12.

Lynn, John H. "Re-Enlistments in the Western Army." *Confederate
    Veteran* 10 (June 1902): 259.

McFerrin, John B. "Religion in the Army of Tennessee." *Home Monthly* 4
    (April–June 1868): 161–62, 211–13, 281–85.

McGrath, John. "In a Louisiana Regiment." *Southern Historical Society
    Papers* 31 (1903): 103–19.

McKee, E. L. "Events of Camp Life in the Army." *Confederate Veteran* 2
    (March 1903): 113.

McMorries, Edward Young. *History of the First Regiment Alabama
    Volunteer, C.S.A.* Montgomery, 1904.

McMurray, W. J. *History of the Twentieth Tennessee Regiment Volunteer Infantry, C.S.A.* Nashville, 1904.

"Marksmanship in the Army." *Confederate Veteran* 4 (January 1896): 14.

"Miss Ella Palmer." *Confederate Veteran* 28 (February 1910): 72.

M'Neilly, J. H. "A Day in the Life of a Confederate Chaplain." *Confederate Veteran* 26 (September 1918): 397–98; (November 1918): 471–72.

———. "49th Tennessee in Battle of Franklin." *Confederate Veteran* 20 (April 1912): 172–73.

Moore, John C. "Shiloh Issue Again." *Confederate Veteran* 10 (July 1902): 316–17.

"More about Re-Enlistments at Dalton." *Confederate Veteran* 10 (September 1902): 399.

Morgan, David B. "In the Army of Tennessee." *Confederate Veteran* 26 (July 1918): 302.

Noll, Arthur H., ed. *Doctor Quintard: Chaplain C.S.A. and Second Bishop of Tennessee.* Sewanee, Tenn., 1905.

Nye, W. S. "Jake Donelson: A 'Cocky' Rebel." *Civil War Times Illustrated* 1 (1962): no page.

Owens, Robert. "Penalties for Desertion." *Confederate Veteran* 2 (August 1894): 235.

Pickett, William D. "Re-Enlistments by the Confederates." *Confederate Veteran* 10 (April 1902): 171.

Porter, George C. "Re-Enlistments in the Army of Tenn." *Confederate Veteran* 10 (August 1902): 351–52.

Rea, R. N. "A Mississippian in the Confederacy." *Confederate Veteran* 30 (August 1922): 287–89.

"Re-Enlistments by the Confederates." *Confederate Veteran* 10 (April 1902): 171.

"Reminiscences of Murfreesboro." *Confederate Veteran* 6 (June 1898): 255.

Rennolds, Edwin H. *A History of Henry County Commands.* Kennesaw, Ga., 1961.

"Resources of the Confederacy." *Southern Historical Society Papers* 2 (September 1876): 120.

Riddell, Thomas R. "Movements of the Goochland Light Artillery." *Southern Historical Society Papers* 24 (1896): 316–27.

Ridley, Broomfield L. *Battles and Sketches of the Army of Tennessee.* Mexico, Mo., 1906.

Ridley, E. L. "Camp Scenes around Dalton." *Confederate Veteran* 10 (February 1902): 66–67.

Roberts, Deering J. "Field and Temporary Hospitals." *Photographic History of the Civil War,* 7:256–72. New York: Thomas Yoseloff, 1956.

————. "Permanent and General Hospitals. *Photographic History of the Civil War*, 7:278–96. New York: Thomas Yoseloff, 1956.

Roberts, Frank S. "In Winter Quarters at Dalton, Ga., 1863–1864." *Confederate Veteran* 26 (June 1918): 274–75.

————. "Review of the Army of Tennessee at Dalton, Ga." *Confederate Veteran* 26 (April 1918): 150.

Robuck, J. E. *Personal Experience and Observation as a Soldier in the Confederate Army*. N.p., 1911.

Roman, Alfred. *The Military Operations of General Beauregard, in the War between the States, 1861–1865; Including a Brief Personal Sketch and a Narrative of His Services in the War with Mexico, 1846–8*. 2 vols. New York, 1884.

Schofield, John M. *Forty-Six Years in the Army*. New York, 1897.

"The Second Tennessee at Chickamauga." In *The Annals of the Army of Tennessee in Early Western History*, ed. Edwin L. Drake, 52–62. Nashville, 1878.

"Service with the Twentieth Tennessee Regiment." *Confederate Veteran* 33 (March 1925): 138–40.

"Severe Discipline." *Confederate Veteran* 1 (December 1893): 374.

Shapard, E. "At Spring Hill and Franklin Again." *Confederate Veteran* 24 (March 1916): 138–39.

Shingleton, Royce. "With Loyalty and Honor as a Patriot: Recollections of a Confederate Soldier." *Alabama Historical Quarterly* 33 (Fall and Winter 1971): 240–63.

Shoup, Francis A. "How We Went to Shiloh." *Confederate Veteran* 2 (May 1894): 137–40.

Silver, James W., ed. *The Confederate Soldier by LeGrand Wilson*. Memphis, 1973.

Smith, Daniel P. *Company K, First Alabama Regiment, or Three Years in the Confederate Service*. Prattville, Ala., 1885.

Smith, Frank. "An Historical Sketch of the 24th Tennessee." Edited by Jill K. Garrett and Marise P. Lightfoot. In *The Civil War in Maury County, Tennessee*. N.p., 1966.

Stanley, Dorothy, ed. *The Autobiography of Sir Henry Morton Stanley*. Boston, 1909.

Stevenson, William G. *Thirteen Months in the Rebel Army*. New York, 1959.

Stout, Samuel H. "Some Facts of the History of the Organization of the Medical Services of the Confederate Armies and Hospitals." *Southern Practitioner* 24 (April 1903): 213.

Sykes, E. T. "Walthall's Brigade: A Cursory Sketch, with Personal Experiences of Walthall's Brigade, Army of Tennessee CSA, 1862–1865." *Publication of the Mississippi Historical Society* 1 (1916): 486–616.

Thompson, Edward Porter. *History of the First Kentucky Brigade.* Cincinnati, 1868.

———. *History of the Orphan Brigade.* Louisville, 1898.

Thompson, William R., ed. "From Shiloh to Port Gibson by William C. Thompson," *Civil War Times Illustrated* 3 (October 1965): 20–25.

———. "From the Defenses of Atlanta to a Federal Prison Camp." *Civil War Times Illustrated* 10 (February 1965): 40–44.

"Three Deserters Shot at Shelbyville." *Confederate Veteran* 16 (March 1908): 128.

Toney, Marcus B. *The Privations of a Private.* Nashville, 1905.

Tower, R. Lockwood, ed. *A Carolinian Goes to War: The Civil War Narrative of Arthur Middleton Manigault, Brigadier General, C.S.A.* Columbia, S.C., 1983.

Urquhart, David. "Bragg's Advance and Retreat." In Robert V. Johnson and Clarence C. Buel, eds., *Battles and Leaders of the Civil War.* 4 vols. 1887–88. Reprint. New York, 1956, 3:600–609.

Vaughn, A. J. *Personal Record of the Thirteenth Tennessee Infantry.* Memphis, 1897.

Walker, C. Irvine. *Rolls and Historical Sketch of the Tenth Regiment, South Carolina Volunteers, in the Army of the Confederate States.* New York, 1881.

Wall, Lillian T., and Robert McBride, eds. "An Extraordinary Perseverance: The Journal of Capt. Thomas J. Taylor, C.S.A." *Tennessee Historical Quarterly* 31 (Winter 1972): 328–59.

Watkins, Sam R. "*Co. Aytch*": *A Side Show of the Big War.* New York, 1962.

———. "Snowball Battle at Dalton." *Confederate Veteran* 2 (July 1894): 204–5.

Watson, William. *Life in the Confederate Army: Being the Experiences of an Alien in the South during the American Civil War.* New York, 1888.

Wiley, Bell I., ed. *Four Years on the Firing Line by James C. Nisbet.* Jackson, Tenn., 1963.

Worsham, W. J. *Old Nineteenth Tennessee Regiment, C.S.A.: June 1861–April, 1865.* Knoxville, 1902.

SECONDARY SOURCES

Books

Andrews, J. Cutler. *The South Reports the Civil War.* Pittsburgh, 1970.

Bailey, Fred A. *Class and Tennessee's Confederate Generation.* Chapel Hill, 1987.

Baird, Nancy D. *David Wendall Yandell: Physician of Old Louisville.* Lexington, Ky., 1978.

Bartlett, Napier. *Military Records of Louisiana*. Baton Rouge, 1964.

Bragg, William Harris. *Joe Brown's Army: The Georgia State Line, 1862–1865*. Macon, 1987.

Brewer, Willis. *Alabama: Her History, Resources, War Record, and Public Men from 1540–1872*. Montgomery, 1872.

Civil War Centennial Commission, ed. *Tennesseans in the Civil War*. 2 vols. Nashville, 1964.

Connelly, Thomas L. *Army of the Heartland: The Army of Tennessee, 1861–1862*. Baton Rouge, 1967.

———. *Autumn of Glory: The Army of Tennessee, 1862–1865*. Baton Rouge, 1971.

Cunningham, H. H. *Doctors in Gray: The Confederate Medical Service*. Baton Rouge, 1958.

Daniel, Larry J. *Cannoneers in Gray: The Field Artillery of the Army of Tennessee, 1861–1865*. University, Ala., 1984.

Daniel, Larry J., and Riley W. Gunter. *Confederate Cannon Foundries*. Union City, Tenn., 1977.

Davis, William C. *The Orphan Brigade: The Kentucky Confederates Who Couldn't Go Home*. Garden City, N.Y., 1980.

Dubose, John W. *General Joseph Wheeler and the Army of Tennessee*. New York, 1912.

Duncan, Louis C. *The Medical Department of the United States in the Civil War*. Gaithersburg, Md., 1987.

Glatthaar, Joseph T. *The March to the Sea and Beyond: Sherman's Troops in the Savannah and Carolina Campaigns*. New York, 1985.

Goff, Richard D. *Confederate Supply*. Durham, N.C., 1969.

Hoffman, John. *The Confederate Collapse at the Battle of Missionary Ridge: The Reports of James Patton Anderson and His Brigade Commanders*. Dayton, 1985.

Horn, Stanley F. *The Army of Tennessee*. Norman, Okla., 1953.

Lacy, Benjamin Rice. *Revivalism in the Midst of Years*. Richmond, 1943.

Lonn, Ella. *Foreigners in the Confederacy*. Chapel Hill, 1940.

McDonald, B. W. *History of the Cumberland Presbyterian Church*. Nashville, 1899.

McDonough, James Lee. *Shiloh—In Hell before Night*. Knoxville, 1977.

———. *Stones River—Bloody Winter in Tennessee*. Knoxville, 1980.

McDonough, James Lee, and Thomas L. Connelly. *Five Tragic Hours: The Battle of Franklin*. Knoxville, 1983.

McDonough, James Lee, and James Pickett Jones. *War So Terrible: Sherman and Atlanta*. New York, 1987.

McMurry, Richard M. *John Bell Hood and the War for Southern Independence*. Lexington, Ky., 1982.

———. *Two Great Rebel Armies: An Essay in Confederate Military History*. Chapel Hill, 1989.

McWhiney, Grady. *Braxton Bragg and Confederate Defeat: Field Command*. New York, 1969.

McWhiney, Grady, and Perry D. Jamieson. *Attack and Die: Civil War Tactics and the Southern Heritage*. University, Ala., 1982.

Madaus, Howard D., and Robert D. Needham. *The Battle Flags of the Confederate Army of Tennessee*. Milwaukee, 1976.

Martin, Bessie. *Desertion of Alabama Troops from the Confederate Army*. New York, 1932.

Mitchell, Reid. *Civil War Soldiers*. New York, 1988.

Norton, Herman. *Rebel Religion: The Story of Confederate Chaplains*. St. Louis, 1961.

Romero, Sidney J. *Religion in the Rebel Ranks*. Lanham, Md., 1983.

Rowland, Dunbar. *The Official and Statistical Register of Mississippi*. Nashville, 1908.

Shattuck, Gardiner H., Jr. *A Shield and Hiding Place*. Macon, 1987.

Sword, Wiley. *Firepower from Abroad: The Confederate Enfield and the LeMat Revolver*. Lincoln, R.I., 1986.

Wiley, Bell I. *The Life of Johnny Reb*. Indianapolis, 1962.

Wommack, Bob. *Call Forth the Mighty Men*. Bessemer, Ala., 1987.

Articles

Bentley, William G. "The Great Snowball Fight." *Civil War Times Illustrated* 5 (January 1967): 22–23.

Breeden, James O. "A Medical History of the Later Stages of the Atlanta Campaign." *Journal of Southern History* 35 (February 1969): 31–59.

Faust, Drew Gilpin. "Christian Soldiers: The Meaning of Revivalism in the Confederate Army." *Journal of Southern History* 52 (February 1987): 63–90.

Jones, Dillard. "Outfitting the Provisional Army of Tennessee: A Report on New Source Materials." *Tennessee Historical Quarterly* 40 (Fall 1981): 257–71.

LaPointe, Patricia M. "Hospitals in Memphis." *Tennessee Historical Quarterly* 42 (Winter 1983): 325–42.

McDonough, James L. "The Battle of Stones River." *Civil War Times Illustrated* 25 (June 1986): 13–51.

McMurry, Richard. "Confederate Morale in the Atlanta Campaign." *Georgia Historical Quarterly* 44 (1970): 226–43.

McNeil, William J. "A Survey of Confederate Soldier Morale during Sherman's Campaign through Georgia and the Carolinas." *Georgia Historical Quarterly* 55 (Spring 1971): 1–25.

McWhiney, Grady. "Braxton Bragg." *Civil War Times Illustrated* 11 (April 1972): 4–7, 42–48.

Meany, Peter J. "Valiant Chaplain of the Bloody Tenth." *Tennessee Historical Quarterly* 41 (Spring 1982): 37–47.

Norton, Henry. "Revivalism in the Confederate Army." *Civil War History* 6 (1960): 410–24.

Prim, G. Clinton. "Born Again in the Trenches: Revivals in the Army of Tennessee." *Tennessee Historical Quarterly* 43 (Fall 1984): 250–72.

Robbins, Peggy. "Desertion: The Great Evil of the War." *Civil War* 8 (September–October, 1990): 30–35, 74.

Taylor, Robert A. "Rebel Beef: Cattle and the Confederate Army, 1862–1864." *Florida Historical Quarterly* 67 (July 1988): 15–31.

Wiley, Bell I. "Billy Yank and Johnny Reb in the Campaign for Atlanta." *Civil War Times Illustrated* 3 (July 1974): 18–22.

———. "Johnny Reb and Billy Yank at Shiloh." *West Tennessee Historical Society Papers* 26 (1972): 5–12.

Index

Adams, Daniel, 25
Alabama artillery batteries: Garrity, 27; Lumsden, 70; Selden, 161; Semple, 91, 105
Alabama cavalry regiments: Fourth, 134; Seventh, 8; Fifty-first, 48
Alabama infantry regiments: First, 89; Seventeenth, 119; Eighteenth, 37, 139; Nineteenth, 68, 84, 104, 112, 129, 156; Twentieth, 33, 120; Twenty-first, 69, 154; Twenty-fourth, 56; Twenty-fifth, 27, 75, 130; Twenty-eighth, 113; Twenty-ninth, 29; Thirty-first, 156; Thirty-second, 25; Thirty-third, 45, 56, 84; Thirty-fourth, 80, 88, 152, 153, 154; Thirty-fifth, 125; Thirty-sixth, 153; Thirty-seventh, 6; Thirty-eighth, 73, 119, 129; Thirty-ninth, 113; Fortieth, 108, 156; Forty-fifth, 3, 58, 137; Forty-sixth, 122; Forty-seventh, 8; Fifty-ninth, 33
Alcoholism, 95–96, 102–3
Alexander, Isaac, 132, 134
Allen, Alfred, 134
Allen, R. A., 165
Ambulances, 75
Ammunition, 48
Amputations, 69

Anderson, Lawrence M., 151
Anderson, Patton, 159
Arkansas infantry battalions: First,
    42
Arkansas infantry regiments: First,
    47, 67, 112; Second, 42, 105;
    Sixth, 42, 127, 136; Seventh, 42,
    107, 108, 110, 155; Ninth, 155;
    Thirteenth, 48; Fifteenth, 89
Arms: shortages of, 39; supply of,
    40; imports, 42, 43, 46; cap-
    tured, 43, 49; wasted, 46
Army of Mississippi, on review, 8–
    9
Army of Northern Virginia, 116,
    134; compared with Army of
    Tennessee, 11, 13, 18, 20, 28, 38,
    99, 126; food supplies for, 55,
    178 (n. 14); venereal disease, 98
Army of Tennessee: on review, 2–8;
    character of troops, 11–13; disci-
    pline, 13, 101–2; literacy, 15;
    intra-army conflict, 17–18; for-
    eigners in, 18–19; politics in, 20;
    view of Lee's army, 20–21; train-
    ing, 24–28; venereal disease, 98–
    99; motivation to fight, 148–50;
    surrender of, 167
Artillery: on review, 6–7; contest,
    25; training, 27
Athey, G. W., 37, 58, 149
Atlanta, Ga., 29, 55, 78
Atlanta, Battle of, 145, 149, 159
Atlanta Arsenal, 46, 47, 49
Atlanta Campaign, 5, 10, 13, 32,
    47, 93, 96, 142; hardships dur-
    ing, 34; rations during, 61; casu-
    alties, 78, 79, 81, 153; religious
    activity during, 119, 124–25; ef-
    fects on morale, 140–46; reac-
    tions to, 152; combat, 153, 156–
    57
Augusta Arsenal, 50
Austin, J. E., 102

Baillie, Melville, 110
Baird, John M. W., 158
Baker, Otis, 94
Bands, 91
Barfield, John, 137
Batchelor, Frank, 132
Bate, William, 3, 5, 37, 80, 106,
    155, 156
Battle, 148–68
Bayonets, 48
Beatty, John (USA), 130, 134
Beauregard, P. G. T., 52, 53, 57
Beers, Fannie, 71
Belmont, Battle of, 65
Bennett House, 167
Berryhill, William, 34, 124, 149
Bigbe, L. W., 138
Black, Hugh, 141
Blacks, soldiers' views on, 14–
    15
Blakemore, George T., 109
Blemiel, Emmeran, 122
Bliss, Robert, 30, 161
Bond, Phillip, 140
Boswell, R. P., 86
Bottom, Henry P., 163
Bowden, William N., 146
Boyd, Alex, 155
Bragg, Braxton, 1, 3, 21, 46, 54, 57,
    71, 109; effects on morale, 101,
    129, 131–33, 136–37; punishes
    soldiers, 107, 110, 112, 114;
    conversion of, 118
Branch, Hamilton, 141, 149, 155
Brand, David, 154
Breckinridge, John C., 24, 25, 40,
    106, 112
Brennan, T. M. & Co., 49
Brewer, Dave, 108
Brown, John C., 72, 120, 159
Brown, Samuel, 81
Brown, W. A., 137, 151
Bruce, J. A., 71
Busk, Martin, 53

Butler, I. W., 105
Butler, Thomas, 18

Camp Brown, 84, 102
Camp Cheatham, 39
Camp life, 83–88
Camp Trousdale, 83, 84, 95
Capers, Elliston, 37
Carroll, William H., 39
Carter, Frank, 129, 149
Catlin, Rufus, 129
Cavalry: on review, 8, 10; training, 27
Chambers, William, 138
Champion Hill, Battle of, 6, 8
Chaplains, 116, 117–19
Chattanooga, Tenn., 30
Cheatham, Benjamin F., 3, 12, 23, 38, 48, 77, 94, 111, 133, 163
Chester, O. D., 157
Chickamauga, Battle of, 1, 4, 5, 27, 28, 58, 61, 106–7, 109, 130, 135, 149; captures at, 46, 50, 75; ammunition expenditure, 48; casualties, 75–77, 163; effects on morale, 136; combat, 152, 153, 154; bravery at, 155; burials, 163
Childress, Polk, 110
Chunn, William, 156
Churchill, Thomas, 3
Clark, John & Co., 49
Cleburne, Patrick, 3, 4, 15, 21, 24, 25, 43, 60, 86, 105, 106, 134, 140
Clements, Henry, 158
Clothing, 32, 37, 174 (n. 24), 175 (n. 34)
Cocker, W. J., 131
Cockfighting, 97
Coffee, 52
Cole, William D., 73, 129
Columbus Arsenal, 50
Colville, R. N., 146

Connelly, Thomas L., xi, 11–12, 21, 22
Connolly, James (USA), 130
Conscription Act, 127, 128
Consolidation of units, 132–33
Cook & Brother, 43
Cooking utensils, 53–54, 57, 61
Cooper, James, 78
Corinth, Miss., 87, 97, 106, 116, 127; sickness at, 66–71; encampment, 84, 85, 86
Cowardice, 104–5, 155–56
Crumpton, W. B., 82
Cummings, Alfred, 57, 120
Cummings, Kate, 69, 76

Daily Rebel Banner, 93
Dalton, Ga., 15, 26, 59, 78, 85, 86, 89, 91, 92, 93, 96, 99, 100, 104, 105, 108, 113, 121, 137, 138, 139; encampment at, 88; snowball fight at, 94; executions at, 112–13; revivals at, 119–23
Daniel, Rufus, 108, 127
Davidson, John, 25, 141
Davidson, John W., 105
Davis, J. N., 90
Davis, Jefferson: visits Army of Tennessee, 20; declares day of prayer, 115
Davis, John, 79
Davis, John J., 27, 80
Davis, William P., 53
Deas, Z. C., 6, 58, 113
Dent, S. H., 90, 141, 146
Desertions, 127–28; punishments for, 104, 107–13; in 1862, 127–28; in 1863, 129–30, 133, 135; in 1864, 137; soldiers' views of, 137–38
Devilbliss, Andrew, 166
Diarrhea, 64, 70, 73, 78, 105
Dickson, J. C., 106

226

Index

Dillon, William S., 97, 108, 133, 154

Disease, 64, 70, 73, 75

Doss, Alexander, 135

Douglas, James, 25, 161

Dysentary, 64, 73

Ector, M. D., 117

Edge, A. J., 138

Eggleston, E. T., 161

Elkin, B. F., 109

Ellis, E. J., 151

Enfield rifles, 42, 43, 45, 46, 47

Estes, William, 117

Executions, 109–14, 188 (nn. 26, 37)

Ezra Church, Battle of, 145, 149, 158

Fackler, Albert, 88

Fagan, William, 107

Fall, Albert, 88

Farris, John, 103

Faust, Drew Gilpin, 117

Featherston, W. S., 8

Fenner, John S., 74

Fiquers, Hardin, 146

Flags, 4, 24

Fletcher, Elliott, 42

Flewellyn, Edward, 75

Florence, Ala., 36, 37, 82

Florida artillery batteries: Marion Light Artillery, 61

Florida Brigade, 5, 81, 120

Florida infantry regiments: First, 56, 151; First and Fourth (consolidated), 91; Second, 113; Third, 112; Fourth, 28, 108; Sixth, 112; Seventh, 91

Floyd, Watt, 155

Foreigners, 18–19

Forrest, Nathan Bedford, 12, 134, 137

Fort Donelson, Battle of, 1, 8, 9, 53, 65, 93, 95, 127, 154

Foster, Samuel T., 34, 147, 152, 168

Frank (mascot), 93

Frank, Joseph A., xii

Franklin, Rube, 108

Franklin, Battle of, 21, 37, 47; casualties, 80–81, 158, 160–61; effects on morale, 146, 149; combat, 159–60; burials, 164

Fraternizing, 157

Fremantle, Arthur J. L., 20, 25, 32, 48, 109

French, Samuel, 9

Furloughs, 138–39

Gadsden, Ala., 37, 80

Gambling, 97

Gander pulling, 93

Georgia artillery batteries: Howell, 7

Georgia cavalry regiments: Fifth, 8

Georgia infantry regiments: Fifth, 92; Twenty-ninth, 73, 80; Thirty-sixth, 137; Thirty-seventh, 137, 156; Thirty-ninth, 137; Forty-first, 29; Forty-second, 37; Forty-sixth, 161; Sixty-third, 5, 80, 112, 141; Sixty-fifth, 60; Sixty-sixth, 112

Gettysburg, Battle of, 134

Gibbons, Israel, 88

Gill, Robert, 13

Gillis, M., 161

Gilmer Hospital, 75

Gist, S. R., 120

Godwin, D. G., 144

Gordon, George W., 94

Graham, E. M., 35

Granbury, Hiram, 38, 160, 167

Green, B. H., 51

Green, Johnny, 85

Gregg, John, 40

Haley, Joel T., 137, 139, 156
Hall, Bolling, 32, 33
Hall, James, 20, 84, 97, 127, 136, 146
Hall, Tom, 110
Hancock, Enoch, 39
Hardee, William J., 3–5, 24, 27, 48, 64, 70, 98, 113, 140
Harris, J. W., 129
Harris, Raymond, 144
Heiman, Adolphus, 95
Hell's Half Acre, 97
Helms, Calathiel, 141
Henry, W. F., 44
Hill, John, 55, 143
Hillyer, Giles, 57
Hindman, Thomas, 5
Hines, J. H., 152
Holmes, Henry, 81
Holt, Hiram, 153–54
Hood, John Bell, 79; baptism of, 122; effects on morale, 143–47; criticizes troops, 157–58
Hospitals, 64–66, 69, 75, 77, 78, 79, 80
Hough, Alfred (USA), 130
Howell, William P., 75
Hunting, 56
Hurst, W. R., 78
Hurt, Robert B., 162

Irish, 18, 128
Ives, Washington, 30, 62, 108, 153

Jackman, John, 27
Jackson, W. H., 10
Jaco, Jeremiah, 142
Jake Donelson (mascot), 93
James, Jasper, 120
Johnson, Charles, 104
Johnson, John, 153, 163
Johnston, Albert Sidney, 1, 39, 40, 52, 65; seeks arms supply, 42; effects on morale, 127

Johnston, Joseph E., 2, 3, 4, 20, 23, 25, 27, 33, 50, 99, 167; seeks food supplies, 57, 59, 60; punishes soldiers, 108, 112–14; baptism of, 122; declares amnesty for deserters, 138; effects on morale, 139, 140–43; removal of, 143–44
Johnston, William Preston, 55
Jones, Henry, 102
Jonesboro, Battle of, 122, 158

Kelly, Daniel, 119
Kelly, Samuel, 105, 141, 144
Kennedy, J. B. G., 93
Kennedy, Robert, 17, 90
Kentucky Brigade, 5, 8, 25, 85, 91, 102
Kentucky Campaign, 17, 18, 31; marches during, 29–30, 31; captures, 43, 49; food shortages during, 54; casualties, 71; discipline problems during, 95, 102
Kentucky cavalry regiments: Third, 45
Kentucky infantry regiments: Second, 25, 93; Third, 67; Fourth, 25, 85, 97; Fifth, 42; Sixth, 25, 112; Ninth, 105
Key, Thomas, 15, 28, 34, 62, 99, 122, 123, 154, 161
Killingsworth, John T., 4
Knighton, John T., 127

LaGrange, Ga., 37
Landis, J. A., 68
Landis, William H., 68
Law, J. G., 127
Lee, S. D., 36, 80, 158
Leeds & Co., 49
Letcher, John, 40
Lewis, Asa, 112
Lewis, C. W., 164
Lice, 17, 85

Liddell, St. John, 25, 32, 56, 123
Longstreet, James, 11
Loring, W. W., 8, 223
Louisiana artillery batteries: Fenner, 92; Washington (Fifth Company), 17, 29, 51, 84, 94, 103,
 121, 129, 150
Louisiana Brigade, 25
Louisiana cavalry regiments: First,
 106
Louisiana infantry battalions: Austin's Sharpshooters, 166; Fourth,
 165; Orleans Guard, 17
Louisiana infantry regiments: First,
 17, 29, 68, 69; Fourth, 127; Eleventh, 51, 70, 88, 102, 104, 116;
 Twelfth, 35; Thirteenth, 18, 24,
 25, 64, 68, 69, 102; Thirteenth
 and Twentieth (consolidated),
 25; Sixteenth, 25, 68; Seventeenth, 16; Nineteenth, 25, 70,
 98, 105, 129; Twentieth, 18, 24,
 25, 163; Twenty-first, 93
Lovell, Mansfield, 40
Lowrey, M. P., 122
Luna, Mark, 116
Lyman, Joseph, 95, 128

McCown, J. P., 25, 117
McCoy, Taylor, 97
McDonald, Fayette, 56
McDonald, Patrick, 103
McGavock, John, 164
McGowan, Alexander, 153
McIntyre, William, 107
Mackey, James T., 40
McKittrick, Samuel, 59
McMichael, Reuben, 16
McMurry, Richard, 126, 140, 144
M'Neilly, James, 121, 159
Macon Arsenal, 50
McWhiney, Grady, 132
Magee, John, 30, 110, 134
Magill, Robert M., 147

Mail, 89–90
Manigault, Arthur M., 3, 7, 13, 17,
 27, 76, 90, 107, 156, 159
Markham, Charles, 107
Martin, A. T., 166
Mascots, 93
Measles, 64, 79
Meckham, A. H., 86, 127, 150
Medical care, 64–82
Mercer, H. W., 5
Miller, Thomas, 102
Mill Springs, Battle of, 41–42
Missionary Ridge, Battle of, 1, 5, 6,
 7, 21, 24, 33, 59, 123, 136; casu-
 alties, 46, 50, 78; rout at, 155
Mississippi artillery batteries:
 Cowan, 34; Jefferson, 103; Stan-
 ford, 25, 26, 151; Turner, 92
Mississippi infantry regiments:
 Third, 8; Sixth, 42, 162; Seventh,
 28; Seventh and Ninth (consoli-
 dated), 94; Ninth, 86, 105;
 Tenth, 76, 94, 155; Fifteenth, 95;
 Twenty-fourth, 34, 108, 132,
 140; Twenty-ninth, 132; Thirty-
 second, 140; Thirty-third, 78;
 Forty-first, 94; Forty-third, 124,
 147; Forty-fourth, 50, 94
Missouri Brigade, 9, 160
Missouri infantry regiments: First,
 108
Mitchell, James, 153
Mitchell, Reid, xii
Montjoy, Jarrett, 45
Montjoy, John W., 45
Moore, William H., 27
Morale, 27, 126–47
Morrow, W. R., 155
Mott, William, 128
Murfreesboro, Battle of, 1, 5, 24,
 105, 132, 149; ammunition ex-
 penditure, 48; captures, 49; casu-
 alties, 71–72, 79, 162–63;
 perceived by Confederates as vic-

tory, 149; combat, 152, 153;
woman at, 154; cowardice at,
155; burials, 163
Music, 91
Myers, Sanders, 7

Napoleon guns, 6, 49, 50
Nashville, Battle of, 147, 154;
losses at, 50; casualties, 82; rout
at, 161
Neal, Andrew J., 27, 133, 136, 143,
156
Newberry, Thomas, 132
New Hope Church, Ga., 156, 164
Noble Brothers & Co., 49
Norrell, William, 80, 156
North Carolina regiments: Thirty-
ninth, 8, 96; Fifty-eighth, 113;
Sixtieth, 112
Northrop, L. B., 52, 53, 57
Nugent, William, 146

Oakland Cemetery, 164
Oladowski, Hypolite, 46, 47
Olden, Van Buren, 129, 133
Owens, Robert, 113
Owens, Thatcher, 88

Patrick, Robert, 18, 146
Patterson, Robert, 74
Peachtree Creek, Battle of, 145,
146, 149, 159; wounded at, 79
Peddy, George Washington, 147
Perryville, Battle of, 1, 5, 31, 43,
149; ammunition expenditure,
48; casualties, 71; perceived by
Confederates as victory, 149;
combat, 151-52; burials, 163
Picket duty, 156
Pillow, Gideon, 133
Polk, Leonidas, 6, 8, 25, 48, 65,
122, 144
Polk, Lucius, 47, 91
Pontoons, 36

Porter, A. Q., 78
Preston, William, 111
Provost, 106-7
Pruitt, Nathaniel, 111
Puckett, J. H., 56
Pugh, Richard, 129, 150, 152
Punishments, 101-14

Quinby & Robinson, 49
Quintard, Charles, 118-19

Rabb, Hezekiah, 45, 134
Rations, 51-63; effect on deser-
tions, 135
Reading & Brother, 49
Reenlistments, 139-40
Reeves, George, xii
Religion, 115-25
Reseca, Ga., 163
Revivals: in 1863, 116-19; in
Dalton, Ga., 119-23; effects of,
123-24
Richmond, Ky., Battle of, 49
Roach, J. F., 107
Roane, Thomas, 35
Roberts, D. J., 80
Roberts, Frank, 3
Roberts, Henry, 109
Robertson, Felix, 103, 106
Robertson, James I., xi, xii
Robertson, Nathan M., 145
Rogers, William, 56, 134
Roher, Walter R., 8, 9
Rowlett, Frank, 91
Ruggles, Daniel, 17
Rulle, John, 19

Sandige, Wright P., 31
Sawyer, Ancel, 76
Schofield, John M. (USA), 147
Scott, Tom, 8
Scurvy, 79
Searcy, James, 32, 52, 153
Searcy, Reuben, 20

Sears, C. W., 10
Selma Arsenal, 46, 47
Semple, Henry C., 105
Settles, Sam, 140
Sex, illicit, 97–100
Shaw, Roderick, 136, 139
Shelbyville, Tenn., 6, 25, 56, 85, 87,
    88, 90, 97, 103, 104, 112, 117,
    118, 124
Shelton, Samuel, 52
Sherman, William T. (USA), 13, 14,
    167
Shiloh, Battle of, 1, 4, 5, 13, 16, 19,
    29, 43, 52, 86, 97, 105, 107, 109,
    111, 128, 129, 149, 151; arms at,
    42, 43; casualties, 66–69, 79,
    162, 163; combat, 150, 153,
    154; reactions to, 152; cowardice
    at, 155; burials, 163
Shoes, 33, 37
Simpson, S. R., 14, 30, 116
Sisters of Charity, 66
Slaughter, John, 154
Smallpox, 74–75
Smith, A. H., 41, 139
Smith, J. Morgan, 17
Smith, Preston, 128
Snowball fight, 94
South Carolina regiments: Tenth, 6,
    47; Nineteenth, 59; Twenty-
    fourth, 37, 62
Sports, 90–91
Springfield rifle, 43, 45, 46, 47
Spring Hill, Tenn., 155
Stanley, Henry, 12
Stanley, William, 34
Stanton, William, 161
Stealing, 103–4
Stephens, W. A., 90, 122, 135, 137,
    156
Stevenson, Carter, 5, 6, 33, 50, 113
Stewart, Alexander P., 5, 6, 42, 48,
    91, 113, 122, 128, 133
Stokes, T. J., 120, 121

Stovall, M. A., 107
Strahl, O. F., 46
Strickland, Oliver, 104
Swor, Pleasant G., 67
Sykes, Columbus, 156

Target practice, 26
Tarlske, A. H., 127
Taylor, I. T., 187 (n. 19)
Tennessee artillery batteries: Bank-
    head, 128; Scott, 25
Tennessee Campaign, 15, 92;
    marches during, 34–36; clothing
    shortages during, 36–37; food
    shortages during, 62–63; casu-
    alties, 80–82; religious activity
    during, 125; effects on morale,
    146–47; cowardice during, 155
Tennessee cavalry regiments: Fifth,
    187 (n. 19); Seventh, 85
Tennessee infantry battalions:
    Twenty-fourth, 124
Tennessee infantry regiments: First,
    43, 83, 86, 118, 137; First and
    Twenty-seventh (consolidated),
    167; Second, 47, 54, 96; Third,
    39, 64, 93, 131; Fourth, 43, 48,
    91, 108, 123, 133, 154; Fifth, 33,
    46, 47, 48, 67, 91, 146, 155;
    Sixth, 28, 44, 53, 160; Sixth and
    Ninth (consolidated), 73; Eighth,
    116, 162; Ninth, 83, 127, 129,
    133; Tenth, 40, 163; Eleventh,
    94, 156; Twelfth, 72, 74, 117,
    128; Thirteenth, 26, 43, 67, 74,
    88, 91, 95, 96, 107, 119, 128,
    132, 167; Fifteenth, 132; Six-
    teenth, 95; Seventeenth, 41, 42;
    Eighteenth, 41, 42; Nineteenth,
    11, 167; Twentieth, 3, 42, 78, 79,
    87, 96, 104; Twenty-first, 103,
    107, 110; Twenty-second, 35,
    128; Twenty-third, 68, 108, 109;
    Twenty-fourth, 61, 66, 91, 111,

128; Twenty-fifth, 56, 105; Twenty-sixth, 73, 109; Twenty-seventh, 28; Thirtieth, 60, 116; Thirty-first, 48; Thirty-second, 73, 155; Thirty-third, 48; Thirty-fifth, 142; Thirty-seventh, 42, 132; Thirty-eighth, 29; Forty-first, 103; Forty-fourth, 65; Forty-fifth, 73, 104; Forty-sixth, 27, 80; Forty-seventh, 42, 43, 84, 128; Forty-eighth, 40, 47, 117; Forty-ninth, 121, 161; Fiftieth, 28; Fifty-first, 35, 41; Fifty-second, 40; Fifty-fourth, 109; Fifty-fifth, 155, 162; One Hundred and Fifty-fourth, 53, 96, 107, 115, 132, 139
Tents, 88
Texas artillery batteries: Douglas, 25
Texas Brigade, 133
Texas cavalry regiments: Eighth (Texas Rangers), 8, 13, 14, 30, 40, 43, 52, 97, 118, 128
Texas infantry regiments: Seventh, 40, 65; Tenth, 120
Thomas, Isham, 135
Tichenor, I. T., 119
Train accidents, 28
Trask, W. J., 144
Treadwell, E. W., 129
Tredegar Iron Works, 49, 50
Trench warfare, 156
Tucker, W. K., 6, 120
Tullahoma, Tenn., 24, 72, 73, 86, 87, 88, 89, 97, 100, 105, 109, 117, 124
Tullos, Columbus, 81
Tupelo, Miss., 37, 54, 84, 96, 103, 108, 110, 128, 147, 188 (n. 24)
Tuscumbia, Ala., 34, 37

Vance, R. B., 117
Vann, Sam, 161
Vawter, Andrew Jackson, 72
Vegetables, 60–61, 73
Venereal disease, 13, 98–99
Vicksburg, Miss., 134

Walker, Calvin H., 9
Walker, James J., 9
Walker, W. H. T., 3, 4–5, 94
Walls, Milton, 166
Ward, J. W., 34, 138, 140
Warrick, Thomas, 84, 88
Wartrace, Tenn., 24, 56, 109, 112, 154
Washington Artillery. See Louisiana artillery batteries
Watkins, Sam, 108, 110, 111
Watson, P. W., 17
Watson, Robert, 58, 95
Waynesboro, Tenn., 34
Weather: effects on soldiers, 34, 87, 154
Weaver, B. P., 37, 157
Weaver, Daniel, 58
Webb, T. M., 124
Wharton, John A., 46
Wheeler, Joseph, 8, 27, 48
Wiley, Bell I., xi, xii, 98, 116, 195 (n. 13)
Williams, James, 84
Winchester, George, 30
Withers, Jones, 5, 17
Woods, S. A. M., 70
Wright, Marcus H., 47, 110
Wyman, B. L., 105, 137, 138

Yandell, David, 66
Young Men's Christian Association, 123

DATE DUE

SEP 1 5 2017			
GAYLORD			PRINTED IN U.S.A.